Encounters with the Self

Encounters with the Self

Don E. Hamachek
Michigan State University

HOLT, RINEHART AND WINSTON, INC.
*New York   Chicago   San Francisco   Atlanta
Dallas   Montreal   Toronto*

Copyright © 1971 by Holt, Rinehart and Winston, Inc.
Library of Congress Catalog Card Number: 75-135128
ISBN: 0-03-077785-2
Printed in the United States of America
1   2   3   4   090   9   8   7   6   5   4   3   2

Preface

This is a book about self-concept. It is about that very private picture each of us carries around which evolves out of who we think we are, what we think we can do, and how best we think we can do it. It is a book about how this phenomenon called the self grows, develops, changes, and expresses itself in behavior. Included in the book are discussions about what it means to understand one's self, a consideration of some of the ways in which we are self-consistent (sometimes without even knowing it), a look at how self-concept is linked to physical growth and development and how it is related to child-rearing practices, an overview of how self-concept is connected to academic adjustment along with some implications for teaching practices, some reflections concerning the encouragement and development of a healthy self-image, and something about the perceptual theory and theorists undergirding some of the major ideas related to self-concept.

The theme of this book is underscored by a simple assumption, namely, the better we know ourselves the more able we will be to forget ourselves, for it is usually those things we do *not* know about ourselves, in terms of personal dynamics, that bog us down from time to time. I do not mean to suggest that this is in any sense a "self-help" or "self-analysis" type of book. It is, however, a book I have attempted to write in a descriptive and explanatory manner as opposed to a style that might be viewed as prescriptive and theoretical. More specifically, I have made a deliberate effort to present the content of this book in such a manner that it could be understood by readers who may be relatively unsophisticated in psychological jargon and terminology. Even more specifically, a goal I had in mind as I planned and wrote this book was to reach a diverse audience with diverse interests, who, among other things, were curious about who they were as individuals and how they got to be the way they are.

It will be no great revelation for you to learn that the things I have chosen to include and record in this volume are things I have been curious about for a long time. My own search for an identity, my own curiosities about self-consistency or lack of it, my own questions about my parents' child-rearing practices and the impact these practices had (and have) on my behavior and self-attitudes, my own queries about the connections between how well or how poorly I did in school and the relation these had to feelings about myself at different points in time—indeed, my own need to have some kind of unifying theme or framework which would facilitate a better understanding of my own and other persons' behavior—these questions and many others stimulated the ideas and organization of the book and made writing it more adventure-like than task-like. (Although I must admit that at times it did not seem too adventure-like.)

The scope of this volume is broad, including as it does ideas about self-consistency, growth and development, child-rearing practices, academic achievement as related to self-concept, and so on, but the ideas all fit under the same theoretical umbrella, which for me, at least, provides the sort of unifying framework and "tying together" I find necessary to operate at some level of effectiveness as a teacher and therapist. The theoretical umbrella evolves from a frame of reference which has been variously called the "phenomenological," "perceptual," "existential," "interactional," or "humanistic" approach. It is a point of view in psychological circles which is sometimes referred to as the "new look" or "third force." More succinctly, it is a point of view which looks at human behavior not only through the eyes of an outsider, but through the eyes of the person doing the behaving. It is a psychology searching to understand what goes on inside a person—his needs, wants, feelings, values, desires, and unique ways of perceiving and understanding that cause him to behave as he does. In an everyday sense, it is the psychology a concerned friend uses as he wonders why we're "feeling so sad"; in a clinical sense, it is what a therapist uses as he probes for the deeper meanings behind what personal experiences mean to the client.

The book has an extensive research base—some chapters more than others. I really do not think that a book related to self-concept has to be just one kind of presentation, and in keeping with this notion I have made a deliberate effort to make room not just for my own and others' personal feelings and speculations about the self, but also to make plenty of room for empirical research findings and conclusions as well.

It is hoped that this book can be a useful source in courses concerned with the preparation of teachers, counselors, mental hygienists, social workers, school psychologists, child development specialists, and researchers interested in understanding man both as he views himself and is acted on by forces outside himself. If you have questions about who you are and how you arrived at being the person you are at this point in time, I would hope that this volume might be one small step en route to answering those questions and stimulating you to read more widely and more deeply in developing insights into yourself and others.

I would like to extend a sincere thank-you to Professors Warren R. Baller (United States International University), Stephen F. Foster (University of British Columbia), Frank T. Severin (St. Louis University), Robert D. Strom (Arizona State University) and to Wayne G. Joosse (Michigan State University) for their critical reviews of the manuscript and very helpful suggestions for its improvement.

D. E. H.

August 1970

Contents

Encounters with the Self

Self-Knowledge is best learned,
not by contemplation, but action.
Strive to do your duty, and you will
soon discover of what stuff you are made.

Goethe (1749–1832)

chapter one

Toward Understanding One's Self

We humans are interesting creatures. Think about it. We can identify what we've done, but we're not always sure why we did it in the first place. We can see where we are, but we're not always certain how we got there. We can usually cite the direction in which we would like to head, but we're not always sure how to go about it. We can tell people our names, but stumble over our identities. We find it easier to describe what we have than to explain who we are. We can characterize what we are against, but we frequently have trouble specifying what we are for. We have the uniquely human talent for being able to think about what we've already thought about, yet still be puzzled. Indeed, in each of our individual pursuits for answers, for values, for whatever you want to call it, we are inescapably confronted with the problem of meaning—with the question of what life is all about.

Ultimately, each of us is faced with three questions which we must answer in one way or another if we are to grow to greater personal maturity:

> *Who am I?*
> *Where am I going?*
> *Why?*

Each of these questions, in its own way, deals with our sense of self, our goals, our values, our strengths and weaknesses, and our way of life or "life

1

style." How we see ourselves and others is reflected to some extent in how we answer these three questions. Some individuals, however, never seem to confront themselves with questions of this sort and, in fact, seem fearful to do so. Let us turn next to some speculations about why this may be.

Reasons for Resisting Personal Growth

FEAR OF MATURITY

Some individuals avoid finding out more about themselves for fear of having to give up a self with which they have grown comfortable or "satisfied." Most people have an initial inclination to resist personal change anyway, but this resistance is even stronger for a person who cannot "fit" new or changed behavior into his current concept of self. For example, a shy, timid, submissive person may not want to see his strengths and assets for fear that he might be expected to be more assertive and socially aggressive. If shyness has become a way of life designed to protect one from the risks of social disapproval (in this case, nothing ventured, nothing lost—in terms of self-esteem), then it may be difficult indeed for a shy person to give up his timidity. Other individuals are reluctant to find out more about themselves because of the threat of having to change in the direction of being more personally mature. Maturity implies many things, among which are a certain degree of independence and autonomy, capacity for self-discipline, certainty about goals and values, and motivation toward some level of personal achievement. All in all, greater maturity means greater responsibility and for some this is a frightening possibility.

FEAR OF SUCCESS

We frequently hear talk about how it is that some people have a fear of failure. For some this is a real fear. But it can only be real for a person *if he wants success to begin with.* Some people have a fundamental fear of success. Why? Because success establishes a precedent, a standard to be lived up to, a performance level to be maintained and this is frightening to an individual who has basic doubts about his ability to sustain a high level of personal performance. For example, I have known students who will invest only a given amount of time to preparation for an exam and then stop. One student expressed it to me something like this: "You see, if I study too hard—I mean really study—then I might get a high grade on the test. But it really wouldn't be because I was smart that I got the high grade; it would be because I studied so hard. Other students in the class might think I was smarter than I really was and what would happen to me the first time I *didn't* do real well? They would probably think I was dumb or

Feeling no sense of responsibility is comfortable, but not very motivating.

something." This particular student persisted in getting C's and an occasional B here and there and in so doing avoided both the stigma of failure and the risk of success.

Fear of success or more mature behavior is expressed in many different ways. One of my colleagues told me of a twenty-year-old girl he had worked with for over five months in therapy. Among the many conflicts this young lady had to work through were her ambivalent feelings about boys. She liked boys; yet she didn't. She wanted to be more successful with boys; yet she didn't. Basically she was afraid of a possible close relationship with a boy, because she dreaded the possibility of not being liked, of being disappointed, let down, and hurt. She was fearful of establishing a close relationship because *she questioned her ability to maintain a close relationship.* Compounding the problem was the fact that she was perhaps thirty pounds overweight. Her therapist discussed the possibility of dieting and exercise, but she resisted both. The dawn of insight broke through during one session when she discovered that being overweight, and hence being less attractive, was one way of assuring that she would *not* be too successful with boys. Being overweight reduced the risk of being hurt, because fewer boys would be attracted to her in the first place. As in the case of the student who studied only minimally to avoid the high grades he didn't believe he could maintain, so, too, did this girl avoid close relationships in which she could be hurt.

Back to our original point. Some persons are fearful of success, fearful of moving on to higher levels of personal realization and personal performance primarily because they doubt their ability to maintain a high standard of performance if they do achieve it. In this sense, fear of success or greater maturity and fear of failure are very much related. The more successful one is, let's say, in terms of fair play, knowledge, sense of perspective, capacity for setting long term goals, the more people expect of that person. And the more people expect of a person the more opportunities or possibilities there are for failing. For some individuals there is just too great a risk in establishing a reputation of competency, too much is then expected. Some persons find refuge and safety in being neither too far behind the pack nor too far ahead of it.

FEAR OF ONE'S BEST

Maslow[1] has noted that although we all have an impulse to improve ourselves, to actualize more of our potentialities, and move further in the direction of human fulfillment, many of us stop short of becoming what we could become because of what he calls a "fear of one's own greatness" or the "evasion of one's destiny" or the "running away from one's best talents." He goes on to observe:

> Not only are we ambivalent about our own highest possibilities, we are also in perpetual . . . conflict and ambivalence over these same possibilities in other people, and in human nature in general. Certainly we love and admire good men, saints—honest, virtuous, clean men. But could anybody who has looked into the depths of human nature fail to be aware of our mixed and often hostile feelings toward saintly men? Or toward very beautiful women or men? Or toward great creators? Or toward our intellectual geniuses? . . . We surely love and admire all the persons who have incarnated the true, the good, the beautiful, the just, the perfect, the ultimately successful. And yet they also make us uneasy, anxious, confused, perhaps a little jealous or envious, a little inferior, clumsy. They usually make us lose our aplomb, our self-possession and self regard.[2]

Why should this be? Why is it that our self-composure frequently takes leave in the face of another person's eminence, or greatness, or intellect, or beauty, or whatever? One reason may be that people who are superior in one way or other make us momentarily more aware of our lesser abilities or skills, without even intending to do so. What usually happens is that we are not conscious of why we feel stupid or ugly or inferior and we sometimes end up being defensive and resentful. That is, we respond as if the person we regard as superior were deliberately trying to make us feel inferior. Hostility, anger, resentment, even jealousy or envy are then understandable consequences.

Understandable as they may be, feelings of this sort are ultimately self-defeating. In the process of being resentful or envious of another man's accomplishments, we sometimes deny that he attained them in any honorable way. So what frequently happens is that we invent excuses for why people who are superior to us happen to be more important or successful or skilled than we see ourselves as being. For example, how many times have you heard comments like: "If I brown-nosed like he did, I'd get A's, too"; or "Sure she dates lots of boys, but look at how aggressive she is"; or "Big deal—I'd have high grades, too, if all I did was study"; or "Well, who wouldn't be beautiful if they could afford to have their hair done once a week like she does!" And so it goes. These are self-defeating feelings because in the process of denying that another person is bright or skilled or accomplished or good-looking, we are also denying the possibility of these qualities existing in ourselves. For example, the student who says, "I'd have high grades, too, if all I did was study," could be making an assertion which is, in fact, true or he could be trying to make it seem as if anyone (including himself, of course) was capable of getting high grades if he studied hard. In either case, the net effect is an effort to make nonattainment of high grades seem less important and less threatening than what actually may be the case. (If high grades were really *not* important to a person, then he wouldn't have to *act* as if they were unimportant by reducing another individual's accomplishments.) Or, as another example, a woman who constantly finds faults in other women's appearances may be doing so because she sees other women looking better than she does and is threatened by the possibility that this could be true. One way of reducing the threat of another woman being more attractive is to exaggerate her flaws and in that way distort the beauty that is there in the first place (or at least detract from it).

We are back to our original point. If we stop responding to people who are in some way superior to us as if they were trying to make us feel inferior, then we are closer to appreciating not only what they have, but what we could be. That is, if we are willing to be very self-aware and self-critical of our *own* inclinations to be defensively reactive, i.e., our own fears or hatreds or inclinations to be threatened by truly good, or beautiful, or ingenious people, we may very likely be less hostile, resentful, and negative to them. We may also find that, as we learn to accept more completely the highest values and qualities in others, we may be able to accept our own high qualities and values in a less frightened way. Of course it can work the other way, too. As we learn to accept our own accomplishments or talents without embarrassment, discomfort, defensiveness, or false humility, we may be better able to accept them in others as well.

What Is the Self?

Interest in the self, what it is and how it develops, is not a recent phenomenon. As a theoretical concept, the self has ebbed and flowed with the currents of philosophical and psychological pondering since the seventeenth century when the French mathematician and philosopher, René Descartes, first discussed the "cognito," or self, as a thinking substance. With Descartes pointing the way, the self was subjected to the vigorous philosophical examinations of such thinkers as Leibnitz, Locke, Hume, and Berkeley. As psychology evolved from philosophy as a separate entity, the self, as a related construct, moved along with it. However, as the tides of behaviorism swept the shores of psychological thinking during the first forty years of this century, the self all but disappeared as a theoretical or empirical construct of any stature. Study of the self was not something which could be easily investigated under rigidly controlled laboratory conditions. As a consequence, the subject was not considered an appropriate one for scientific pursuit. Nonetheless, the concept was kept alive during the early part of the twentieth century, by such men as Cooley,[3] Mead,[4] Dewey,[5] and James.[6] During the period since World War II, the concept of self has been revived and has exhibited remarkable vitality. For example, Allport writes:

In very recent years the tide has turned. Perhaps without being fully aware of the historical situation, many psychologists have commenced to embrace what two decades ago would have been considered a heresy. They have re-introduced self and ego unashamedly and, as if to make up for lost time, have employed ancillary concepts such as self-image, self-actualization, self-affirmation, phenomenal ego, ego-involvement, ego-striving, and many other hyphenated elaborations which to experimental positivism still have a slight flavor of scientific obscenity.[7]

THE EGO

Although there is no single, universally accepted definition of the self, many psychologists accept a distinction between two aspects of the self— one inferred by an external observer and one of which the person himself is aware. The *inferred self*, that is, the personality structure that represents the core of decision-making, planning, and defensiveness, can be understood best by an external observer (who in fact, may detect unconscious features of which the individual is unaware). This dimension of the self is commonly called the *ego*, a term borrowed from Freud, though not adhering exactly to the Freudian definition. The ego, specifically, is a construction from behavior, a hypothetical construct that, though it cannot be directly observed, can be *inferred* from one's behavior. For example, we speak of a person as having a weak or a strong ego based on how we have observed that person behave under given conditions. The ego is the primary agent of personality which is inferred on the basis of certain observed effects. In a sense, our concept of ego is similar to our concept of electricity, i.e., even though we cannot see electricity we can still know what it does by defining it in terms of its functions and effects. Just as we can assess electric current as weak or strong, in terms of its effects on fuses, gauges, or light bulbs, so we can estimate one's ego as being strong or weak in terms of certain behavioral consequences.

In the language of psychoanalytic psychology, personality is usually thought of as having three distinct components: the *id*, the *ego*, and the *superego*. The id is unconscious and is the source of basic urges and impulses. The id, according to Freud, "has no organization and unified will, only an impulsion to obtain satisfaction for the instinctual needs in accordance with the pleasure principle . . . the id knows no value, no good and evil, no morality."[8] In a manner of speaking, it is that part of each of us that demands vengeance if we are hurt or immediate gratification if we are in need. The superego is synonymous with conscience and is at the other extreme of what has been termed the id. Freud has defined the superego as "the representative of all moral restrictions, the advocate of the impulse toward perfection; in short, it is as much as we have been able to apprehend psychologically of what people call the 'higher' things in human life."[9] It is that part of each of us which may say, "No, you shouldn't," if vengeance is our goal or "No, you mustn't," if immediate gratification of an impulse is our objective. This is where one's ego comes into play. The ego is that part of personality which is in contact with external reality. It is responsible for perceiving inner and outer reality, for regulating behavior, and for controlling our impulses. Think of it this way: the ego is the personality's executive secretary whose job it is to screen and temper the demands and impulses of the id and superego prior to those demands and impulses being expressed in behavior. When we say that a person has a weak ego, we are also saying that he finds it difficult to check his impulses, or he has low frustration tolerance, or he has a hard time postponing gratification, or he can be easily hurt, or any combination of these possibilities. In other words, a strong ego can more successfully hold id-superego demands in check in order to achieve a healthy balance between what one wants and what one can have. In short, the ego perceives, reality-tests, selects, and rejects behavior patterns. It is responsible for learning and for the control and suppression of basic impulses.[10]

THE SELF

Whereas the ego is constructed from behavior and inferred by others, the self, as we will use it here, is that part of each of us of which we are consciously aware. Acquiring a self-concept involves a slow process of differentiation as a person gradually emerges into focus out of his total world of awareness and defines progressively more clearly just who and what he is. Jersild is probably as clear as anyone about what the self is when he says:

> A person's self is the sum total of all he can call his. The self includes, among other things, a system of ideas, attitudes, values, and commitments. The self is a person's total subjective environment; it is the distinctive center of experience and significance. The self constitutes a person's inner world as distinguished from the outer world consisting of all other people and things.[11]

As the *self* has evolved in psychological literature, it has come to have two distinct meanings. From one point of view it is defined as a person's attitudes and feelings about himself, and from another it is regarded as a group of psychological processes which influence behavior and adjustment. The first meaning can be looked at as a *self-as-object* definition, as it conveys a person's attitudes, feelings, and perceptions of himself as an object. That is, it is as if one could stand outside of himself and evaluate what he sees from a more or less detached point of view. In this sense, the self is what a person thinks of himself. The second meaning may be called the *self-as-process* definition. In other words, the self is a doer, in the sense that it includes an active group of processes such as thinking, remembering, and perceiving.

It is through the door of the self that one's personality is expressed. How the self is expressed is a complex phenomena meaning different things to different people. It is one person's brashness and another person's shyness; it is one person's sympathetic giving and another person's selfish hoarding; it is one person's trusting nature and another person's suspiciousness. An individual's image of himself is constructed from his conception of the "sort of person I am." All of us have beliefs about our relative value and our ultimate worth. We feel superior to some persons but inferior to others. We may or may not feel as worthy or as able as most other individuals, and much of our energy is spent trying to maintain or modify our beliefs about how adequate we are (or would like to be).

William James, a psychologist both of and beyond his time, has observed that how a person feels about himself depends entirely on what he *backs* himself to be and do. For example in a famous passage James wrote:

> I am not often confronted by the necessity of standing by one of my empirical selves and relinquishing the rest. Not that I would not, if I could, be both handsome and fat and well-dressed, and a great athlete, and make a million a year, be a wit, a bon-vivant, and lady-killer, as well as a philosopher, a philanthropist, statesman, warrior, and African explorer, as well as a "tone-poet" and saint. But the thing is simply impossible. The millionaire's work would run counter to the saint's; the bon-vivant and the philanthropist would trip each other up; the philosopher and lady-killer could not keep house in the same tenement of clay . . . to make any one of them actual, the rest must more or less be suppressed. . . . So the seeker of his truest, strongest, deepest self must review the list carefully, and pick out the one on which to stake his salvation. All other selves thereupon become unreal, but the fortunes of this self are real. Its failures are real failures, its triumphs real triumphs, carrying shame and gladness with them. . . .
>
> I, who for the time have staked my all on being a psychologist, am mortified if others know more psychology than I. But I am contented to wallow in the grossest ignorance of Greek. My deficiencies there give me no sense of personal humiliation at all.[12]

I think it is clear from the above quotation that how James felt about himself depended, in large measure, on how he saw himself ranking in comparison to others *who also backed themselves to be psychologists.* In other words, we might generalize that our feelings of self-worth and self-esteem grow in part from our perceptions of where we see ourselves standing in relation to persons whose skills, abilities, talents, and aptitudes are similar to our own. For example, if a math major "backs" himself to be an excellent math student, but can get only C's or if an athlete "backs" himself to be an excellent athlete, but can make only the third team, then each will either have to rationalize their sub-par performances or lower their expectations for themselves or go on to something else in which greater success is more possible. As soon as one's performance in what he backs himself to be is less than his minimum level of self-imposed expectations, then the loss of self-esteem will be greater than its gain. As high self-esteem usually comes from being able to do one or two things at least as good as, if not a trifle better than most other people it would be difficult to maintain, not to mention enhance, self-esteem if one saw himself consistently finishing somewhere behind the group with which he was comparing himself.

Self-imposed expectations refer to our personal levels of aspirations and these expectations are very much connected to our feelings of self-esteem because they help establish what we regard as either success or failure. What is a success or enhancing experience for one can be a failure or deflating experience for another. For example, I remember a C I received in an undergraduate course which I regarded as particularly difficult. That C, however, was quite consistent with my expectations and level of aspiration for performance and I felt it was a minor, if not a major, success. On the other hand, a friend of mine who also received a C in that course viewed this as a total failure, because his expectations and level of aspiration were not lower than a B. In other words, by getting that C I maintained my self-esteem, because it was an even money return on my personal investment in the course. My friend lost a measure of self-esteem, *because the return was less than his personal investment.* By starting out with different amounts of personal investment, we had different expectations for a personal return in order to maintain our original investments. In a similar vein, both of us could have enhanced our self-esteem if we had received a grade which *exceeded* our original levels of aspiration.

Although each person's level of aspiration determines to a large extent what he interprets as failure or success, and hence what either adds to or takes from his self-esteem, another factor worth considering is one's history of successes and failures. For example, to fail at something is more tolerable and less apt to threaten our self-esteem if we have had a history of success in that particular endeavor. Some cases in point: a girl who has had many boyfriends is not likely to sour on boys if she loses one, but a girl with few boyfriends could; a team with a 10–0 record is not apt to give up after losing the eleventh game, but a 0–10 team might; a .350 baseball player is not particularly discouraged when he strikes out, but a .150 player is; a student with a long string of above average grades is not likely to quit school if he fails his first course, but a below average student who fails his tenth course might. In other words, the impact of falling short of one's personal aspirations stands to be a less self-deflating experience, if one's list of successes in that endeavor exceeds his tally of failures.

How Does the Self Become Known?

Ever since William James, it has been customary to speak of an infant's consciousness as a "big, blooming, buzzing confusion." Although the accuracy of this description may never be determined, it nonetheless seems pretty certain that the infant's consciousness includes no awareness of himself as an individual. In fact, the newborn infant apparently does not even know where his own body leaves off and his environment begins. Since we cannot directly assess the nature of a child's growing awareness, we must appraise the stages through which a child becomes aware of himself largely through an inferential process.

BEGINNINGS OF AWARENESS

Self-awareness develops slowly as the child recognizes the distinction between self and not-self, between his body and the remainder of his visible environment. Only gradually does he learn to recognize and sort out his body parts, name, feelings, and behavior as integral parts of a single *me* and build a cluster of beliefs about himself. His serendipitous discoveries of the various parts of his body and the recognition of his own voice are the beginnings of his growing awareness of personal properties and resources. It seems likely that a child's body-awareness furnishes a common core around which self-reference becomes organized, although later he does learn to distinguish self from the physical body. From his behavior we can reasonably infer that soon after he is born he is flooded with a wave of sensory impressions—sensations that exist in his body when he's hungry, sensations from the surface of his body when it is hot or cold, sensations that reach him through his eyes and ears, and probably also sensations of taste and smell. As near as can be judged from a child's earliest reactions, he is not at first able to make a clear distinction between his early sensory experiences and the stimuli which elicit them. For example, if you touch a hot stove you know what is causing the pain. When something hot touches an infant he probably doesn't know where the pain comes from. The birth of self-awareness very likely occurs when a child begins to make a distinction between his sensations and the conditions which produce them.

As a growing child's experience broadens, his sense of personhood gradually extends to include things outside of himself with which he feels personal involvement. When we think of *me* or *my*, we may include such things as our home, possessions we own, groups we are loyal to, the values we subscribe to, and, most particularly, the people we love. The process of identification is an important part of coming to know and expand one's definition of self. Allport describes this process more fully:

> A child . . . who identifies with his parent is definitely extending his sense of self, as he does likewise through his love for pets, dolls, or other possessions, animate or inanimate. . . .

> As we grow older we identify with groups, neighbors, and nation as well as with possessions, clothes, and home. They become matters of importance to us in a sense that other people's families, nations, or possessions are not. Later in life the process of extension may go to great lengths, through the development of loyalties and interests focused on abstractions and on moral and religious values.[13]

INFLUENCE OF SOCIAL ROLES
AND OTHERS' EXPECTATIONS

To some extent, a person's sense of identity is influenced by other peoples' appraisal of the social roles he happens to be in. For example, if the group regards an individual as a leader, a solid Joe, a follower, a good athlete, or a social rum-dum, he is likely to regard himself in the same way. In other words, a person tends to adopt the values and attitudes that are expected of one in his position. In so doing, he begins to get a certain kind of feedback; this in turn reinforces how he feels about himself. I recall a student I had some years ago who was elected chairman of a group of about fifteen students whose assignment it was to work as a total group on a research paper which the chairman would present to the whole class. The lad chosen was a shy, quiet sort of person, I thought, but he did such a remarkable job of presenting the paper that the entire class broke into spontaneous applause when he concluded. (I think it may be that most students are so prepared to be bored by dull presentations made by their peers that violations of their expectations are welcome reliefs indeed.) After class I expressed to the young man what a great job I thought he had done and he responded with something like this: "You know, I was scared to death. I didn't think I could do it! But then I got to thinking about it and I figured that if they wanted me to be a chairman, I'd *act* like a chairman—even if I had to fake it. And you know, that's what I did—faked it. From our first meeting on I just took charge like I had all the confidence in the world. And you know, a strange thing happened. The other kids in the group began to treat me as if I really *was* confident. They seemed to expect me to have answers and be able to organize and pretty soon I didn't know if I was faking it or if that's the way I really felt." Not only did this student learn that he had potential leadership abilities, which was an important discovery in itself, but *he also learned that how he behaved influenced how others behaved toward him.* Although, in this boy's words, he had to "fake" the initial leadership behavior, it may be important for us to remember that all the faking in the world would not have helped his cause if he did not have leadership potential to begin with. By "faking it" he discovered in himself latent qualities which had always been there.

The idea of a person responding in terms of what he thinks another person expects of him is not a new one, but it is receiving increasing attention as a phenomenon in psychological research. For example, Rosenthal[14] and Friedman,[15] have demonstrated that at least one very important variable which has not been controlled in past psychological experimentation is the variable of *what the experimenter expects to happen.* In other words, the result the scientist *expects* to get is more likely to occur than any other.

Haimowitz, has extended the "expectation for behavior" idea to an examination of how criminals are "made" and writes:

> Gradually, over the years, if he (the Criminal) comes to expect of himself what his neighbors expect of him, he becomes a professional criminal. . . . As a professional criminal, he has standards to live up to, friends who will help him when in trouble, . . . tell him where the police are lax and where strict. . . . At twelve, fourteen, sixteen, or eighteen he has come to a conclusion about his career that ordinary boys may not make until they are twenty or even forty. And he could not have drifted into this career without the help of his family and neighbors who sought a scapegoat and unwittingly suggested to him that he become an outlaw.[16]

The basic unit of interaction that concerns us here is a simple one. One person acts and in so doing intentionally or unintentionally expresses a part of his self, something of what he is, or thinks he is, or hopes he is. A second person responds to the first person's behavior. Very frequently the second person's reactions convey approval or disapproval, acceptance or rejection. The effects of these different responses to behavior soon become quite apparent. Behavior that results in attention or approval or affection tends to be repeated more and more frequently. Behavior that leads to withdrawal or indifference or rejection occurs less and less frequently. There are, of course, exceptions to this general tendency as, for example, when a person behaves in order to obtain a response, any response, in order to bring attention to himself or take it away from someone else.

However, because of the human capacity for self-consciousness the process of developing a sense of self is not a matter of simple reinforcement. That is, an individual's behavioral patterns arouse responses within himself leading to perceptions of himself which become stable. As an illustration, if a student has had reasonably good success in school and has high personal expectations for maintaining a high achievement level, he is not likely to respond to the expectations that his less achievement-oriented buddies may have for him to study less often. On the other hand, if it is more important for a student to be socially accepted than it is to get high grades, then that student may, in fact, be more susceptible to the shifting whims of others' expectations. Riesman[17] has described these different modes of responding to either internal or external expectations as *inner-directedness* or *other-directedness*.

An important first step along the road of self-understanding is the ability to be able to discriminate between those expectations which come from inside the self and those which come from outside the self. Rogers,[18] for example, speaking from his many years of experience as a psychotherapist, has noted that when an individual moves away from compulsively "meet-

Sometimes it is difficult not to listen to others' expectations.

ing others' expectations," he becomes free to listen to his own expectations and to become the person he *feels* he wants to be.

Just as it is likely that a certain behavior can arouse certain expectations in the minds of others for future behavior of a similar sort, it is also possible that perceived expectations may trigger behavior which may not have been produced if those expectations had not been there in the first place. Let's untangle this with a few examples. A ninth-grade girl I counseled some years ago told me of an incident with her mother which may help make this idea of expectations clearer. She brought home her first ninth-grade report card with three C's and a D in math. Her mother looked at it and said something like, "The way you think when numbers are involved it's no wonder you got a D. Besides, I was never any good in math so I'm not surprised you're not either. You'll probably be lucky to pass." The girl received a somewhat similar response from her father and the matter was dropped. As a consequence of this feedback (and other feedback like it), the girl nurtured the impression that she was expected to do poorly. That is, her mother and father did not *expect* her to do well in math. In other words, her behavior (a D in math) evoked certain expectations ("You'll be lucky to pass.") for this girl's future behavior, which she began to believe as being true.

Let's take another example. During an interview I had with a seventeen-year-old delinquent boy who had just been returned to the reformatory, I asked him why he had gotten into so much trouble while he was back home for three weeks. He screwed up his face and replied, "Man, what did you expect. The whole neighborhood knew I was at this place for nine months. Man, I wanted to do good—I tried, but even my grandfather wouldn't hardly talk to me. Some of the parents in the neighborhood—some with kids in more trouble than me—wouldn't even let their kids talk to me. They would say something like there goes that kid from the vocational school, watch out for him. They had their minds made up before they even looked to see if I had changed. Hell with them. They want me to be bad—I'll *be* bad." In other words, it was clear to this boy that people in his neighborhood *expected* him to play the role of the delinquent boy and he ended up behaving in terms of what he perceived their expectations to be for him. True, his delinquency history determined their expectations, but their expectations facilitated the very behavior they were opposed to in the first place. This doesn't excuse the boy's behavior, but it does help us understand it. Expectations for behavior have a strong influence on what kind of behavior is expressed. Since this is one of the themes basic to this book, more will be said about this in subsequent chapters.

INFLUENCE OF SOCIAL INTERACTION

The self grows within a social framework. If, for example, you were to make a list of as many personality characteristics you could think of, you would find that each is influenced in some way or other by social interaction. Some, like friendliness or shyness are social by definition; that is, one cannot be friendly or shy except in relation to other people. Other characteristics, like creativeness or independence, are less social by definition. Although one can be creative or independent in solitude, it is difficult to see how one could acquire such traits apart from social interaction.

Mead, in describing the social interaction processes involved in the development of the self writes:

> The self arises in conduct, when the individual becomes a social object in experience to himself. This takes place when the individual assumes the attitude or uses the gesture which another individual would use and responds to it himself or tends to so respond. . . . The child gradually becomes a social being in his own experience, and he acts toward himself in a manner analogous to that in which he acts toward others.[19]

This description may be made clear by a single example. Let's say that a child play-acts being mother or father. In his play, he talks to himself as his mother and father have talked to him, and he responds to this imaginary talk of his mother and father. Eventually, the end result of speaking to himself as others have spoken to him is that he comes to perceive himself as a social object to which other people respond. He learns to conceive of himself as having characteristics which are perceived and encouraged by others. For example, as a young child grows he learns that words such as cute, good, bad, intelligent, dumb, heavy, lazy, shy, etc., are attributed to him as a person; it is through his long immersion in an interpersonal stream of continual reflected appraisals from other people (particularly people who *matter* to him) that he gradually develops a picture of himself which he then strives to maintain.

Perhaps we can appreciate the importance of social interaction if we look at an example in which there was virtually no interaction at all. Davis[20] reported the case of Anna, a five-year-old child, who was found tied to a chair in a secluded room. She had apparently been kept there for several years by her grandfather who found her unbearable because she was a second illegitimate child. When found she was unable to move or talk. Her leg muscles had atrophied to the point that her flaccid feet fell forward. She was malnourished and showed no response to sound or sight. Within three days of being taken out of this isolated environment she was able to sit up if placed in a sitting position and could move her arms and hands. She was massaged, placed on a high vitamin diet, and given lots of attention. At first she neither smiled nor cried and was almost expressionless, although later she began to smile if coaxed and showed signs of temper if physically restrained. Ten days after the first visit, the examiners found the child more alert and able to fix her attention. She showed taste and visual discrimination, smiled more often, and began to display ritualistic motions with her hands and a series of tricks that any infant performs. Two months after being found, Anna ceased to improve. In nine months she had learned little. She could not chew or drink from a glass or control her bodily processes, and she could barely stand even when holding on to some support.

At this time Anna was placed in a foster home in the keeping of a warm, supporting foster mother. Within a month of this placement she had learned to eat, hold a glass, and feed herself. Improvement continued until she understood many instructions and babbled, although she could not use words. Motor ability increased, but her initiative was low. Again she seemed to hit a plateau and was placed in a home for retarded children. In 1942 she was speaking at about the level of a two-year-old. She reflected signs of being socialized, used a spoon, comformed to toilet habits, loved her dolls, and spoke a few simple sentences. She died shortly thereafter at an estimated age of ten and one-half.

Records revealed that as a baby she had appeared normal, indeed attractive. The matter of hereditary endowment is open to speculation, for the mother was dull mentally, and there was doubt as to her father's identity. Nonetheless, there is little doubt but that Anna's lack of social interaction and environmental stimulation contributed heavily to her retarded growth as a total human being.

Social interaction is the medium of exchange through which one hones his perceptions of the outside world, develops his interpersonal skills, extends his intelligence, and acquires attitudes about himself. As Tenenbaum[21] and Deutsch and Brown,[22] among others, have demonstrated in their research with the disadvantaged, impoverished children who grow up with restricted cultural and social opportunities suffer both intellectually and emotionally. Suffice it to say, interaction with others is an important social vitamin in one's daily nourishment of an expanding self-awareness.

Mechanisms To Defend the Self

Whether we are always aware of it or not, each of us uses certain "defense" mechanisms to help us "preserve" or "protect" our self-systems. Indeed, our effectiveness in using certain defenses has a lot to do with how successful we are in meeting the daily stresses and strains of living. Although defense mechanisms are necessary, they can prove debilitating, if one uses them, however consciously or unconsciously, to avoid assuming responsibility, to abstain from taking risks now and then, or to manufacture excuses for persisting in behavior which may be immature and self-defeating.

As each person's self is the integrating core of his personality, threats to its worth or adequacy are quickly viewed as potential intimidations to that individual's very center of existence. Defense mechanisms help us perserve our integrity and sense of personal worth when we find ourselves in ego-involved stress situations. For example, the fan who proudly announces, "my team won today," may find some measure of importance by "identifying" himself with a successful team (Have you ever noted how an entire student body exhibits a kind of "collective chest puffing" after their team wins a big one?); the student who flunks an exam may "project" the blame for his performance onto the instructor's lack of fairness or the poor construction of the test; the student who cheats on an exam may "rationalize" that everyone else cheats and he might as well, too. The protection of self from possible devaluation and thus from anxiety is the very essence of the defensive functions of these mechanisms.

The use of defense mechanisms is a normal human reaction, unless they are used to such an extreme that they begin to interfere with the maintenance of self-esteem rather than aiding it. In a sense, the self, like a soldier busy defending himself against an enemy's charge, may break down under the very weight of its defensive activities. In addition, these mechanisms, necessary as they are, have certain drawbacks. They are not usually adaptive in the sense of realistically coping with problems. For example, a person who continually rationalizes away his blunders is not likely to profit from his mistakes on subsequent occasions. Defense mechanisms involve a fair degree of self-deception and reality distortion. Furthermore, they function on relatively unconscious levels and therefore are not subject to the usual checks and balances of more conscious processes. In fact, we usually resent having someone call our attention to them because once they become conscious they do not serve their purposes as well.

Defense mechanisms can be best understood in view of the *objective* they serve, which is to safeguard the integrity and worth of the self. Thus, it is only as we conceive of an active, dynamic self which struggles to maintain a certain stability that they make sense. Once we view the "self" in this framework, we may be better able to understand our ability to protect the self by utilizing defense mechanisms to change the so-called "facts" so that they fit our personal needs.

With this small introduction, let us now turn to a consideration of the more important of these defense mechanisms along with a brief discussion of how each functions.

DENIAL OF REALITY

Sometimes we manage to avoid disagreeable realities by ignoring or refusing to acknowledge them. This inclination is exemplified in a great many of our everyday behaviors. We turn away from unpleasant sights; we refuse to discuss unpleasant topics; we ignore or disclaim criticism; and sometimes we refuse to face our real problems. A vain woman may deny a vision problem in order to avoid wearing glasses; an insecure middle-aged man may deny his years by pursuing younger girls; or a low self-esteem student may deny his competency by attributing a high grade on a test to "luck." Parents, for example, are notoriously blind when it comes to the defects of their offspring. I recall one mother, whose ten-year-old boy had been diagnosed as brain-damaged by a team of experts, who asserted that his "head was just developing slower than the rest of him, that's all." The common adages, "None is so blind as he who will not see," and "Love is blind," perhaps illustrate even more clearly our tendency to look away from those things which are incompatible with our wishes, desires, and needs. This mechanism does, indeed, guard us from painful experiences. However, like the proverbial ostrich who buries his head in the sand, denial may also get in the way of our "seeing" things which might otherwise facilitate progress toward more effective living and greater maturity of self.

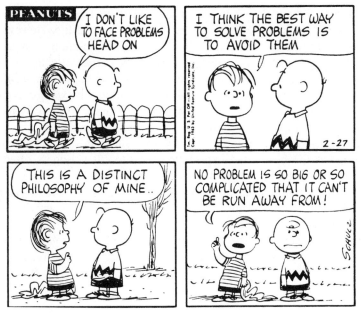

It may sound fine in theory, but it seldom works in practice.

FANTASY

Not only do we frequently deny unpleasant reality, but we are also inclined to "embellish" our perceptions so that the world is seen more as we would like it to be. Fantasy is stimulated by frustrated desires and grows primarily out of mental images associated with need gratification. It can be productive or nonproductive. Productive fantasy can be used constructively in solving problems, as in creative imagination, or it can be a kind of nonproductive wish-fulfilling activity which compensates for a *lack* of achievement rather than stimulating or promoting achievement. James Thurber's *The Secret Life of Walter Mitty* is a classic example of how one can achieve wished-for status by imagining that he is rich, powerful, and respected. Einstein, on the other hand, had mental pictures or "fantasies" which led to productive hypotheses, formulas, and solutions.

Many of our fantasies are ready-made for us in the form of magazines, books, movies, and soap operas. Not infrequently we escape from our own self-perceptions by identifying ourselves, fantasy fashion, with the hero or heroine, bravely facing and surmounting their problems with them, and sharing in their adventures or triumphs.

The capacity to remove ourselves temporarily from unpleasant reality into a more affable world of fantasy has considerable therapeutic value.

Fantasy may, for example, add the dash of excitement and interest we need to motivate us to greater efforts toward our goals in real life. However, the individual who *consistently* turns to fantasy as his solution to a troublesome reality is in danger psychologically. It is particularly under conditions of extreme frustration and deprivation that our fantasies are likely to get out of hand and during times of this sort we should be wary of solutions conjured by the mind's eye. For example, Bettelheim[23] found that at the concentration camps of Dachau and Buchenwald, "the longer the time a prisoner had spent in camp, the less true to reality were his daydreams; so much so that the hopes and expectations of the old prisoners often took the form of eschatological and messianic hopes."

Nonetheless, there is substantial evidence to suggest that fantasizing and daydreaming is not only normal, but an almost universal activity among people of both sexes.[24] It is when a person uses it as a permanent and not a temporary escape that he is apt to get himself into trouble. It is one thing to build a castle in the sky; it is quite another to try to live in it.

COMPENSATION

Compensation is an attempt to disguise the existence of a weak or undesirable characteristic by emphasizing a more positive one. This defensive reaction takes many forms. For example, a physically handicapped individual may attempt to overcome his handicap directly through increased effort and persistence. The heroic and successful efforts of the fine actress, Patricia Neal, following her stroke is an example of what sheer effort and persistence can accomplish. Usually, however, compensatory reactions are more indirect. That is, there is an effort to either substitute for the defect or to draw attention away from it. As illustrations, the girl who regards herself as unattractive may develop an exceptionally winning personality; the uncoordinated boy may turn from athletics to scholastics; the mediocre, insecure nobody may become the Chief Imperial Wizard of the Ku Klux Klan. Indeed, a whole science of cosmetics and dress has developed which seems to have as its major objectives the modification or alteration of the human anatomy, its features, expressions, and protrusions. The short man is made to look tall, the fat girl thin, the colorless one glamorous, the flat one curvaceous, and so on.

Not all compensatory behaviors are desirable or useful. For example, a person who feels unloved may become sexually promiscuous or homosexual; the boy who feels inferior may become the neighborhood bully; the person who feels insecure may eat or drink too much; the individual who feels inadequate may brag too much.

We constantly compare ourselves with others and frequently gauge our worth in terms of how we see ourselves in relation to other people's status, achievements, and possessions. This can lead to strong motivation toward at least average, and if possible, superior achievement. In meeting these conditions, compensating behaviors may help, but where they become exaggerated or take antisocial forms, they hinder rather than assist a person express his potential.

INTROJECTION (INTERNALIZATION)

Introjection is a process in which a person internalizes threatening situations. That is, he incorporates into his own personality structure the achievements or qualities of those who threaten him. We can see examples of this in the behavior of a young child as he gradually learns and accepts as his own the various social boundaries and value attitudes of his parents. By becoming like his parents, it is then possible for him to regulate his own behavior in terms of internalized values and protect himself from possible infractions of rules, thus avoiding social retaliation and punishment. The saying, "If you can't beat them, join them," reflects the use of this mechanism in everyday life. This "identification with the aggressor" behavior is primarily a defense mechanism of the weak against the strong. Prisoners, for example, often attempt to reduce the threat to their existence by becoming "informers" or otherwise cultivating the favor of guards whom they hate and fear. The dynamics behind a threatened prisoner's frantic efforts to win a guard's favor are basically no different than those of a frightened, intimidated college student who goes out of his way to be friendly to a professor who terrifies him. Fundamentally the thinking is, "If I'm on his side maybe he won't be harsh on me. Or better still, maybe he won't give me a low grade." Whether it is the frightened prisoner or the intimidated student the dynamics are the same, namely, a total effort to incorporate, to "introject," those characteristics of that person who is seen as most threatening.

PROJECTION

Projection is a means by which we (1) relegate the blame for our own shortcomings, mistakes, and transgressions to others, and (2) attribute to others our own unacceptable impulses, thoughts, and desires. It is perhaps most commonly apparent in our tendency to blame others for our own mistakes. The athlete who fails to make the team may feel sure the coach was unfair; an exwife may conclude: "It's all his fault"; a bruised seven-year-old may exclaim, "It wasn't my fault, he hit me first"; the baseball player called out on strikes may suggest that the umpire not delay in consulting an ophthalmologist, and so it goes. Fate and bad luck are particularly overworked targets of projection. Even inanimate objects are not exempt from blame. The golfer who whiffs his tee shot may examine his driver as if expecting to find a hole in it or the three-year-old who tumbles from his hobby horse may accuse it or someone of deliberately throwing him off. Sometimes a person may ascribe ethically unacceptable desires and impulses to others while remaining blithely unaware of their internal origins within himself. For example, the individual with suppressed homosexual leanings may be the first to spot a wide assortment of homosexual tendencies or characteristics in other males. Or the girl who is frightened by her own very strong sexual urges may accuse men of "always being on the make."

Such projections help maintain our feelings of adequacy and self-esteem in the face of failure, and probably develop from the early realization that placing the blame on others for our own mistakes helps us to avoid social rejection and disapproval. This can, however, be carried to extremes. Some individuals are so busy looking for faults and shortcomings in *other* people that they never get around to examining their own, which ultimately deprives them of growing to higher levels of maturity.

RATIONALIZATION

Rationalization has two primary defensive objectives: (1) it helps us invent excuses for doing what we don't think we should do but want to do anyway, and (2) it aids us in softening the disappointment connected to not reaching a goal we had set for ourselves. Typically, it involves thinking up logical, socially acceptable reasons for our past, present, or future behavior. With not too much effort we can soon think of a reason for not getting up for an eight o'clock class ("It'll probably be a dull lecture anyway."), for going to a movie instead of studying ("There really isn't *that* much to do."), for smoking heavily ("The lung cancer and smoking relationship isn't conclusive and besides they'll soon have a cancer cure anyway.").

We have endless ways for justifying our behavior and protecting our adequacy and self-esteem. How many parents, for example, are honest enough to admit that the child they just spanked got spanked because they (the parents) were angry, without having to mask it with "It was for his own good," or "It hurt me more than it did him." Or how many students are honest enough to admit they cheated because they didn't know the material rather than cover it with "Everyone else does, so I *have* to in order to pass." If a parent had to face his anger or if a student had to face his lack of savvy, each would probably feel ashamed and guilty. Hence, the rationalizations, the excuses.

Sometimes, of course, it is difficult to know where an objective consideration of facts leaves off and rationalization begins. Two good behavioral symptoms of excessive rationalization are: (1) hunting for reasons to justify behavior and beliefs, and (2) getting emotional (angry, guarded,

Some people's rationalizations never seem to end.

"up-tight") when someone questions the reasons we offer. Should these re-actions occur, it is usually a good time to take pause and examine how factual our reasons really are. The price of excessive rationalization, of course, is self-deception, for if we accept reasons for our behavior which are not true ones, we are less likely to profit from our errors. Carried to extremes this could lead eventually to the development of false beliefs or delusions sustained in the face of contradictory evidence.

REPRESSION

Repression is a defensive reaction through which painful or dangerous thoughts and desires are excluded from consciousness. It has often been labeled as selective forgetting, but it is more in the nature of selective remembering. It is a way of protecting one's personal equilibrium by for-getting experiences which are upsetting. Repression is by no means always complete. Vague feelings of unworthiness, insecurity, and guilt often are signs of incomplete repression. Along this line I recall a client of mine who struggled for several months working through the nagging guilt feel-ings he always experienced whenever he felt sexually attracted to a girl.

He knew it was in some way related to his childhood and his mother's attitudes, but he didn't know exactly how. During one of our sessions, as he was sorting through his buried file of memories, he recalled a time when he was eight years old when his mother caught him and a seven-year-old neighbor girl in the basement, both with pants down, exploring each other. He was spanked, admonished for being a terrible, nasty boy, and sent directly to bed. So painful was that experience that he soon "forgot" it, but it served nonetheless as an unconscious hatchery from which guilt was spawned whenever he had any kind of sexual feeling about a girl. It was the key to insight, and once he had unlocked that memory and was able to look at it in connection with a mother who had neurotic fears about sex, he was in a better position to examine his own fears.

The repression of undesirable impulses and experiences not only demands considerable energy, but it also hinders healthy personality integration. A more realistic confrontation of problems is always more conducive to good mental health and positive self-development.

REACTION FORMATION

Reaction formation refers to the development of conscious attitudes and behavior patterns which are opposite to what one really feels and would like to do. It is a way of suppressing impulses and desires which a person thinks might get him into trouble, if he actually carried them out. Reaction formation can be recognized by its extreme and intolerant attitudes, which are usually far out of proportion to the importance of the situation. For example, self-appointed guardians of the public's morals who voluntarily devote their time to reading "dirty" books and magazines, investigating burlesque shows, and who are generally obsessed with censoring all things related to sex, alcohol, and other alleged vices are frequently found to have unusually high impulses in the same direction themselves. Indeed, the most aggressive crusaders are very often fighting their own suppressed impulses as well as condemning the expression of such impulses in others.

In everyday behavior, reaction formation may take the form of being excessively kind to a person we do not like, or of developing a "who cares how other people feel" attitude to conceal feelings of loneliness and a craving for acceptance, or of assuming an air of bravado when one's adequacy is threatened, e.g., "That test tomorrow doesn't frighten me . . . much."

Reaction formation has adjustive value insofar as it helps us to maintain socially approved behavior and to control unacceptable impulses. On the other hand, this mechanism, too, is self-deceptive and can lead to exaggerated and rigid fears or beliefs which could lead to excessive harshness or severity in dealing with the values of others and ourselves.

DISPLACEMENT

Displacement refers to the shift of emotion or fantasy away from the person or object toward which it was originally directed to a more neutral or less dangerous person or object. For example, the man upbraided by his boss may suppress the anger he feels toward the boss because he knows he would be in deep trouble if he expressed his feelings. So what does he do? He comes home and hollers at his wife for not having dinner ready and yells at the children for being too noisy. Not infrequently the smallest incident may serve as the trigger which releases pent-up emotional feelings in a torrent of displaced anger and abuse. A young housewife had been admonished by her husband for not being more efficient and later in the same day lost her purse while shopping. On her way home she was halted by a patrolman for speeding. That was the final straw. She exploded with a volley of abuse on the startled officer with questions ranging all the way from "Haven't you anything better to do than chase women?" to blaming him generally for the city's traffic condition which he should have been working on rather than harassing busy, civic-minded citizens for barely exceeding the speed limit.

Through a process of symbolic association, displacement can be extremely indirect and complex. For example, "beating" a disliked rival at a game or in an athletic match may symbolically represent his destruction. Under the guise of "I just want to help" many a next-door neighbor has indulged in destructive and vindictive gossip as a means of expressing anger, resentment, and hostility.

Displacement is a valuable mechanism because it enables one to vent dangerous emotional impulses without risking loss of love and possible retaliation, and without the necessity of even recognizing the person for whom such feelings were originally intended. By displacing his bottled-up anger on his wife and children, the man maintains his feelings of respect and cordiality toward his domineering boss. The wife who released her rage on the patrolman can more easily avoid ambivalent feelings toward a husband who demands she be more tidy.

Unfortunately, displacements can become too deviant and can result in continual avoidance of situations which could be more efficiently handled by a more direct approach. On the whole, one is psychologically better off when he learns to express and discuss his feelings with the person at whom the feelings are intended in the first place, rather than aim them at someone who does not even know what they're all about.

EMOTIONAL INSULATION

In emotional insulation, the individual attempts to reduce his needs and fears by withdrawing into a sort of shell of passivity. As a consequence of prior hurts and disappointments, we sometimes learn to garrison ourselves not only by lowering our level of aspiration but by curbing the extent of our emotional involvement in the achievement of our goals. For example, the girl disappointed in her first real love may be extremely cautious about allowing herself to get emotionally involved on subsequent occasions. She may experience difficulty in "letting herself go" in the sense of entering into a close emotional relationship. Sometimes persons who have been badly bruised in the school of hard knocks develop a kind of emotional scar tissue and are often unable to either give or receive affection. Although persons of this kind may appear to be unusually self-sufficient, they are frequently victims of intense feelings of loneliness and anxiety.

Another way of emotionally insulating ourselves is to avoid competitive activities in which we may not rate favorably with others. For example, some persons will not engage in sports such as golf, bowling, or tennis, or card games such as bridge or poker unless they excel in them. In this way it is possible to minimize the possible "loss of face" that might result from doing less well than others.

Getting emotionally involved in the business of living does, indeed, involve certain "calculated risks." For example, there is always the possibility that the person we give our affection to may reject us or be taken from us by death. A healthy person operates on the assumption that the rewards of emotional involvement are worth the risks, even though he also knows that he shall inevitably experience pain and disappointments in life, too.

Used in mild dosages, emotional insulation is an important defense against too much hurt and disappointment. However, when used to the extent that a person becomes "an island onto himself," it can curtail a person's healthy and active participation in life and lead to eventual shallowness and blunting of emotional involvement. When one "dares not to hope" he ceases to grow.

REGRESSION

Regression is behavior involving a retreat, in the face of stress, to the use of behavioral patterns appropriate at earlier levels of development. It usually involves modification of behavior in the direction of more primitive, infantile expressions. For example, when a new addition to the family is brought home from the hospital, it is not uncommon for the older child, who may feel that his status is threatened, to regress or "go back" to bedwetting, baby-talk, thumb-sucking, demands for mother's attention, and other infantile behaviors. As other examples, the frustrated adult may return to the temper tantrums or sulkings which got him his way when growing up, a wife may run home to mother whenever there is discord, or a person may "cry like a baby" when experiencing great emotional pain.

Regression can perhaps be better understood if we remember a child's gradual shift from a position of helplessness and dependency on parents to one which demands increasing independent behavior and responsibility. This developmental process from dependency to independency is an arduous task, and it is common for all of us, confronting a harsher and more demanding adult world, to yearn now and then for the carefree and sheltered days of infancy and childhood. Consequently it is not surprising that in the face of severe stress we may retreat periodically from our adult status to an earlier level of growth and adjustment.

Regression is, however, more comprehensive than merely resorting to earlier behavior patterns when new ones have failed. In regression a person retreats to a less demanding personal status—one which involves lower personal goals and expectations and more readily accomplished satisfaction. For example, a wife who runs home to mother after an argument with her husband could be substituting her "little girl" need for mother's support for the more mature behavior involved in working the problem through with her husband. That is, by behaving like a hurt little girl, less is expected of her and the satisfactions are in the immediate reduction of anxiety.

Regression has its useful purposes, but, like other defensive mechanisms, when used as a primary mode of adjustment it can serve as a giant roadblock in one's route to more mature behavior.

SUBLIMATION

Sublimation involves the acceptance of a socially approved substitute goal for a drive whose normal channel of expression is blocked. This is a broader meaning than Freud gave the term, restricting the use of the mechanism to sexual motivation. It has, however, more meaning and wider significance when applied to different forms of motivation. There are, for example, many ways in which motives can be sublimated. As an illustration, curiosity about people, which can express itself in undesirable ways (voyeurism, sexual conversation, gossip, nosiness about the affairs of others) and lead to feelings of guilt, can be sublimated into art and medicine, where the human body can be viewed without conflict or reprisal, or it can be sublimated into counseling or psychology, where behavior and motives can be discussed at will. As another example, a young man with strong aggressive impulses may find suitable expression for those impulses in being a very assertive basketball player or maybe in being a hardnosed linebacker.

The defensive functions of sublimation are somewhat different from those of compensation because the motivation is different. Whereas compensation is founded on some kind of inadequacy, sublimation is directed more towards the reduction of guilt feelings associated with such motives as aggression, sex, curiosity, cruelty, and the maternal drive. A classic illustration of sublimation is the redirection of the maternal drive through teaching, social work, and recreation work, all of which provide opportunities for a wholesome expression of the desire for and love of children.

DEFENSE MECHANISM IN RETROSPECT

Understanding one's self involves, among other things, an awareness of the mechanisms we use to preserve the self. It is worth remembering that defense mechanisms are learned adjustive behaviors, that they function on relatively unconscious levels, and that they involve a certain amount of reality distortion and self-deception. Defense mechanisms serve the aims of adjustment by reducing conflict and frustration, and particularly because they stand in guard of the self, they function as a bulwark against more serious disturbances. Consequently they can be considered quite normal and desirable, except when they are used to an excessive degree and operate at the expense of a person's ultimate adaptive efficiency and continued personal progress toward greater maturity.

In Perspective

This chapter has introduced you to the nature of the self, ideas about how it becomes known, influences of self-awareness and social interaction on the growth of self, reasons for resisting personal growth and the functions and purposes of the defense mechanisms we use to preserve and protect the self.

One's concept of himself is a very personal possession. How we view ourselves is determined partially by how we perceive ourselves as *really being*, partially through how we view ourselves as ideally wanting to be, and partially through the expectations we perceive that others have for us. These are complex interrelated perceptual processes, no one of which is more important than the other. Depending on the individual, each of these three perceptions contributes more or less to our feelings of selfhood. For some, expressing their *real* self, whatever it may be, is most important and they struggle to stay as close in tune to the harmony of that inner self as is possible. For others, striving to become that ideal self is the guiding star which gives them their sense of purpose and direction. For still others, looking to and obeying the expectations of the world around them is their most satisfying mode of self-expression.

Social interaction is the primary medium through which we come to know ourselves. Self-awareness develops as we compare and contrast our physical bodies, skills, attitudes, and achievements to those of other people.

Some persons are concerned primarily with physical qualities and so this becomes their measuring stick for self-esteem. (I am stronger, handsomer, more beautiful, or more agile; therefore I am adequate.) Others are concerned primarily with qualities of the mind and so this becomes their barometer of self-esteem. (I know more answers, or I can solve more problems, or I am more creative; therefore I am adequate.)

Although complete, total knowledge about one's self is probably neither necessary nor possible, it is, nonetheless, possible to come closer to an understanding of our upper and lower limits, our private fears and guarded hopes, our secret dreams and wildest ambitions if we remain open to who we think we are, where we would like to go, and why we are headed in that direction to begin with.

[1] A. H. Maslow, "Neurosis as a Failure of Personal Growth," *Humanitas.* 1967, 2: 153–169.

[2] Maslow, p. 164.

[3] Charles H. Cooley, *Human Nature and Social Order.* New York: Charles Scribner's Sons, 1902.

[4] G. H. Mead, *Mind, Self and Society.* Chicago: University of Chicago Press, 1934.

[5] John Dewey, *Democracy and Education.* New York: The Macmillan Company, 1916.

[6] W. James, *Principles of Psychology, I.* New York: Henry Holt & Co., 1890.

[7] G. W. Allport, *Becoming.* New Haven: Yale University Press, 1955, pp. 104–105.

[8] Sigmund Freud, *New Introductory Lectures on Psycho Analysis.* W. J. H. Sprott, trans. New York: W. W. Norton & Company, Inc., 1933, pp. 104–105.

[9] Freud, p. 95.

[10] H. Hartmann, "Comments on the Psychoanalytic Study of the Child," in Anna Freud and others (Eds.), *The Psychoanalytic Study of the Child,* Vol. I. New York: International Universities Press, 1947, pp. 11–38.

[11] Arthur T. Jersild, *In Search of Self.* New York: Teachers College Press, Columbia University, 1952.

[12] James, p. 91.

[13] Allport, p. 45.

[14] Robert Rosenthal, *Experimenter Effects in Behavioral Research.* New York: Appleton-Century-Crofts, 1966.

[15] Neil Friedman, *The Social Nature of Psychological Research: The Psychological Experiment as a Social Interaction.* New York: Basic Books, Inc., 1967.

[16] Morris L. Haimowitz, "Criminals Are Made, Not Born," in M. L. Haimowitz and N. R. Haimowitz (Eds.), *Human Development, Selected Readings.* New York: Thomas Y. Crowell Company, 1960, p. 374.

[17] David Reisman, *Faces in the Crowd.* New Haven: Yale University Press, 1952.

[18] C. R. Rogers, *On Becoming a Person.* Boston: Houghton Mifflin Company, 1961, pp. 163–198.

[19] G. H. Mead, *Mind, Self, and Society: From the Standpoint of the Social Behaviorists.* Chicago: University of Chicago Press, 1934, p. 48.

[20] Kingsley Davis, "Extreme Social Isolation of a Child," *American Journal of Sociology.* 1940, 45: 554–565.

[21] S. Tenenbaum, "The Teacher, the Middle Class, the Lower Class," *Phi Delta Kappan.* 1963, 45: 82–86.

[22] M. Deutsch and B. Brown, "Social Influences in Negro-White Intelligence Differences," *Journal of Social Issues.* 1964, 20: 24–35.

[23] Bruno Bettelheim, "Individual and Mass Behavior in Extreme Situations," *Journal of Abnormal and Social Psychology.* 1943, 38: 417–452 (p. 443).

[24] Floyd L. Ruch, *Psychology and Life* (Brief 6th ed.). Glenview, Ill.: Scott, Foresman and Company, 1963, p. 203.

References of Related Interest

Bennis, Warren G., E. H. Scheim, F. I. Steele, and D. E. Berlew (Eds.), *Interpersonal Dynamics: Essays and Readings on Human Interaction* (rev. ed.). Homewood, Ill.: The Dorsey Press, 1968.

Berne, Eric, *Games People Play.* New York: Grove Press, Inc., 1964.

Bois, J. S., *The Art of Awareness.* Dubuque, Iowa: William C. Brown Company, Publishers, 1966.

Borgatta, E. F., and W. W. Lambert (Eds.), *Handbook of Personality Theory and Research.* Skokie, Ill.: Rand McNally & Company, 1968.

Brennan, James F., "Self-Understanding and Social Feeling," *Journal of Individual Psychology.* 1967, 23: 53–57.

Erikson, E. H., "The Problem of Ego Identity," *Journal of the American Psychoanalytic Association.* 1956, 4: 56–121.

Grebstein, Lawrence C. (Ed.), *Toward Self-Understanding.* Glenview, Ill.: Scott, Foresman and Company, 1969.

Hamachek, Don E. (Ed.), *The Self in Growth, Teaching, and Learning.* Englewood Cliffs, N.J.: Prentice-Hall, Inc., 1965, Part I.

Hamachek, Don E. (Ed.), *Human Dynamics in Psychology and Education.* Boston: Allyn and Bacon, Inc., 1968, Part V, "Toward Understanding What Happens within One's Self."

Hass, Kurt, *Understanding Ourselves and Others.* Englewood Cliffs, N.J.: Prentice-Hall, Inc., 1965.

Hilgard, Ernest R., "Human Motives and the Concept of Self," *American Psychologist.* 1949, 4: 374, 382.

Jourard, Sidney M., *Personal Adjustment* (2d ed.). New York: The Macmillan Company, 1963, Chap. 7, "Defense versus Growth of Self."

Leuba, Clarence, *Personality: Interpersonal Relations and Self-Understanding.* Columbus, Ohio: Charles E. Merrill Books, Inc., 1962.

Major, Jacqueline (Ed.), *The Search for Self.* New York: The Macmillan Company, 1968.

Maltz, Maxwell, *Psycho-Cybernetics*. Englewood Cliffs, N.J.: Prentice-Hall, Inc., 1960.

Maslow, A. H., *Toward a Psychology of Being* (2d ed.). Princeton, N.J.: D. Van Nostrand Company, Inc., 1968.

Maslow, A. H., *Motivation and Behavior*. New York: Harper & Row, Publishers, 1954.

Matsou, Floyd W., *Being, Becoming, and Behavior*. New York: George Braziller, Inc., 1967.

Sechrest, Lee, and J. Wallace, Jr., *Psychology and Human Problems*. Columbus, Ohio: Charles E. Merrill Books, Inc., 1967, Chap. 9.

Strecker, Edward A., E. A. Appel, and J. W. Appel, *Discovering Ourselves* (3rd ed.). New York: The Macmillan Company, 1958.

Symonds, P. M., *The Ego and the Self*. New York: Appleton-Century-Crofts, 1951.

Wylie, Ruth C., *The Self Concept*. Lincoln, Neb.: The University of Nebraska Press, 1961.

chapter two

The Self
and Perceptual
Processes:
Theory and Theorists

The theme underlying this book grows from a frame of reference which has variously been called the "phenomenological," "perceptual," "existential," "interactional," or "humanistic" approach. It is point of view in psychological thought which is sometimes referred to as the "new look" or "third force." Actually, it is a point of view which seeks to understand man in terms of how he views himself. It looks at human beings not only through the eyes of an outsider, but through the eyes of the person doing the behaving. It is a psychology searching to understand what goes on inside a person in terms of how his needs, feelings, values, and unique ways of perceiving influence him to behave as he does. In an everyday sense, it is the psychology a concerned friend uses as he wonders why we're "feeling so sad"; in a clinical sense, it is what a therapist uses as he probes for the deeper meanings behind what personal experiences mean to the client.

A fundamental thesis of the perceptual point of view is that behavior is influenced not only by the accumulation of our past and current experiences, but even more importantly it is influenced by the *personal meanings we attach to our perceptions of those experiences.* In other words, our behavior is more than simply a function of what happens to us from the outside, it is also a function of how we feel about ourselves on the inside. There is little question but that a person's past experiences can have a vast influence on his current behavior. Although we cannot change what happened to us yesterday, we *can* change how we *feel* about it today. We cannot change the event, but can modify the perceptions we have *about* the event. Therapy, for example, does not "cure" a person in the sense of removing his problems, but it does assist an individual towards *new perceptions* of the problems so they can be coped with more effectively.

Perception, defined, refers to the process by which we select, organize, and interpret sensory stimulation into a meaningful and coherent picture of the world. Which brings us logically to our next topic for consideration.

The Nature of Perceptual Processes

Combs and Synggt[1] have developed the idea that each person behaves in a manner consistent with his "perceptual field," which is a more or less fluid organization of personal meanings existing for every individual at any given instant in time. Perceptual field has also been called one's private or personal world, one's psychological field or life-space, or one's phenomenal field. The last term, which is appearing more frequently in psychological circles these days, is derived from the Greek, *phainesthai*, which means "to appear," or "to appear so," or "as it appears." In its original usage, a phenomenon was "that which is known through the senses and immediate experience" rather than through deductions. This is still the case. That is, to a phenomenologist, reality lies not in the event but in the phenomenon, which is to say, in a person's *perception* of the event. The idea of how perception can influence behavior is nicely illustrated in the following example cited by Combs:

> Several years ago a friend of mine was driving in a car at dusk along a Western road. A globular mass, about two feet in diameter, suddenly appeared directly in the path of the car. A passenger screamed and grasped the wheel attempting to steer the car around the object. The driver, however, tightened his grip on the wheel and drove directly into the object. The behavior of both the driver and the passenger was determined by his own (perceptions). The passenger, an Easterner, saw the object in the highway as a boulder and fought desperately to steer the car around it. The driver, a native Westerner, saw it as a tumbleweed and devoted his efforts to keeping his passenger from overturning the car.[2]

Each person in the car behaved according to what he "saw." The behavior of each was determined not by what the "objective" facts were, but by their "subjective" interpretations of the facts. It turned out that the driver was correct: it wasn't a boulder, but the passenger, at the instant of behaving, responded in terms of what he *thought* the facts were and not what they *actually* were. In other words, when the passenger grabbed the wheel, *he* was right, and he behaved accordingly. Our perceptions usually have the feeling of "being right" at the instant of behaving. This may not be true in retrospect as we look back over things we did yesterday, or last week, or five years ago, but at the time we acted it very likely seemed to us that the things we did, the thoughts we had, and the feelings we felt were legitimate, valid, and rational. For example, consider the following incident reported by Shlien[3] about a twenty-eight-year-old sociology graduate student who was wearily on his way home by bus after midterm examinations. In the graduate student's own words, this is what happened:

After an hour or so, the bus stopped in a small town, and a few passengers got on. One of them was a blonde girl, very good looking in a fresh but sort of sleazy way. I thought that she was probably a farm girl, and I wished she'd sit by me. By God, she did. She was really comely, if you know what I mean, and she smiled a bit so I felt sure she'd be approachable. Oh boy, what luck. I didn't want to be too eager, and I was still exhausted so we just smiled then sort of dozed off for a little while, hoping to recuperate by the time the driver turned out the lights and meanwhile enjoying my fantasies about the prospectus for the rest of the trip. The last thing I remember was smiling at her and noticing that when her skirt slipped up on her knee as she reached up to the back of the seat, she didn't pull it down. Wow! About four hours later we were pounding along the road in complete darkness when I opened my eyes. Her leg, the outside of it, was against mine, and the way it pressed and moved with the motion of the bus woke me up. This was more than I'd dreamed of. I was terribly excited, and when I stirred a little the steady pressure of leg didn't move away. By this time, I had a terrific erection, and the more I thought about this cute little babe pressing against me, the worse it got. I was just about to reach out and touch her when we pulled into a gas station for a stop, and when the light came through the window, *she* wasn't there at all! She must have left while I was asleep. A fat man with a growth of beard and a dead cigar dropping ash on his vest was sprawled next to me, sound asleep. It was *his* leg pressing against me, and he was so fat and slovenly that even when I drew myself away, his sloppy flesh stayed against me. I was so dumbfounded—disappointed too, and the funny thing—I lost that erection almost immediately, got up and moved to another seat. What a letdown.[3]

Just as it is true that we may find our perceptions (hence, our behavior) in error as we review them in retrospect, we may also discover that our most carefully considered plans for the future can also be inaccurate. That is, looking forward at this moment to the situation we will be in next week or next year, we may plan very carefully what will be first and appropriate to do and even feel confident about the outcome.

New evidence sometimes helps to change perceptions.

When the time comes, however, we may end up behaving very differently than we thought (or hoped) we would because things "seem" different at the moment. The exam you take today, for example, that you "saw" yourself prepared for yesterday, may radically change your perceptions of how ready you actually may be. So, behavior has to be revised to be consistent with new perceptions.

We organize, we "see" our environment—initially a physical, then a sensory environment—in such a way so that it has personal meaning for us. It is full of objects, circumstances, and events that are perceived as beautiful or ugly, good or bad, positive or negative, experiences to be approached or avoided. The perceptual world of each of us is organized in ways that are dictated not only by the construction of our central nervous systems, but also in accordance with the symbolic backgrounds and self-concepts which each of us brings to our perception of "reality."

INFLUENCE OF NEEDS AND VALUES

Each of us is continually motivated to maintain and enhance how we feel about ourselves. Whether we are successful or not depends on the sort of perceptions we're able to make in the course of our lifetimes. Our perceptions enable us to be aware of the world around us and to behave in ways which result in the satisfaction of our fundamental needs for personal adequacy. We might expect then, that an individual's needs and values would strongly influence his perceptions. This is exactly what proves to be so.

Out of all the phenomena we might perceive, we usually perceive what is meaningful to us and consistent with the needs we feel at the moment. For example, experiments on food deprivation in which participants were kept off food for varying periods of time have shown repeatedly that as hunger increases, so, too, do erroneous perceptions of food. In classes you may have had which lasted into the lunch hour, have you noted how your mind sometimes flashes more and more food images across your mental screen? Osgood[4] describes this nicely from his own personal experience as follows: "An office that I pass each day is numbered 400D; inevitably, when the hour is near mealtime, I perceive this as FOOD. The car I used to drive had the euphemistic label SILVER STREAK on its dashboard; inevitably when the hour was near mealtime, I would read this as SILVER STEAK." And of course we're all familiar with the common desert scene of the parched, dehydrated man pulling himself across the hot sands toward some watery illusion created in answer to a desperate need for body fluid.

The influence of needs on perceptions has also been demonstrated under more rigorous laboratory conditions. For example, Levine and others,[5] presented food-deprived subjects with pictures of various objects distorted behind a ground-glass screen and found that those who had gone three to nine hours without eating saw more food objects than did those who had eaten forty-five minutes to two hours before the experiment. McClelland and Atkinson[6] deprived Navy men of food for periods ranging from one to sixteen hours. The investigators then pretended to flash food pictures on a screen, but actually projected nothing. All of the subjects were unaware of the relation between their hunger and the perceptual test they were taking. Under the general set to see objects, the hungrier men had a greater frequency of food perceptions than the less hungry ones. The differences in the number of food responses were particularly large between the one-hour and sixteen-hour groups. The experimenters also found that as the hours of food deprivations increased so, too, did the apparent *size* of the perceived food objects.

Rogers[7] has emphasized that a person's need for self-consistency also influences perception. If, for example, a person has learned to regard homosexual behavior as an abnormality "too disgusting to even think about" then any feeling within himself which could possibly be construed as homosexual (because "normal people just don't feel that way") has to be adjusted so it is consistent with how he sees himself. A young man, who had recently been confronted by a homosexual, told me during one of our counseling sessions: "I don't know whether I was frightened by his proposition or my feelings of maybe going along with it. All I know is that it makes me nervous to even think about being a queer, so I told him to get the hell out of my room."

Even psychologists, who should know about such things, are not immune to the affect of needs on perception. In a study of the evaluations of other people by clinical psychologists, Weingarten[8] found that psychotherapists saw more problems in their clients in those areas in which the clinicians themselves had problems. Even when the purpose of the investigation was brought to their attention, they persisted in seeing in the clients they examined the problems they wrestled with themselves!

Similarly, values are determinants of our perceptions and behavior. We more readily perceive those things, experiences, and people we value, prize, and esteem. For example, have you ever noticed your ability to spot the person you care for in a crowd of people, or your ability to quickly see *your* name on an entire page of names. Or have you noticed your inclination to buy more food than you really need when exceptionally hungry? The need for something, in this case, food, seems to have the affect of increasing its value potential.

The influence of one's values on perceptions has also been demonstrated in research. A case in point is Vroom's[9] findings which suggest that an individual tends to perceive his own values and attitudes in persons for whom he has a negative attitude. Apparently we do not like to see characteristics we value in ourselves as being part of a disliked individual's personality. Could it be that if we see certain of our own values exhibited in a person we do not like, that these same values seem to us less important or less real or less good in ourselves?

Postman and others[10] have been able to demonstrate that personal values are determinants of an individual's perceptual selectivity. First they measured the value orientation of twenty-five students with a value scale. Then they flashed words representing the six values one at a time on a screen with increasingly longer exposures until they were recognized by each student. Their general finding was that the more closely a given work reflected a value already held by the student, the more rapidly he was able to recognize it. For example, subjects with dominant religious values would recognize on very brief exposure such words as "priest" or "minister" while taking longer to perceive economic words such as "cost," "price," or "bonds." In other words, there seemed to be a predisposition, or readiness, to see more quickly words reflecting one's personal values. In another study, Bruner and Goodman[11] found that values exert other kinds of influence on perception. They asked ten- and eleven-year-old boys from wealthy and poor families to guess the size of various denominations of coins (1, 5, 10, 25, 50 cents) by having them vary the diameter of a circle of light to the size of a specified coin. When asked to adjust the light to the size of a remembered nickel or dime or half dollar, all the children tended to overestimate the size of the coins, with the overestimation increasing with the increased value of the coin. The poorer boys, however, overestimated to a greater extent than boys from more prosperous families. The hunch here is that perhaps because perceived size is related to perceived value, the personal value of the coins was greater for the poorer boys.

A very lifelike example of how social values influence perception was reported by Hastorf and Cantril[12] and dealt with the perceptions of Princeton and Dartmouth students to a rough and tense football game between the two schools. Each group of students was asked questions about which side was responsible for the "roughness" or "dirtiness" of the game. When asked which team "started it," only 36 percent of the Dartmouth students said Dartmouth did, while 86 percent of the Princeton students blamed Dartmouth; 34 percent of the Dartmouth students saw the game as "rough and fair"; while only 3 percent of the Princeton students could make the same judgment, tending almost unanimously to see it as "rough and dirty" with the Dartmouth team responsible for the dirt. When later shown the complete movie for the game, Princeton players "saw," on the average, about 10 rule infractions by Dartmouth players. On the other hand, Dartmouth players "saw" less than half that much foul play on the part of their own team. (Alas, the report failed to mention who won.)

INFLUENCE OF BELIEFS

By and large, people tend to behave in a manner which is consistent with what they believe to be true. In this sense, seeing is not only believing; seeing is behaving! A fact is not what is; a fact is what one believes to be true. When man believed that the earth was flat he avoided its edges; when he believed that blood-letting would drain out the evil spirits and cure a patient he persisted in this practice despite the fact that people died before his very eyes. When man believed that phrenology could help him, he had his head examined (literally). There is even evidence to suggest that when a researcher believes that his hypothesis is true, he is more apt to find evidence supporting that hypothesis than if he didn't believe it was true.[13] And so it goes.

Kelley[14] conducted an experiment which very clearly shows the influence of beliefs on behavior. Students in a college class were presented with brief written descriptions of a guest lecturer prior to his appearance in class. The descriptions were almost the same except for one phrase, which in one case described him as a "rather cold" person and in the other case as a "very warm" person. Some students received the "warm" and some the "cold" description. They did not know that two different descriptions had been distributed.

After hearing his lecture the students who had received the "warm" description rated the lecturer as more considerate of others, more sociable, more popular, better natured, more humorous, and more humane than did students who had received the "cold" description. The findings directly reflect how implicit beliefs regarding what traits go with warmth and coldness can influence what one "sees" in another person.

Kelley also found that the warm-cold variable affected the amount of interactions that the students engaged in with the guest lecturer. Fifty-six percent of the students who received the "warm" description participated in class discussion, but only thirty-two percent of the students who received the "cold" description did so. This was the case even though the students were sitting in the same room hearing the same lecture. Thus do our beliefs about people sway our reactions to them and influence the course of interpersonal behavior.

Bills and McGehee[15] found that the students who learned and retained the most in a psychology experiment were inclined to believe things such as, "Psychology experiments are useful and will eventually help us to completely understand people," and "Psychology, in general, is a valuable, quantitative science with many practical aspects." On the other hand, students who quickly forgot the material were those who held beliefs such as "Psychological experiments are a total waste of time," and "Psychology, in general, is nothing but a witch hunt."

Our beliefs influence our perceptions, nurture our assumptions, and to a large extent determine our behavior. We do not easily give up that which we believe to be true. The church of our youth and the first political party to which we gave our allegiance usually continue to be our choices. Perceptions of one person by another person can be as varied as the assumptions on which the perceptions are based. An interesting example of how different beliefs can influence different perceptions was reported by Stachnik and Ulrich[16] in a paper in which they described the divergent perceptions of Barry Goldwater by psychiatrists after he received the 1964 Republican nomination for President. *Fact* magazine sent a questionnaire to all 12,356 psychiatrists registered in the American Medical Association asking, "Do you believe Barry Goldwater is psychologically fit to serve as President of the United States?" Not all answered, but of the 2,417 who did reply, 571 said they did not know enough about him to answer, 657 said they thought him psychologically fit, and 1,189 said he was not. Consider some examples of how dramatically the perceptions of Goldwater differed. One psychiatrist said, "I not only believe Barry Goldwater is psychologically fit to serve as President, but I believe he is a very mature person." On the same subject, however, another psychiatrist observed, "I believe Mr. Goldwater is basically immature . . . He has little understanding of himself or why he does the things he does." It is also interesting to note that diametrically opposing views regarding Goldwater's fitness were defended with rock-like conviction. For example, a Connecticut psychiatrist concluded:

> I believe Goldwater is grossly psychotic . . . he is a mass murderer at heart and a suicide. He is amoral and immoral, a dangerous lunatic. Any psychiatrist who does not agree with the above is himself psychologically unfit to be a psychiatrist.

A Georgia psychiatrist was just as adamant, but had a different belief about Goldwater:

> I value my reputation as a psychiatrist, but I am willing to stake it on the opinion that Barry Goldwater is eminently qualified—psychologically and in every other way—to serve as President of the United States.

The authors suggested, tongue-in-cheek(?), that among other things "A Republican seeking psychiatric counsel should be sure to see a Re-

© *1962 United Feature Syndicate, Inc.*

Sometimes those things we really believe in are hard to give up.

publican psychiatrist since this apparently enhances the probability of receiving a favorable diagnosis. . . ."

Beliefs are difficult to change. This is even more true for persons who have strong prejudices,[17] which, after all, are nothing more than beliefs which have become so fixed as to become permanent props in one's personality structure. Perhaps the point that beliefs change slowly can be illustrated by the yarn about the man who believed he was dead. His psychiatrist, after hearing his story, suggested that during the next week he repeat thrice daily, "Dead men don't bleed." When the man returned the next week the psychiatrist asked the man if he had followed his advice. Assured that he had, the psychiatrist took a needle and pricked the man's finger and squeezed out a drop of blood. "Well," said the psychiatrist, "What do you think about that?" The man regarded his finger with some care, looked up at the psychiatrist with a puzzled expression and answered, "I'll be darned. Dead men *do* bleed!"

INFLUENCE OF SELF-CONCEPT

Perception is a selective process and the picture that one has of himself is a vital factor in determining the richness and variety of perceptions selected. It makes a great deal of difference how one perceives, let's say, the Pope if one sees himself as a Jew, Protestant, or Catholic. Depending on one's concept of self, an exam is perceived as either something to avoid failing or something to pass with as high a grade as possible; a class discussion is viewed as either something to actively engage in or something to sit quietly through for fear of saying the wrong thing; front seats of classrooms are seen as either vantage points for better seeing and hearing or as potentially dangerous spots where one could be more easily seen and, heaven forbid, called on! It depends on how one perceives himself.

There is another consideration related to the impact of self-concept on perception and that is connected to its possible boomerang effect. For example, a student who views himself as poor in math not only internalizes that perception, but he is also likely to *project* it in his behavior. That is, he "projects" the "I can't do math" perception outside of himself by either, (1) avoiding math courses, and/or (2) by being so tense in the math courses he does take that he trips over his own anxiety trying to work problems he doesn't think he can solve in the first place. Through either course of action it is possible to perpetuate a negative self-image. By avoiding math, the student is in effect saying, "I'm too dumb to take math," which serves to reinforce the negative attitude with which he started. By taking math with the "I can't do it," feeling he is apt to increase the likelihood of overstimulating his anxiety to the point of not being able to think clearly when it counts. Naturally enough this usually leads to poor performance and ultimately leads to further evidence to support his negative self-concept. This is what is meant by the boomerang effect. The very process of *beginning* with a negative attitude usually guarantees that it will be projected in behavior in such a way as to "bring back" to the person evidence that he really cannot do what he thought he couldn't do in the first place. It ends up being a self-fulfilling prophecy. Of course, the boomerang effect can also work in the other direction. It is possible to start with a more positive attitude and accumulate evidence to support and maintain a more favorable self-perception.

I am not for a moment suggesting that how one performs or behaves is a simple matter of saying "I can" or "I can't" and therefore it will be true. Behavior is far more complex than that. Each of us has certain aptitudes and skills which equip us to do a few things a little better than some and some things a little better than most. The task before any person desiring to grow more competent is to keep himself as open as possible to experiences and opportunities which could broaden and expand his perception of self. By sampling new experiences and by testing one's self in as wide a variety of ways as possible, one not only increases the possibility of discovering those things which he does a little better than most, but he also decreases the possibility of being deflated by things he's not particularly good at. Most of us are better than we give ourselves credit for being and taking on new challenges now and then is one good way to find that out.

PERCEPTIONS CAN BE MODIFIED

As difficult as it is to change perceptions once they are acquired and incorporated into one's self-system, there nonetheless is abundant evidence to suggest that perceptions toward one's self and others can be modified. For example, studies in psychotherapy have shown us that if a therapist is genuine, accepting, and empathically understanding of a client's private world, then the client is better able to alter his self-perceptions in the direction of becoming more confident and self-directing, more mature and socialized, more healthy and integrated.[18]

On the other hand, clinical studies of "brainwashing" techniques used by the Chinese communists on American prisoners during the Korean conflict have shown that it is possible to break down a man's confidence, destroy the concept he has of himself, and, in general, distintegrate his personality structure to the point of apathetic resignation.[19]

As another illustration, research has demonstrated that some members of a group will report perceptions which are contrary to the evidence of their senses. They will, for example, report that Figure A covers a larger area than Figure B, when their visual perceptions *plainly indicate that this is not true.* Experiments by Asch,[20] later refined and improved by Crutchfield,[21] have shown that when a person is *led to believe* that other members in a group see B as larger than A, then he is inclined to go along with this judgment. More than that, he frequently does so with a real belief in his false perception.

Perception can be dramatically altered by setting up conditions which produce vivid hallucinations and other abnormal reactions in a thoroughly normal, awake individual. For example, in sensory deprivation experiments at McGill University[22] it was discovered that if all sensory input was cut off or reduced, abnormal perceptions resulted. If healthy subjects lie relatively motionless, to reduce kinesthetic stimuli, with eyes covered to eliminate light, with hearing muffled by foam-rubber pillows as well as being in a quiet cubicle, and with tactile sensations reduced by cuffs over the hands, then within forty-eight hours many subjects experience weird perceptual processes and hallucinations resembling that of a psychotic individual.

Anyone who has ever had a drink or two (or three or four) at a party has first-hand evidence of how perceptual processes can be temporarily modified via the introduction of alcohol into the blood. For example, recent research indicates that when an individual has had a given amount to drink, he is inclined to distort the subjective probability of success and begin to perceive various alternatives as less serious than they really are.[23] What would normally be regarded as high risk-taking behavior is no longer perceived as such at all. As actual ability decreases, the feeling of competency increases. Interesting to note in regard to risk-taking is how the party behavior of imbibing individuals is inclined to get more socially daring and aggressive as the evening wears on. From alcohol to "truth serum" to chemotherapy practiced in psychiatric wards to drugs for the normal person, there are many ways of changing psychological and perceptual states. We may take a drug to mobilize our anxiety to cram for an exam or a drug to reduce our anxiety before an exam. And of course drugs such as marijuana, heroin, LSD, and its many variants are known to have enormous effects on one's perceptual processes—many times very destructive effects.

Perceptions can be modified or changed by conditions both inside and outside the self. The changes can be for better or for worse and they can be either temporary or permanent. What we see may be real or imagined and whether we perceive when we are drunk or sober, manic or depressed, anxious or tranquil, we persist in behaving in a manner which, at the moment of behaving, is consistent with what we perceive to be true.

THINGS ARE NOT ALWAYS WHAT THEY SEEM

When we look at things from our own point of view they don't always square with how they may be perceived by another person. For example, I recall an incident involving a youthful art teacher who admonished one of her first-grade pupils for drawing a cow the way he did because, after all, "Cows just don't look like that." The little boy frowned a bit, examined his cow closely, looked up at the teacher and said, "Maybe they don't, but I bet if you were down here with me they would."

Shlien[24] has reported a story about a psychologist which perhaps best illustrates some of the things about perception we have been talking about: influence of needs, impact of self-concept, behavior which is consistent with perceptions, the possibility of misinterpreting behavior if we examine it only from our own point of view, etc. It goes like this.

The parents of a small boy were worried. He was quiet, sensitive, lonely, and acted afraid of other children. The parents wanted some professional advice before the child entered school and so invited a psychologist friend of theirs to the house for an afternoon and dinner so he could observe the boy under more natural conditions. Upon arriving, the psychologist asked all the appropriate questions about history and be-

The way we see things may be different from someone else's view.

havior and then took a spot on the balcony where he watched, unseen, the boy play in a garden by himself. The boy sat pensively in the sun, listening to the neighborhood children shout. He frowned, rolled over on his stomach, kicked the toes of his white shoes in the grass, sat up and looked at the stains. Then he saw an earthworm. He stretched it out on a flat stone, found a sharp edged chip, and proceeded to saw the worm in half. Many impressions were taking shape in the psychologist's mind, and he made some tentative notes to the effect: "Seems isolated and angry, perhaps over-aggressive, or sadistic, should be watched carefully when playing with other children, not have knives or pets." Then he heard the boy talking to himself. He leaned forward and strained to catch the words. The boy finished his separation of the worm, his frown disappeared, and he said, "There. Now you have a friend."

Humanistic Social Psychological Theory

The theoretical orientation or position we will examine in the remainder of this chapter is one which focuses on man as a social being who is influenced and guided by the personal meanings he attaches to his experiences. In its most simple terms, it is an orientation which seeks to understand man by studying man. A man can understand astronomy only by being an astronomer; he can understand entomology only by being an entomologist (or perhaps an insect); but he can understand a great deal about psychology merely by being a man, *by being the object of his own study*. This may seem to be a self-evident point of view, an obvious direction for psychology to take, but, alas, this has not always been the case. Why? Perhaps the following observation by a clinical psychologist may help us understand:

Because of our need to compete with the physical sciences, behavioral sciences have skipped over, by and large, the naturalistic stage from which other disciplines developed. We have not been people-watchers as biologists were bird- and bug-watchers. We have moved too quickly into the laboratory and looked only at special populations of people under special circumstances; we have thought we could derive generalizations about human behavior without first gaining the kind of understanding that could come only from years of performing normal tasks. Very few of us make any attempt to use our scientific training to investigate what people are really like when they are being themselves. When one examines the literature in the behavioral sciences, one seldom has the feeling, "that's what it's like to be me." The *person* is usually missing and the findings have no reality or meaning for us because we cannot find *ourselves*.[25]

As if in answer to the need to put man back into the behavioral sciences, humanistic psychology has emerged as a major orientation to the study of man. The humanistic orientation represents "the third force" in psychology, insofar as it endeavors to go beyond the points of view of behaviorism and psychoanalysis, the two most dominant perspectives within the broad arena of psychology. The humanistic point of view does not see itself as competitive with the other two systems; rather it attempts to supplement their observations and to introduce further perceptions and insights.

Since humanistic psychology, phenomenology, and existential psychology are frequently used in the same breath by those who identify with any frame of reference that discusses a psychology of the self, it might be well if we take a look at the meaning of each of these terms, their relationships to each other and to perceptual psychology.

Let's begin with existentialism. This is basically a twentieth-century philosophy which stresses an individual's responsibility for making himself what he is. It is an introspective theory which expresses the individual's intense awareness of his own existence and freedom to choose among alternatives for behaving. A main tenet of existentialism is the idea that man struggles to transcend himself, to reach beyond himself. In this sense, the idea of transcendence boils down to man's capacity for "dynamic self-consciousness."[26] Not only can a person think, but he can also think about (criticize and correct) his thinking. Not only can a person feel, but he can have feeling about his feeling. Man is not only *conscious*, he is self-conscious.

We have already noted that to a phenomenologist, reality lies not in the event but in the phenomena, that is to say, the person's *perception* of the event. This is not so different from the existential point of view that suggests that man is the determiner of his own nature and definer of his own values. For the phenomenologist, one's perceptions grow out of his experiences; for the existentialist, one's "essence" or "being" grows out of his capacity to make choices. Both of these points of view regard man to be the measure of all things and that the reality he responds to is his own. This is in opposition to the more deterministic points of view (psychoanalytic or behavioristic) that maintain that man's "being" is shaped primarily by forces outside of himself.

Humanistic psychology fits comfortably in the company of phenomenology and existentialism inasmuch as it is an orientation which centers on human interests and values. It is concerned with the sort of human experiences and expressions which psychology has long neglected, e.g., love, creativity, sense of self, higher values, becoming, spontaneity, warmth, meaning, fair-play, transcendental experiences, psychological health, and related concepts. It is, in the best sense of the word, an expression of what psychology still means to the average, intelligent layman, that is, the functioning and experience of a total human being.

Bugental[27] has suggested five basic postulates for humanistic psychology that outline the scope of this frame of reference for understanding human behavior.

1. *Man, as man, supersedes the sum of his parts.* In other words, man is more than the accumulative product of various part-functions. I suppose that this is something like saying that Beethoven's *Fifth Symphony* is more than the summation of individual musical notes that went into composing it.

2. *Man has his being in a human context.* The unique nature of man is expressed through his relationship to his fellows and, in this sense, humanistic psychology is always concerned with man in his interpersonal potential.

3. *Man is aware.* This suggests that whatever the degree of consciousness, man is aware of himself and his existence. He does not move from one experience to the next as if they were discrete and independent episodes unrelated to each other. How a man behaves in the present is related to what happened in his past and connected to his hopes for the future.

4. *Man has choice.* Phenomenologically, choice is a given of experience. When man is aware, he can choose and thereby become not a bystander but a participant in experience.

5. *Man is intentional.* Through his choice of this or that, of going here or there, man demonstrates his intent. He "intends" through having purpose, through valuing, and through seeking meaning in his life. Man's intentionality, his "conscious deliberateness," is the basis on which he builds his identity and distinguishes himself from other species.

Bugental[28] has also articulated five basic characteristics of the humanistic orientation in psychology, which are as follows:

1. Humanistic psychology cares about man.
2. Humanistic psychology values meaning more than procedure.
3. Humanistic psychology looks for human rather than nonhuman validation.
4. Humanistic psychology accepts the relativism of all knowledge.
5. Humanistic psychology relies heavily upon the phenomenological orientation.

In summary, we might say that existentialism focuses on man's *existence*; phenomenology is concerned about man's here and now *perceptions* of his existence, and humanistic psychology studies the *personal meaning man assigns to his perceptions of his existence.*

Humanistic Social Psychological Contributors

Many great names in psychology are either directly or indirectly related to a humanistic social-psychological orientation to the study of human behavior. Contributors such as Erik Erikson, Gordon Allport, Harry Stack Sullivan, Erich Fromm, A. H. Maslow, Carl Rogers, Arthur Combs, Donald Syngg, Kurt Lewin, Otto Rank, Karen Horney, Hadley Cantril, Alfred Adler, George H. Mead, Charles H. Cooley, and William James, among others have each made significant contributions to the point of view we are considering. (Basic references to each of these theorists are suggested at the end of this chapter.)

Although there is neither sufficient space nor necessity to detail the contributions of each contributor, what we will do is to consider a cross-section of their theoretical points of view to get some idea of the variety of interpretations possible within a humanistic social psychological framework.

C. H. COOLEY (THE LOOKING-GLASS SELF)

C. H. Cooley[29] was one of the earliest social psychologists to explore the idea of self. He recognized that the social milieu from which a person comes contributes heavily to how a person views himself. With this idea in mind, he developed a theory of the self that was concerned primarily with how the self grows as a consequence of interpersonal interactions. From this he posited the concept of "the looking-glass self" that is perhaps best expressed in his own words:

> In a very large and interesting class of cases the social reference takes the form of a somewhat definite imagination of how one's self . . . appears in a particular mind, and the kind of self-feeling one has is determined by the attitude toward this attributed to that other mind. A social self might be called the reflected or looking-glass self.
>
> > Each to each a looking glass
> > Reflects the other that doth pass.
>
> The self that is most important is a reflection, largely, from the minds of others. . . . We live on, cheerful, self-confident . . . until in some rude

hour we learn that we do not stand as well as we thought we did, that the image of us is tarnished. Perhaps we do something, quite naturally, that we find the social order is set against, or perhaps it is the ordinary course of our life that is not so well regarded as we supposed. At any rate, we find with a chill of terror that . . . our self-esteem, self-confidence, and hope, being chiefly founded upon the opinions of others, go down in a crash. . . .[30]

We can see here, in the process of self-appraisal by an individual, the importance of his accurate perception and interpretation of the reaction of the other person to him.

GEORGE H. MEAD (SOCIALLY FORMED SELF)

A somewhat more sophisticated view of the self was developed by G. H. Mead,[31] who, as Cooley did, felt it necessary to root the self in the social conditions relevant to the individual and to derive the content of the self from the interaction between the individual and his social world. Mead's self is an *object of awareness*, rather than a system of processes. That is, a person comes to know himself and respond to himself as he sees others responding to him. Mead's self is a *socially* formed self which grows in a *social* setting where there is *social* communication. He further suggests that a person can have as many selves as there are numbers of social groups in which he participates. For instance, a person may have a family self that reflects the values and attitudes expressed by his family, a school self which represents the expectations and attitudes expressed by his teachers and fellow students, and many other selves.

HARRY STACK SULLIVAN (REFLECTED APPRAISALS)

Closely related to the social interaction ideas of Mead and Cooley is the theoretical position of Sullivan,[32] a psychiatrist who developed what has been called an interpersonal theory of personality development. As Sullivan sees it, from the first day of life, the infant is immersed in a continual stream of interpersonal situations in which he is the recipient of a never-ending flow of "reflected appraisals." It is through his assimilation of these reflected appraisals that the child comes to develop expectations and attitudes toward himself as an individual. If these appraisals have been mainly derogatory, then the self-image is apt to be disparaging and hostile. If, on the other hand, the reflected appraisals have been chiefly positive and constructive, then one's feelings about himself are more inclined to be positive and approving.

ALFRED ADLER (LIFE PLAN OR LIFE STYLE)

The essential pillar of Adlerian psychology,[33] in terms of which the rest of it takes on meaning, is his conception of a "life plan" of the individual, or the purpose, the goal, the "end in view" which determines behavior. Adler's self is a highly personalized, subjective system through which a person interprets and gives meaning to his experiences. Unlike Freud, who made the unconscious the center of personality, Adler (who, by the way, was one of Freud's earliest pupils) stressed *consciousness* as the center of personality. He viewed man as a conscious being ordinarily aware of his reasons for behavior. More than that, he is a self-conscious individual, who is capable of planning and guiding his actions with full awareness of their meaning for his own self-realization.

Adler saw every person as having the same goal, namely that of superiority, but he also saw that there were countless different "life styles" for achieving that goal. For example, one person may try to become superior through developing his intellect, another may strive to be a Don Juan, and still another bends all his efforts to achieving the body beautiful. The intellectual, the lady-killer, the muscleman each has an individual life style. The intellectual seeks knowledge, the Don Juan women, the muscleman strength. Each arranges his life in such a way so as to achieve the end of being more or less superior to those seeking similar goals.

From Adler's point of view, a person's life style is determined largely by the specific inferiorities, either fancied or real, that a person has. An individual who is, let's say, small, physically inferior, and feels unnoticed may shape his whole life in terms of this relationship. (It is not uncommon, for example, to find that many "musclemen" did, in fact, start out in the "90-lb. weakling" category.) Or it may be a voice defect, a facial blemish, a physical handicap, or some other characteristic which is the primary feature determining a person's total reaction to his environment. The important matter is that the individual sets up a certain "life plan" that is directed in such a way as either to overcome the defect or compensate for it. It is this setting up of a goal or direction in life that gives meaning to events which might not otherwise make sense. Adler's conception of the nature of personality coincides nicely with the humanistic idea that man can be the master, and not the victim, of his fate.

KAREN HORNEY (MOVING TOWARD, AGAINST, AND AWAY FROM PEOPLE)

Like Sullivan and Adler, Horney was another psychiatrist who reacted to Freud's instinctivistic and genetic psychology. Horney's ideas spring from her primary concept of basic anxiety, which she defined as:

. . . the feeling a child has of being isolated and helpless in a potentially hostile world. A wide range of adverse factors in the environment can produce this insecurity in a child; direct or indirect domination, indifference, erratic behavior, lack of respect for the child's individual needs, lack of real guidance, disparaging attitudes, too much admiration or the absence of it, lack of reliable warmth, having to take sides in parental disagreements, too much or too little responsibility, overprotection, isolation from other children, injustice, discrimination, unkept promises, hostile atmosphere so on and so on.[34]

Any one or combination of these experiences could predispose an individual to adopt certain strategies of adjustment in order to satisfy a neurotic need or needs growing from disturbed human relationships. Horney developed a list of ten needs, any one of which could be acquired as a consequence of trying to untangle the problem of disturbed human relationships. She calls these needs "neurotic" because they are irrational solutions to the basic problem:[35]

1. *The neurotic need for affection and approval.* This need is highlighted by an indiscriminate need to please others and to do what others want. This sort of person wants the good will of others and is extremely sensitive to signs of rejection and unfriendliness. "If I am rejected I am unworthy."
2. *The neurotic need for a "partner" who will take over one's life.* This individual has a dread of being deserted or left alone and tends to "overvalue" love in the sense of seeing love as the magic potion to solve all problems. "If I am loved I am worthwhile."
3. *The neurotic need to restrict one's life within narrow borders.* Such a person is more inclined to save than to spend, fears making demands on others, and feels a strong necessity for remaining inconspicuous and in the background as much as possible. "If I am cautious I will not be hurt or disappointed."
4. *The neurotic need for power.* This need expresses itself in craving power for its own sake, in an essential disrespect for the feelings and individuality of others and in a basic fear of uncontrollable situations. There is also a strong belief in the omnipotence of intelligence and reason along with a denial of powers of emotional forces and even contempt for expressions of emotion. Such persons dread "stupidity" and bad judgment and believe that most anything is possible through the sheer exertion of will power. "I rely primarily on my ability to think and reason; emotional people are weak people."
5. *The neurotic need to exploit others.* This person evaluates others primarily in terms of whether or not they can be exploited to be used. "Do they have power, position, or authority to do something for me?"

6. *The neurotic need for prestige.* This sort of person's self-evaluation is dependent on the amount of public recognition he receives. "If I am recognized by many people, I feel worthwhile."

7. *The neurotic need for personal admiration.* Here we have a person with an inflated image of himself, a need to be admired not for what he possesses or presents in the public eye but for the imagined self. Self-evaluation is dependent on living up to his image and on admiration of it by others. "Even though it is difficult being something I am not, it is worth it for the admiration I receive. Besides, what would happen if people saw me as I really am?"

8. *The neurotic ambition for personal achievement.* In this case there is usually a relentless driving of one's self to higher and higher levels of achievement, usually accompanied by an intense fear of failure. Self-esteem is dependent on being the very best, particularly in one's own mind. "If I fail I could never accept myself and neither would others; I had better fight for the number one spot."

9. *The neurotic need for self-sufficiency and independence.* Having experienced personal pain in attempts to find warm, satisfying relationships with people, this person turns to distance and separateness as his major source of security. Usually there is a fear of being hurt and so the person acts as though other people were not needed. "If I don't get close to people no one can hurt me."

10. *The neurotic need for perfection and unassailability.* This sort of person usually has a deep fear of making mistakes and being criticized and so tries to make himself impregnable and infallible. He is constantly in search of flaws in himself so that they can be covered up before they become too obvious to others. "If I am perfect, who can criticize me?"

From Horney's point of view, these ten needs are the sources from which inner conflicts develop. The neurotic's need for power, for example, is insatiable: the more he acquires the more he wants. He's never satisfied. In a similar vein, the need for independence can never be fully satisfied because another part of the personality cries out to be loved and accepted. The search for perfection is a lost cause from the beginning. In one way or another, all of the above needs are unrealistic and self-defeating.

Horney later classified these ten neurotic needs under three headings: (1) moving toward people, (2) moving away from people, and (3) moving against people.[36] Each of these interpersonal response traits represents a basic orientation toward others and oneself. Consider some examples of each of these three types.

A person whose predominant interpersonal trait is one of *moving toward people*:

. . . shows a marked need for affection and approval and an especial need for a "partner"—that is, a friend, lover, husband or wife who is to fulfill all expectations of life and take responsibility for good and evil. . . . (He) needs to be liked, wanted, desired, loved; to feel accepted, welcome, approved of, appreciated; to be needed, to be of importance to others, especially to one particular person.

A person whose predominant interpersonal response trait is one of *moving against people* perceives:

. . . that the world is an arena where, in the Darwinian sense, only the fittest survive and the strong annihilate the weak. . . . a callous pursuit of self-interest is the paramount law. . . . He needs to excel, to achieve success, prestige or recognition in any form.

For the person whose interpersonal response trait is *moving away from people*:

The underlying principle . . . is never to become so attached to anybody or anything that he or it becomes indispensable. . . . Another pronounced need is for privacy. He is like a person in a hotel room who rarely removes the "Do Not Disturb" sign from his door. . . . His independence, like the whole phenomenon of detachment of which it is a part, has a negative orientation; it is aimed at *not* being influenced, coerced, tied, obligated.

The three types could be summarized as follows: The *compliant* type worries about how he can make people like him so they won't hurt him. The *aggressive* type considers the best defense to be the best offense. The *detached* person has the philosophy that if he doesn't get close to people then he won't get hurt too badly.

Horney suggests that the essential difference between a normal and a neurotic conflict is one of degree. For example, she states, ". . . the disparity between the conflicting issues is much less great for the normal person than for the neurotic."[37] In other words, everyone has these conflicts to some degree, but some people, usually because of early experiences with rejection, neglect, overprotection and other expressions of unfortunate parental treatment, possess theirs in exaggerated form.

CARL ROGERS (THE FULLY FUNCTIONING PERSON)

Rogers'[38] self-theory and ideas about the fully functioning individual represent a synthesis of phenomenology as developed by Combs and Snygg, social interaction theory as represented in the writings of Mead and Cooley, and of Sullivan's interpersonal theory.

The principle conceptual ingredients of Rogers' self-theory are the following: (1) the *organism*, which is the total person, (2) the *phenomenal field*, which is the totality of experience, and (3) the *self* which is a differentiated portion of the phenomenal field and consists of conscious perceptions and values of the "I" or "me."

The self, which is the nuclear concept in Rogers' theory, has numerous features, the most important of which are these: (a) the self strives for consistency, (b) a person behaves in ways which are consistent with the self, (c) experiences that are not consistent with the self are perceived as threats and are either distorted or denied, (d) the self may change as a result of maturation and learning.

The nature of these concepts and their interrelationships are discussed in a series of nineteen propositions formulated by Rogers in his book, *Client-Centered Therapy*. To give you a feeling for how these propositions are related to Rogers' ideas about the self and how it functions, seven of the most basic propositions are as follows:[39]

1. Every individual exists in a continually changing world of experience of which he is the center. In this sense, each person is the best source of information about himself.

2. Each individual reacts to his perceptual field as it is perceived and experienced. Consequently, knowledge of the stimulus is not sufficient for predicting behavior; one must know how the person is perceiving the stimulus and what it *means* to him.

3. Each individual has a basic tendency to strive, to actualize, maintain, and enhance the experiencing organism.

4. As a result of interaction with the environment, and particularly as a result of evaluational interactions with others, one's picture of himself is formed—an organized, fluid, but consistent conceptual pattern of perceptions of characteristics and relationships of the "I" or the "me."

5. Perception is selective, and the primary criteria for selection is whether the experience is consistent with how one views himself at the moment.

6. Most ways of behaving which are adopted by the individual are those that are consistent with his concept of self.

7. When a person perceives and accepts into one integrated system all his sensory and visceral experiences, then he is in a position to be more accepting and understanding of others as separate and *different* individuals. For example, a person who feels threatened by his own hostile or sexual feelings may tend to criticize or move away from others whom he perceives as behaving in sexual or hostile ways. On the other hand, if he can accept his own sexual or hostile feelings he is likely to be more tolerant of their expression by others.

Out of this self theory and from his many years as a practicing psychotherapist, Rogers had developed some ideas of what it means to be a "fully functional person." For the most part, his ideas evolved from his very personal experiences with his clients as he was able to observe them developing a "self" which was uniquely their own. According to Rogers, a person en route to becoming "fully functioning" usually exhibits characteristics such as the following:[40]

1. He tends to move away from facades. That is, he moves away from a self that he is *not* and moves towards the self that he really *is*.
2. He tends to move away from "oughts." In other words, he ceases to guide his conduct in terms of what he "ought" to be or "ought" to become.
3. He tends to move away from meeting others' expectations and moves more toward meeting his *own* expectations.
4. He tends to move away from pleasing others and begins to be more self-directing.
5. He tends to be more accepting of himself and able to view himself as a person in the process of "becoming." That is, he is not upset by the fact that he does not always hold the same feelings toward a given experience or person, or that he is not always consistent. The striving for conclusions or end states seems to decrease.
6. He tends to move toward being more open to his experiences in the sense of not having to always blot out thoughts, feelings, perceptions, and memories which might be unpleasant.
7. He tends to move in the direction of greater acceptance of others. That is, as he is more able to accept the experiences of others.

A. H. MASLOW (SELF-ACTUALIZATION)

Maslow's[41] unique contribution to the humanistic social psychological viewpoint lies in his preoccupation with healthy people rather than sick ones, and his feeling that studies of these two groups generate different types of theory. He feels that psychology has focused too intently on man's frailties and not enough on his strengths; that in the process of exploring man's sins it has neglected his virtues. Where is the psychology, Maslow asks, that takes into account such experiences as love, compassion, gaiety, exhilaration, and well-being to the same extent that it deals with hate, pain, misery, guilt, and conflict? Maslow has undertaken to supply the other half of the picture, the brighter, better half, and to round out a portrait of the whole man.

Maslow has offered a theory of human motivation which assumes that needs are ordered along a hierarchy of priority of prepotency. That is, when the needs that have greatest prepotency and priority are satisfied, the next need in the hierarchy emerges and presses for satisfaction. He assumes that each person has five basic needs, which are arranged in hierarchical order from the most potent to the least potent as follows:[42]

1. The physiological needs, i.e., hunger and thirst
2. The safety needs
3. The love and belongingness needs
4. The esteem needs
5. The self-actualization needs, i.e., the desire for self-fulfillment, for becoming what one has the potential to become.

In order to study what makes healthy people healthy, or great people great, or extraordinary people extraordinary, Maslow has made intensive clinical investigations of people who are, or were, in the truest sense of the word, self-actualizing, in the sense of moving in the direction of achieving and reaching their highest potentials. People of this sort are rare, indeed, as Maslow discovered when he was selecting his group. Some were historical figures, such as Lincoln, Jefferson, Walt Whitman, Beethoven, William James, F. D. Roosevelt, while others were living at the time they were studied, like Einstein, Eleanor Roosevelt, Albert Schweitzer, along with some personal acquaintances of the investigator. Upon studying healthy, self-actualizing individuals, Maslow was able to sort out fifteen basic personality characteristics which distinguished them from, how shall we say, "ordinary" people. This is not to suggest that each person he studied reflected all fifteen self-actualizing characteristics, but each did, however, exhibit a greater number of these characteristics and in more different ways than might be expected in a less "self-actualized" person. Maslow describes the features which distinguish "self-actualizing" people as follows:[43]

1. They are realistically oriented.
2. They accept themselves, other people, and the natural world for what they are.
3. They are spontaneous in thinking, emotions, and behavior.
4. They are problem-centered rather than self-centered in the sense of being able to devote their attention to a task, duty, or mission that seemed peculiarly cut out for them.
5. They have a need for privacy and even seek it out on occasion, needing it for periods of intense concentration on subjects of interest to them.
6. They are autonomous, independent, and able to remain true to themselves in the face of rejection or unpopularity.
7. They have a continuous freshness of appreciation and capacity

A desire to be alone and away from other people is a need we all have from time to time.

to stand in awe again and again of the basic goods of life, a sunset, a flower, a baby, a melody, a person.

8. They have frequent "mystic" or "oceanic" experiences, although not necessarily religious in character.

9. They feel a sense of identification with mankind as a whole in the sense of being concerned not only with the lot of their own immediate families, but with the welfare of the world as a whole.

10. Their intimate relationships with a few specifically loved people tend to be profound and deeply emotional rather than superficial.

11. They have democratic character structures in the sense of judging people and being friendly not on the basis of race, status, religion, but rather on the basis of who other people are as individuals.

12. They have a highly developed sense of ethics and are inclined to choose their behavior with reference to its ethical implications.

13. They have unhostile senses of humor, which are expressed in their capacity to make common human foibles, pretensions, and foolishness the subject of laughter, rather than sadism, smut, or hatred of authority.

14. They have a great fund of creativeness.
15. They resist total conformity to culture.

An impressive list to be sure, and one of the most detailed conceptions of self-actualization yet developed.

In Perspective

This chapter has introduced you to the nature of perceptual processes and how needs, values, beliefs, and self-concept variables can influence perception. In addition, we have looked at some ways in which perceptions can be modified or changed by conditions both inside and outside the self. Although things may not always be what they seem, we nonetheless behave in a manner which is more or less consistent with what we perceive to be true.

Each of the contributors who have been discussed in relation to this humanistic social psychological orientation tends to espouse a "dynamic" view of human behavior in the sense of seeing man as an active, choosing, conscious organism whose behavior is shaped by both internal and external forces. Moreover, they represent points of view that give man credit for not only assigning personal meaning to his perceptions and experiences, but for adjusting his behavior so it is consistent with his personal meanings. This is not to suggest that one's perceptions and, hence, his personal meanings are always correct. Hardly. Most of our personal and interpersonal problems arise not from disagreements about reality, but from distortions and misperceptions of reality. In order to be as accurate as possible in our perceptions, we must develop as much insight as we can into ourselves as individuals and the ways in which our needs, values, and beliefs influence how we perceive the world in which we live.

Thus, if a person is to behave effectively and appropriately, his perceptions of reality must be fairly accurate. When one's perceptions of himself and/or others is inaccurate, he is more likely to undertake actions which have little chance of success. Indeed, he could seriously reduce his opportunities for engaging in many things he might otherwise do and enjoy if it were not for his misperceptions.

The need for knowing one's self is basic and universal in human experience, not confined to the heroic few or to the giants among men. The need which has been variously labeled "self-acceptance," "self-love," "self-understanding," and the like is neither innate nor indistinct in function and origin. It is basically a need for an image of one's self that is accurate enough to be workable and acceptable so a person can enjoy experiencing and expressing it.

If one is to move in the direction of what Søren Kierkegaard called "being that self which one truly is," then each individual must constantly explore, redefine, and reevaluate himself in light of new experiences, shifting social conditions, and changing perceptions of himself and others.

[1] Arthur W. Combs and D. Snygg, *Individual Behavior* (rev. ed.), New York: Harper & Row, Publishers, 1959, pp. 16–36.

[2] Combs and Snygg, p. 20.

[3] John M. Shlien, "Phenomenology and Personality," in S. M. Wepman and R. W. Heine (Eds.), *Concepts of Personality*. Chicago: Aldine Publishing Co., 1963, p. 295 (used by permission).

[4] C. E. Osgood, *Method and Theory in Experimental Psychology*. New York: Oxford University Press, 1953, p. 286.

[5] R. Levine, I. Chein, and G. Murphy, "The Relation of the Intensity of the Need to the Amount of Perceptual Distortion, a Preliminary Report," *Journal of Psychology*, 1942, 13: 283–293.

[6] D. C. McClelland and S. W. Atkinson, "The Projective Expression of Needs: I. The Effect of Different Intensities of the Hunger Drive on Perception," *Journal of Psychology*. 1948, 25: 205–222.

[7] C. R. Rogers, *Client-Centered Therapy*. Boston: Houghton Mifflin Company, 1951.

[8] Evica M. Weingarten, "A Study of Selective Perception in Clinical Judgment," *Journal of Personality*. 1949, 17: 369–406.

[9] Victor H. Vroom, "Projection, Negation, and The Self-Concept," *Human Relations*. 1959, 12: 335–344.

[10] L. Postman, J. S. Bruner, and E. McGinnis, "Personal Values as Selective Factors in Perception," *Psychological Review*. 1948, 55: 314–324.

[11] J. S. Bruner and C. C. Goodman, "Value and Need as Organizing Factors in Perception," *Journal of Abnormal and Social Psychology*. 1947, 42: 33–44.

[12] A. Hastorf and H. Cantril, "They Saw a Game: A Case Study," *Journal of Abnormal and Social Psychology*. 1954, 49: 129–134.

[13] Robert Rosenthal, *Experimenter Effects in Behavioral Research*. New York: Appleton-Century-Crofts, 1966.

[14] H. H. Kelley, "The Warm-Cold Variable in First Impressions of Persons," *Journal of Personality*. 1950, 18: 431–439.

[15] R. E. Bills and B. R. McGehee, "The Effect of Attitude Toward Psychology in a Learning Experiment," *Journal of Personality*. 1955, 23: 499–500.

[16] Thomas J. Stachnik and R. Ulrich, "Psychiatric Diagnoses: Some Cracks in the Crystal Ball," *Psychological Reports*. 1965, 17: 989–990.

[17] T. W. Adorno, E. Frenkel-Brunswik, D. J. Levinson, and R. N. Sanford, *The Authoritarian Personality*. New York: Harper & Row, Publishers, 1950.

[18] Carl R. Rogers and R. F. Dymond (Eds.), *Psychotherapy and Personality Change*. Chicago: University of Chicago Press, 1954.

[19] Edgar H. Scheim, "Reaction Patterns to Severe Chronic Stress in American Army Prisoners of War of the Chinese," *Journal of Social Issues*. 1957, 13: 21–30.

[20] Soloman E. Asch, *Social Psychology*. Englewood Cliffs, N.J.: Prentice-Hall, Inc., 1952, pp. 450–483.

[21] Richard S. Crutchfield, "Conformity and Character," *American Psychologist*. 1955, 10: 191–198.

[22] W. H. Beston, H. Woodburn, and T. H. Scott, "Effects of Decreased Variation in the Sensory Environment," *Canadian Journal of Psychology.* 1954, 8: 70–76.

[23] A. I. Teger, S. Katkin, and D. G. Pruitt, "Effects of Alcoholic Beverages and Their Congener Content on Level and Style of Risk Taking," *Journal of Personality and Social Psychology.* 1969, 11: 170–176.

[24] Shlien, pp. 324–325.

[25] Richard E. Farson (Ed.), *Science and Human Affairs.* Palo Alto, Calif.: Science and Behavior Books, 1965, p. 13.

[26] Van Cleve Morris, "Existentialism and Education," *Educational Theory.* 1954, 4: 252–253.

[27] J. F. T. Bugental, "The Third Force in Psychology," *Journal of Humanistic Psychology.* 1964, Spring: 23–24.

[28] Bugental, pp. 24–25.

[29] C. H. Cooley, *Human Nature and The Social Order.* New York: Charles Scribner's Sons, 1902.

[30] Cooley, pp. 20–21.

[31] G. H. Mead, *Mind, Self, and Society.* Chicago: University of Chicago Press, 1934.

[32] H. S. Sullivan, *The Interpersonal Theory of Psychiatry.* New York: W. W. Norton & Company, Inc., 1953.

[33] A. Adler, *Practice and Theory of Individual Psychology.* New York: Harcourt, Brace & World, Inc., 1927.

[34] Karen Horney, *Our Inner Conflicts.* New York: W. W. Norton & Company, Inc., 1945, p. 41.

[35] Karen Horney, *Self-Analysis.* New York: W. W. Norton & Company, Inc., 1942, pp. 45–60.

[36] Horney (1945), pp. 48–95.

[37] Horney (1945), p. 31.

[38] Rogers (1951).

[39] Rogers (1951), pp. 483–520.

[40] Carl R. Rogers, *On Becoming a Person.* Boston: Houghton Mifflin Company, 1961, pp. 163–198.

[41] A. H. Maslow, *Motivation and Personality.* New York: Harper & Row, Publishers, 1954.

[42] Maslow, pp. 80–92.

[43] Maslow, pp. 203–228.

References of Related Interest

Allport, G. W., *Pattern and Growth in Personality.* New York: Holt, Rinehart and Winston, Inc., 1961.

Angyal, A., *Foundations for a Science of Personality.* New York: Commonwealth Fund, 1941.

Bugental, James F. T. (Ed.), *Challenges of Humanistic Psychology.* New York: McGraw-Hill, Inc., 1967.

Cantril, H., "The Place of Personality in Social Psychology," *Journal of Psychology*. 1947, 24: 19–56.

Diggory, James C., *Self-Evaluation: Concepts and Studies*. New York: John Wiley & Sons, Inc., 1966.

Erickson, E. H., *Childhood and Society*. New York: W. W. Norton & Company, Inc., 1955.

Fieandt, Kai von, *The World of Perception*. Homewood, Ill.: The Dorsey Press, 1966.

Fromm, E., "Value, Psychology, and Human Existence," in A. H. Maslow (Ed.), *New Knowledge in Human Values*. New York: Harper & Row, Publishers, 1959.

Fromm, E., *Escape From Freedom*. New York: Holt, Rinehart and Winston, Inc., 1941.

Goldstein, K., *The Organism*. New York: American Book Co., 1939.

Hall, C. S., and G. Lindzey, *Theories of Personality*. New York: John Wiley & Sons, Inc., 1957.

Hochberg, Julian R., *Perception*. Englewood Cliffs, N.J.: Prentice-Hall, Inc. 1964.

James, W., *Psychology: The Briefer Course*. New York: Harper Torchbooks—The Academy Library, 1961.

Kneller, George F., *Existentialism and Education*. New York: Philosophical Library, Inc., 1958.

Lewin, K., *Field Theory in Social Science*. New York: Harper & Row, Publishers, 1951.

Maddi, Salvatore R., *Personality Theories: A Comparative Analysis*. Homewood, Ill.: The Dorsey Press, 1968.

May, R. (Ed.), *Existential Psychology*. New York: Random House, Inc., 1961.

Patterson, C. H., "Phenomenological Psychology," *The Personnel and Guidance Journal*. 1965, XLII: 997–1005.

Severin, F. T. (Ed.), *Humanistic Viewpoints in Psychology*. New York: McGraw-Hill, Inc., 1965.

Snygg, Donald, "The Need for a Phenomenological System in Psychology," *Psychological Review*. 1941, 48: 404–424.

Thévenaz, Pierre, *What Is Phenomenology?* Chicago: Quadrangle Books, 1962.

Tiryakian, Edward A., "The Existential Self and the Person," in C. Gordon and K. Gergen (Eds.), *The Self in Social Interaction*. New York: John Wiley & Sons, Inc., 1968, pp. 75–86.

Weintraub, D. J., and E. L. Walker, *Perception*. Belmont, Calif.: Brooks/Cole, 1966.

Wepman, J. M., and R. W. Heine, *Concepts of Personality*. Chicago: Aldine Publishing Co., 1963.

chapter three

Nature and Expressions of Self-Consistency

Personality is many things in one. It is a multiple system of interrelated ideas, attitudes, beliefs, experiences, and feelings seeking expression and focus in a single source. Yet, in spite of the myriad of experiences and people who have touched and influenced your life to this point in time, you are a unique personality unlike any other. You may or may not like your personality, but it is, nonetheless, you as you know you. Chances are pretty good that how any of us behave today is more or less consistent with or similar to how we behaved yesterday and also to how we will, in all probability, behave tomorrow. Although a person may wear other hats, assume different roles and behavior for short periods of time, he ultimately expresses that self which he truly is. *A person cannot help but be himself.* Which is the whole point of this chapter.

Unity, Consistency, and Behavior

It is questionable whether total unity of personality is ever achieved in terms of an individual developing a completely consistent, unified self-image. Even though such unification of personality as exists seems to be only a matter of degree, psychological evidence suggests that each of us develops certain primary dispositions and response styles which we can be counted on to more or less consistently reflect in the general course of our behavior. We commonly detect more consistency in our own and other people's behavior than we can always put our finger on and have the lurking suspicion that there is more overall consistency than that which meets the eye. One author wryly observed, for example, that ". . . we not only see people as being all of one piece, but we treat them as if they are, and we often punish them if they are not."[1]

The fact is, we have a strong inclination to perceive, expect, and assume personal consistency of behavior on the part of others in our social environment. There are several good reasons for this. In the first place, there is much less personal strain and anxiety if the social environment is not in a constant state of change. In the second place, the appropriateness of our behavior toward another person is in direct proportion to the correctness of our conceptions of him. "Correct" conceptions, of course depend on the other person's behaving in a more or less consistent manner. Indeed, there is evidence to suggest that when a person behaves inconsistently, he is not as well-liked. For example, one study demonstrated that, over a variety of conditions, a predictable person comes to be liked and an unpredictable one produces a negative reaction.[2]

On the whole, the world of social perception tends to be fairly stable; it is through our abilities to conceptualize that the complex flux of interpersonal relationships is simplified and made comprehensible. For example, as we are exposed to facts and information about another, these perceptions are ordered, synthesized, and integrated into a mind's eye concept of the sort of individual we believe that other person to be. Noting a person's self-effacing manner and submissive behavior, for example, may lead us to conceptualize or picture this person as "shy." This concept is then used as the label for a cluster of observations which serves as the keystone for what we regard as "understanding" the other person. When conceptual judgments are made they tend to remain intact and unchanging. Once we label a person as shy, aggressive, deceptive, friendly, or whatever, we do not easily give up that perception. Even if later information grossly contradicts our perception of what we believe another person is like, it may be either distorted or misperceived so that it fits what we believe to be true. For example, research has shown that when persons receive contradictory information about another, they often misconstrue new information so that what they hear or see is internally consistent with what they already believe to be true about the other person.[3] In ways like this, persons tend to be seen as stable and consistent.

Not only is it important to be able to predict, to count on a certain consistency in others' behavior, but it is crucial that we see threads of consistency in our own behavior as well. You will recall that in Chapter One we discussed the importance of being able to answer the "Who am I" question as the first step toward understanding one's self. The capacity to know who one is and what one stands for is the cornerstone on which behavioral consistency is built. Just as there is less personal strain and anxiety if the social environment is not in a constant state of change, so, too, is it less taxing and anxiety-provoking if one's own personality is not constantly shifting. Being able to predict one's self with reasonable accuracy is comforting because it serves to free a person from unnecessary fretting and worrying about how he might behave under certain conditions. It is when we cannot predict how we might behave or what we might say or be that we get most anxious. A young male client of mine expressed the problem in the following way during our initial interview:

> The thing that bothers me most is me. Isn't that stupid? I don't even know who me is. Every now and then I think I know, but I keep changing. My girl—I should say, my ex-girl—broke up with me because she says I was always breaking my promises. Couldn't trust me, she said. I think she's right, actually. I did break promises. The thing I don't know is how I can keep a promise if I can't even tell when I'm making it whether or not I can keep it. Isn't that stupid—I can't even tell that.

The boy was right, of course; it is difficult to carry out a promise (which is, after all, an explicit declaration that one will do or refrain from doing something which he himself specifies) if he doesn't know himself well enough to make that sort of declaration (prediction) in the first place.

The fact is, our everyday experiences have taught most of us that it is possible to make predictions about one's behavior. Many times our soothsayings ring true, which suggests a certain unity of personality. This unity grows out of our need to be consistent with our "self" concept. However, our predictions are not always correct because, of all things, we are not always perfectly consistent. Indeed, most people have the experience of being astonished from time to time by their own behavior and say things in retrospect like "I don't know how I could have done such a thing," or "I couldn't have been myself when I said that." A student could have succumbed to the temptation to cheat; this is contrary to his self-image and he is literally puzzled as to how he could have done such a thing. The genial, warm, and somewhat self-effacing person who lashes out in vicious anger may have great difficulty understanding what happened and why he expressed himself in such a manner. However, the very rarity of such occurrences points to the personal need for unity and consistence in behavior.

Behavioral Consistency and Self-Concept Theory

William James was among the first to speak about the importance of inner consistency. He distinguished between the essentially healthy person

Reflecting certain behavior patterns with some degree of consistency is common for most people.

whose inner constitution is "harmonious and well balanced from the out-set" and the "sick souls" whose "spirit wars with their flesh. They wish for incompatibles, wayward impulses interrupt their most deliberate plans, and their lives are one long drama of repentance and of effort to repair misdemeanors and mistakes."[4] For James the only hope for these "divided selves" was in the "normal evolution of character," which involved the "straightening out and unifying of the inner self."

Prescott Lecky was one of the first psychologists to develop the idea that the "normally" functioning human being strives for consistency in all aspects of his life. He looked at personality as an organization of ideas which he felt were consistent with one another. Lecky suggested that one overpowering motivation in life is to sustain the unity of this system, an idea which is strongly reflected in the following quote:

Behavior expresses the effort to maintain integrity and unity of the organization. . . . In order to be immediately assimilated, the idea formed as the result of a new experience must be felt to be consistent with the ideas already present in the system. On the other hand, ideas whose inconsistency is recognized as the personality develops must be expelled from the system. There is thus a constant assimiliation of new ideas and the expulsion of old ideas throughout life.[5]

Another psychologist, Carl Rogers, has observed that the integration of various aspects of an individual into a unified concept of self "is accompanied by feelings of comfort and freedom from tension."[6] He goes further to say that one major way of preserving the unity of the self-system is by filtering one's experiences so that they are either ". . . (a) symbolized, perceived and organized into some relationship to the self, (b) ignored because there is no perceived relationship to the self-structure, (c) denied symbolization or given a distorted symbolization because the experience is inconsistent with the structure of the self."[7] This proposition states, in effect, that perception is selective, and the primary criteria for selection is whether the experience is consistent with one's self-picture.

A somewhat related approach is found in the neo-Freudian concept of *identity*. For example, Erikson has made this concept the core of a modern version of psychoanalytic theory and has observed that it is especially during adolescence that one attempts to bring the sense of one's own identity in closer unity to one's social relationships. Erikson writes:

> The sense of ego identity is the accrued confidence that one's ability to maintain inner sameness and continuity . . . is matched by the sameness and continuity of one's meaning for others.[8]

Extending Erikson's idea a step further, Allport suggests that one's ability to maintain inner sameness and continuity is more likely to occur when one is ego- or "self"-involved in whatever the experience at hand happens to be. As Allport states it:

> . . . thoughts and behavior have greater consistency when they relate to what we consider to be warm, central, and important in our lives than they have when they are not so related.[9]

Research evidence tends to support this view. For example, public opinion polls show that people who feel strongly about an issue will be quite consistent in endorsing all the propositions that are related to the issue. If they feel less strongly involved (less "self"-involved) they are more likely to be variable and inconsistent.[10] They are, in a word, less predictable.

As you can see, the value of "inner sameness" has been stressed by many psychologists who have been curious about the relationships between self-concept and behavioral consistency. This line of thinking identifies a healthy personality with a complete and unified self-image. We must remember that self-image includes not only a view of "What I am" but also "What I would like to be" and "What I ought to be." By bringing these three dimensions of the self together a person approaches a greater degree of unification and consistency of behavior.

In short, self-concept theory strongly suggests that a person will "act like" the sort of individual he conceives himself to be. As he encounters new experiences he accepts or rejects them in terms of their compatibility with his present evaluation of himself and thereby maintains his individuality and reduces conflict. Just as a person, as a result of experience, forms attitudes which he organizes into a consistent self-system, which he defends against attack even if it calls for disregard or falsification of the evidence, so the person, also as a result of his experiences, forms attitudes toward himself. Although all attitudes are important determinants of behavior, attitudes involving the self are much more central and basic than those in which a person is less ego-involved. Self-attitudes are usually more potent in determining the course of behavior.

Behavioral Consistency as Related to Primary Motives and Dominant Values

Each person has certain primary motivations or dominant values around which his self-system is organized. It is through the process of being internally consistent to those motivations and values that we can see overt expressions of behavioral consistencies.

Hartshorne and May[11] presented findings which were in apparent contradiction to the idea of self-consistency when they found from their studies of deceit that a child who cheated in one situation did not always cheat in another, although an outside observer might have expected him to do so. They concluded that there is no general personality factor such as honesty, but that honesty is specific and situational, a position which is contrary to the behavioral consistency idea postulated by self-concept theory. The key to the contradiction lies in the fact that it is only to the person doing the observing that the child's behavior is unpredictable. From the child's point of view, his behavior stems from and is determined by a set of dominant values distributed along a definite hierarchy of prepotency. For example, a person might keep money dropped on the sidewalk by a stranger but would never think of doing this if it were lost by a cherished friend. The explanation for the inconsistency in behavior could be that loyalty is more a dominant value for the person in question than is honesty. Hence, he behaves in an honest fashion because he is loyal, not because he is honest.

Since most situations to which we react are complex happenings, they bring into play a multiplicity of motives and values. Usually, however, the dominant value system prevails and the resulting behavior is logical, if not always justifiable, from the standpoint of the behavior. For example, the student who cheats in one instance but not another may still be self-consistent. If his dominant values center on the attainment of high grades, he may feel he *has* to cheat if he suspects he is in serious grade trouble. If, on the other hand, he places honesty above high achievement in his hierarchy of values, he might sooner fail than cheat and even feel a bit self-righteous about passing up what he considers to be a golden opportunity to copy from someone else's paper during an exam. (Along this line, I am reminded of a student who approached me after an exam and complained bitterly about the rampant cheating he saw going on among three other members of the class, all of whom sat near him. He concluded with the time-honored observation that "They're just cheating themselves." As he turned to leave, heavily burdened with the cross he was bearing, he remarked, "I may fail this test, but at least I flunked on my own!") Of course, to pursue the example a step further, if a student's dominant value *is* honesty and he *does* cheat, then he would have to deny or rationalize his dishonesty or feel the heavy weight of guilt. In general, when a person continually behaves in a manner which is inconsistent with his primary motives and dominant values, he is usually in trouble from a psychological point of view. When an individual's behavior is inconsistent with the kind of person he either thinks he should be or wants to be, he may be in need of some kind of therapeutic assistance in integrating his system of values so as to reduce internal conflict.

The fact is, each person projects a certain personality "style" which makes him more or less identifiable and predictable to others. The deeper we know a person, the more predictable he may become to us, particularly if we understand his primary motivations and dominant values.

Sometimes we are wrong in our observations and predictions about another person, not necessarily because he behaved inconsistently, but because our perceptions of him were in error. For example, consider the story of G. B. Shaw's *Pygmalion* (the Broadway musical, *My Fair Lady*) in which Eliza Doolittle, an ignorant little flower girl, is taken on by Professor Higgins for speech training. He not only teaches her to speak in an educated manner, but he finds that she unquestioningly obeys his every order. If he tells her to act like a servant, she does so; like a lady, and she does. On the surface, it seems that Eliza has no consistency at all in her personality. Underneath, however, there is one unifying explanation for her conduct: she is in love with the good professor. Her love is her primary motivation; when we view her behavior in this light we can see that her behavior lacked unity because of a misperception on our part

and not because of her inconsistency. Although she was absurdly inconsistent in her manners of speech and behavior, she was highly consistent
in her love for Professor Higgins. Once we know this we are tapping a
deep primary value, which, from Eliza's point of view, unifies much of
her behavior.

Another example of how behavioral consistency can be misconstrued
by mistaken perceptions is cited by Allport:

> There is the case of a thirteen-year-old girl who was referred for coun-
> seling because she used excessive makeup on her face. This habit seemed
> sadly at variance with her scholarly nature. Her teacher felt something
> must be "wrong." The apparent split in the girl's personality was readily
> explained. She had a heavy crush on her teacher, who was herself
> scholarly and enjoyed a high natural complexion. The little girl was
> entirely (consistent) in her striving to be like her beloved teacher.[12]

In every personality there are primary motives of major significance and
some of minor significance. Occasionally a primary motive is so outstanding in a life that it deserves to be called a *cardinal* motive. Allport has
suggested that such a master quality could also be called ". . . the
eminent trait, the ruling passion, the master-sentiment, the unity-thema,
or the radix of life."[13] Tolstoy's passion for the "simplification of life," or
Schweitzer's guiding ideal of "reverence for life," or Martin Luther
King's struggle to make his "dream" a reality might be examples of
cardinal motives which brought a high degree of unity to behavior. Sometimes, however, we have to look hard for that one cardinal motive which
might unify what otherwise seems like inconsistent behavior.

Take the case of Tom, a college senior who has trouble sustaining
long-term relationships with girls. When he is on a date he is warm,
giving, and empathic, but during the week he is cold, rejecting, and
nonfeeling to the same girls he dates. Does this contradiction in behavior
mean that he lacks primary motives or dominant values? Not at all. He
has two opposed primary motives, one which is warm and giving, and
another which is cold and rejecting. Different situations arouse different
primary motives. Pursuing the case further, the duality is at least partly
explained by the fact Tom has *one* primary motive from which these
contrasting behaviors proceed. The outstanding fact about his personality
is that he is a self-centered egotist who is friendly, warm, and giving only
when he thinks this behavior will serve his own best interest. This cardinal
self-centeredness expresses itself in warm, congenial behavior when he
wants something or in cold, distant behavior when he does not. Most
girls he dated were quick to sense the expediency of his motives and
simply refused to be used by him in this selfish manner. Hence, his difficulty
establishing long-term relationships with girls.

Failing to see a person's deeper motives may lead us to serious misperceptions about his behavior.

The consistency of a motive is a matter of degree. As you can see in the above example, there must be some demonstrable relationship between separate behaviors before its existence can be inferred. The existence of contradictory behaviors does not necessarily mean that a person is behaving inconsistently; it may mean only that we have failed to spot correctly the deepest (most cardinal) motive that is operating.

GENOTYPICAL, PHENOTYPICAL, AND PSEUDO MOTIVES

This last point brings us to a useful distinction suggested by Lewin[14] and elaborated further by Allport.[15] Descriptions of behavior in terms of the "here and now" are *phenotypical*. For example, in the example above, Tom can be either warm and giving or cold and rejecting. These are phenotypical descriptions. Explanatory accounts, which seek deeper motives, are *genotypical*. To take Tom as a case in point again, he has both warm and cold ways of behaving (phenotypical), but these opposing responses are rooted in a more fundamental or primary motive (genotypical) that has been diagnosed as self-centeredness.

It would not be accurate to conclude that phenotypical or primary motives are not true motives. Although they may not reflect the nucleus of a person's basic personality structure, they at least show some consistency in behavior. For example, whether we know that Tom's primary motive was self-centeredness or not, we might still be able to detect that at certain times he was consistently warm and accepting and at other times consistently cold and distant. Getting to the genotypical motive helps us understand the otherwise contradictory and opposing phenotypical motives.

Sometimes our judgments about another person can be totally erroneous. We may, for example, regard a father who buys many gifts for his children as being a *caring* and *generous* person. But what if he is merely trying to buy their favor and affection? In this instance we are not even dealing with a phenotypical motive, for the father has no inclination at all for generosity or caring. The phenotypical or secondary motive is bribery (not generosity or caring) and the underlying genotype (primary motive), for all we know, may contain as its core a feeling of insecurity about whether people generally and his children specifically could ever love him if he didn't first bring them gifts. This is an example of *pseudo motives*, errors of inference, misjudgments that result from drawing conclusions about another person based solely on appearances.

A quite common error of inference, for example, many parents make is in regard to what seems to be the contradictory behavior of their children when the children are in school as opposed to when they are home. As a case in point, a mother approached me after a meeting recently and wondered what was wrong with her nine-year-old boy. She went on to explain that at school he was "a reasonably quiet, well-mannered little boy who behaved pretty well," but that at home he was "unruly, noisy, and frequently sassed both his mother and father." He was, the mother concluded "two different boys." And she wanted to know, "Why?" The boy was, unquestioningly, showing phenotypically contrary behaviors. That is, at school his primary motive seemed to be to behave well; at home it was to behave poorly. Was there a deeper, more genotypical motive? Later, after several counseling sessions with both the mother and the father it turned out that there was indeed. The boy was starved for attention and he found that one way to get it was to be good at school and bad at home. Although his surface behavior seemed inconsistent (good at school, bad at home), both behaviors were quite consistent with the underlying genotypical or primary motive of getting attention. (The parents discovered, by the way, that the reason he misbehaved at home is that they never showed much attention to him when he was good—a heavy price to pay for good manners. Needless to say, they set out to change their behavior that very evening.)

It is only through being careful, disciplined, critical, yet sensitive observers of behavior that we can come close to an accurate diagnosis.

Personality Style and Expressions of Consistency

Earlier it was mentioned that each person projects a certain personality "style" which makes him more or less "knowable" to others. When we talk about personality style, we are referring to the sum total of all that one is and does, to his *characteristic patterns of perceiving and responding*. Each painter and composer has a style all his own; so, too, each musician, ball player, teacher, novelist, housewife, and mechanic. From style alone it is possible to recognize the novels by Hemingway, the musicals of Rodgers and Hammerstein, the paintings of Picasso, or the cooking of one's wife. Each of these activities carries its own unique mark. Although Picasso's art may resemble the art of many others, no one but Picasso can paint exactly like Picasso. A person himself is the fundamental and unique unit of all activity. An artist, it is said, is not a special type of man; but every man is a special type of artist. Each person's artistry, if you will, is projected in his personality style and the purpose of the following discussion will be to show some of the evidence that indicates how various perceptual styles and response styles are ultimately linked to the organized unity of the individual personality.

© 1967 United Feature Syndicate, Inc.

Sometimes a person is consistent in ways he would just as soon change.

EXPRESSIVE VERSUS COPING BEHAVIOR

Before we examine how different people express different kinds of consistency, it may be useful for us first to consider the distinction which Allport[16] makes between *expressive* and *coping* behavior. Everything we do conveys both a coping and an expressive effort. Allport suggests that we can ". . . think of coping as the *predicate* of action (what we are doing); expression as the *adverb* of action (how we are doing it)."

There are at least three important differences between coping and expressive behavior. (1) Coping is more apt to be determined by the demands of the situation; expressive behavior reflects deeper personal motives. (2) Coping can be more readily controlled while expressive behavior is often more difficult to change and often uncontrollable. (For example, changing our style of handwriting or voice inflection, which is expressive behavior, can be kept up for only a short time.) (3) Coping behavior is typically conscious, even though it may employ automatic skills; expressive behavior generally springs from our unconscious.

As an example, take handwriting, which is a product of both coping and expression. On the one hand, we deliberately set out to convey our thoughts, we use some of the conventions of writing we learned in school, and we adapt to the paper and pen available to us. All these reflect coping behaviors. At the same time, we project our personal style in the slant of our writing, the size of our letters and margins, in the pressure we exert on the paper, and so on. All of these are expressive behaviors in the sense that our own unique life styles and primary motives surge into our performances.

As soon as we do something according to convention or in some prescribed manner, then the opportunity for expressive behavior is reduced. For example, the radio announcer must use his voice as an instrument of coping; the result is less expressive individuality. Expressive behavior is most likely to occur in those things we do spontaneously, unconsciously, and of our own accord. That is, most people develop highly characteristic and consistent styles of talking, writing, sitting, walking, gesturing, laughing, and relating to others. At a distance we spot a friend by his gait. We recognize the presence of a friend in a crowded theatre by his laugh. Over the phone we identify who greets us, not so much from what he says as from his voice and manner of speaking. Our expressive behavior is perhaps the most irrepressible part of our natures. Our coping behavior is variable and it depends on *what* we have to do. But *how* we do it carries the mark of our particular and individual personality styles.

It is important to keep in mind that what is revealing about one person's expressive behavior does not necessarily reveal the same thing in

another person. This means that various expressive behaviors are of un-
equal importance in different people. For example, some faces are open
books and some are "poker faces." For some people gestures are merely
conventional, whereas for others they are highly spontaneous and individual. Sometimes the color or style of dress or perhaps the handwriting
seems "just like" the person, and in other cases they seem entirely nonex-
pressive. One person reveals himself consistently and primarily through the
way he talks, another, through his posture and gait, and a third through
his style of dress or ornamentation. Allport has suggested that "every
person has one or two leading expressive features which reveal his true
nature."[17] If this is so, and there is evidence to support that it is, then what
we first have to do is to become as aware as possible of the various ways in
which people reveal themselves in expressive behaviors.

At the same time, we need to keep in mind that any expressive behavior
may have some compensatory deception built into it. In other words, it is
not enough to rely on the obvious interpretation (the face-validity) of an
expressive behavior. Self-defensiveness and other countercurrents may
be seriously affecting how the other person behaves. We can never be
totally certain what the expressive aspect of an act signifies because the
unity of expression is a question of degree, just as the unity of personality
is a matter of degree. There are few uncomplicated one-to-one relationships. We might hunch, for example, that an "introverted" (quiet, shy,
withdrawn) person would "logically" express his doodling in small, or
tight, or constricted lines. What does research say about this? Consider
the following:

> Two psychologists asked a group of subjects to draw doodles and then
> measured the area covered in their doodlings. As you might suspect, the
> introverted subjects, on the average, drew small and tight doodles. But
> there were marked exceptions. Some drew expansively large ones. Also,
> as you might suspect, extroverted (out-going, confident) subjects tended
> to draw large doodles, but some of them scribbled in a remarkably small
> and tiny manner. The explanation for these confusing results is that the
> deviants were found to be, by other measurements, highly *anxious* people.
> Their *expressive* behavior was an effort to compensate for the underlying
> feeling. For example, the anxious introvert *compensated* for his anxiety
> by exaggerated drawings; the anxious extrovert *compensated* in the oppo-
> site way.[18]

These findings should not surprise us. We all know cases such as the insecure adolescent who exhibits a rough, tough, "bully" attitude, which he
hopes will mask his feelings of inferiority or insecurity. His behavior may
be very specific to certain situations, or it may have become a daily expression of his personality style. Whatever the case, we should remain

Nonanxious introvert

Anxious introvert

Anxious extrovert

Nonanxious extrovert

Figure 3.1 Illustrative expressive doodles. (From M. A. Wallach and R. C. Gahm, "Personality Functions of Graphic Restriction and Expansiveness." *Journal of Personality*, 1960, 28, 73–88, by permission.)

alert to the possibility of compensatory deception existing in expressive behaviors.

PERCEPTUAL STYLE AS RELATED TO PERSONALITY

What we see in our outer worlds is related to how we feel about our inner selves. In many, if not most, of our interpersonal experiences we show a consistent tendency to be either passively or aggressively rigid or actively and flexibly adaptive. As we discussed in Chapter Two, what we "see" and what we "hear" depend in large measure on who we are and how we feel about ourselves. As William James long ago pointed out, if four men go to Europe—a politician, an artist, a businessman, and a playboy— they will see, hear, note, and remember entirely different scenes and events.

George Klein[19] was among the first to demonstrate that people develop characteristic ways, which he called "perceptual attitudes," of dealing with how they see things, irrespective of content and sensory modality. A person's perceptual style is an important source of unity and consistency within the personality. Consequently, one's perceptual style is a factor making for a characteristic way of dealing with the environment which eventually comes to be an identifying feature of the unique personality. How do personality and perceptual style interact? Consider the following experiment by Holzman and Klein:

A group of subjects were presented with square designs and asked to judge each for size. At first only squares 2 and 5 inches on a side were presented. Later the 2-inch square was omitted and a 7-inch square substituted. Eventually, the 3-inch square was replaced by an 8-inch one, the 4-inch square by a 9-inch one, and so on. Thus without their knowledge, the subjects were required to deal with gradually changing sizes. The results were surprising. Some subjects were realistic and accurate and held closely to the actual sizes presented, while others apparently fell into a rut and continued to repeat a judgment when it was no longer appropriate. The extent of this lag is made even more dramatic by the fact that toward the end of the experiment some subjects were judging a 13-inch square to be only 4 inches on a side.[20]

Klein proposes a "leveling-sharpening" continuum of perceptual functioning to describe this difference among individuals. *Levelers* are individuals who characteristically hold tight to their categories of perception and judgment and tend to ignore changes. *Sharpeners*, by contrast, are alert to changes and more able to spot fine nuances and small differences. He also found that levelers had more difficulty finding a simple figure embedded in a more complex design, more trouble finding hidden faces in puzzle pictures, and they reported less contrast in figures of differing brightness. Thus there seems to be some evidence for asserting that these individuals have a perceptual style which characterizes them in many different situations. Personality studies have found that "levelers" tend to avoid competition, to seek relationships in which they could be dependent on others, and to be self-oriented, self-abusing, and passive. "Sharpeners" are inclined to be more competitive, exhibitionistic, and to have high achievement needs.

From different approaches different investigators, including Klein, have made a single central discovery. To put it simply, some people are unable to change their mental "set" (their minds, judgments, perceptions, first conclusions) even when confronted with new information or changing conditions. For example, Witkin[21] and his co-workers identified what he called *field-dependent* and *field-independent* persons. He found that the field-independent mode of perceiving focuses on the figure or "central object of perception" and resists the influence of the background. Field-dependent perceiving is markedly influenced by variations in the background. Tested individuals vary in their tendency to be field-dependent or field-independent, but—and this is important for us—a given individual's perceptual style tends to remain constant over a variety of test situations. For example, in one experiment the subject sat in a tilted chair and was asked to adjust a movable rod so it would be vertical. The field-dependent person tended to keep the rod parallel to his own body and line of sight. He could not abstract the "true vertical" from his own position and line of sight. The field-independent person was better able to correct for his own position and handle the pointer as the external conditions changed. Another task called for a similar judgment of the vertical in a small room tilted off the horizontal. Still another involved finding an embedded figure buried in a complex figure (See Figure 3.2). The "field-independent" were not disturbed by the tilted framework and could find the embedded figure easily, whereas the "field-dependent" subjects had great difficulty with both tasks.

Now let us look at the personalities of the field-dependent—those who are strongly influenced and controlled by the situation in which they find themselves. Witkin and his associates found that adults who were field-dependent were inclined to be passive and submissive to authority, to be afraid of their sexual and aggressive impulses, and to have low self-esteem and self-acceptance. In general, they are people who are very dependent on environmental supports. Field-independent people, on the other hand, tended to be independent in their social behavior, rather accepting of their hostile and sexual impulses, and better able to control them. They were generally less anxious, more self-confident, and more accepting. Other research reviewed by Elliot[22] indicated that field-dependent

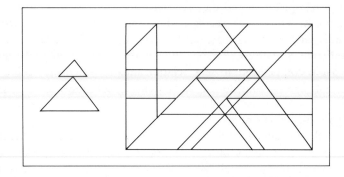

Figure 3.2 The embedded figures task. This task, devised by Gottschaldt, requires that the person locate the simple figure at left in the complex figure at right. A test using many of these has been employed in studies of perceptual style. (From K. Gottschaldt, "Ueber den Einfluss der Ehrfahrung auf die Wahrnehmung von Figuren." *Psychologische Forschung,* 1926, 8: 261–317.)

people tend to rate high on gregariousness and conventionality, whereas field-independent people tend to rate high on measures of interpersonal hostility, creativeness, and originality.

Our everyday experiences have taught us that some people are inclined to see everything as black or white, or all good or all bad. Some people have a high need for a two-plus-two-equals-four type answer to their questions, while others are more tolerant of ambiguity and uncertainty. Frenkel-Brunswik[23] tested for tolerance of ambiguity in a strictly perceptual sense by presenting pictures in a series which gradually changed from one percept to another (e.g., cat to dog). The subjects who were judged as being "intolerant of ambiguity" were those who held onto the original percept for a considerable time, then switched to the other, but were unable to admit that the picture might be either object. It *had* to be one or the other. Frenkel-Brunswik found that these individuals tended toward extremes in their emotional reactions as well as in their perceptual style.

Particularly interesting in this connection is the discovery that people who are rigid (who are "levelers," field-dependent) in their perceptual style and thinking tend to be prejudiced against Negroes, Jews, Catholics, and other groups. It is as if they cannot tolerate ambiguity or something different from what they know of any sort: neither in their perceptions, in their ways of thinking, nor in "taking chances" with ethnic or religious groups other than their own.[24]

A person's perceptual style does, indeed, seem to be related to his total personality. It affects a person's percept of himself, his view of others, and his adjustment to situations. For example, a person who is insecure, feels inadequate, self-distrustful, and who feels threatened by life generally, tends to have a congruent perceptual style which is rigid, field-bound, concrete, and passive. In contrast, the more active, confident, secure, relaxed individual is better able to perceive and think across a broader range of ideas and circumstances and is on the whole, better adapted to the objective demands of the situation in which he finds himself.

How does it happen that people develop such differing perceptual styles? To a large extent it depends on how they were raised. For example, working with ten-year-olds, to whom perceptual tests similar to Witkin's had been given, it was found that the background and training of the field-dependent (less secure) and field-independent (more secure) children differed markedly. Field-dependent children were found to have mothers who were more restrictive, more concerned with dominating their children, and inclined to discourage curiosity and to encourage conformity. The mothers of field-independent children tended to encourage individuality, responsibility, exploring behavior, and independence.[25]

When considering the relationships between personality and perceptual preferences, Barron[26] has suggested that we are dealing with two types of perceptual preferences. One of them is a perceptual style which chooses that which is stable, regular, balanced, predictable, clear-cut, traditional, and follows some general abstract principle, which in human affairs is personified as authority. The other perceptual style is that which chooses what is complex, which is to say unstable, asymmetrical, unbalanced, whimsical, rebellious against tradition, and even at times irrational, disordered, and chaotic. To see things predominantly one way or the other is a sort of perceptual decision related to one's total personality style. For example, in our private world of experience, we may attend to its ordered aspects, to regular sequences of events, to a stable center of the universe (God, the church, the state, the home, the parent, etc.) or we may attend primarily to its complex aspects, to the eccentric, the relative, and the arbitrary aspects of the world (briefness of individual life, hypocrisy of the "system," accidents of circumstance of fate, the impossibility of total freedom, and so on).

A perceptual style which enables a person to see the world as orderly and predictable can have two kinds of consequences. At its best, the decision to see things in an orderly and predictable way could reflect personal stability and balance, a sort of easygoing optimism combined with religious faith, a friendliness towards tradition, custom, and ceremony, and a respect for authority. We might expect people to be this way who are open, trusting, and independent.

At its worst, a perceptual decision in favor of order and predictableness could reflect a need to reject all that threatens the order, a fear of anything that might "rock the boat." Such a decision is associated with stereotyped thinking, rigid and compulsive morality, and a distrust of angry and sexual impulses. Personal stability depends essentially upon exclusion of impulses and experiences that do not fit easily into some preconceived system. We might expect people to be this way who are somewhat closed-minded, suspicious, and dependent.

A perceptual style which enables a person to see the world in its various shades of complexity can also have two consequences. At its best, an inclination to see the complexities of daily living could reflect an inclination for originality and creativeness, a greater tolerance of the unusual and the different, and a willingness to work at a reasonable balance between the inner and outer complexity in a higher order synthesis. The goal is to attain the psychological analog of mathematical elegance, to allow one's self to absorb the greatest possible richness of experience, while searching for some unifying pattern or theme. We might expect people to be this way who were creative, sensitive, even flighty.

At its worst, a perceptual style in favor of complexity could lead to grossly disorganized behavior, nihilism, despair, disintegration, and surrender to chaos. One's personal life becomes a simple acting out of the meaninglessness of the universe and the apparent insolubility of the problem. We might expect people to be this way who have a sense of futility, who seem aimless, and who feel little sense of responsibility.

RESPONSE STYLES AS RELATED TO PERSONALITY

Just as it is true that each of us has a certain perceptual style which contributes to our unique and unified personality, so, too, does each of us reflect certain characteristic "response styles" that indicate something of the nature of our feelings about ourselves and others. Response styles have many outlets and can be expressed in one's general tension level, his handwriting, facial expressions, his voice and speech, posture, gesturing habits, and even by the way he walks. None of these behaviors are random and unrelated to the personality of the behaving person and in the discussion to follow we will try to indicate how even somatic or visceral or motor expressions are more or less consistent with an individual's personality and feeling.

VISCERAL OR SOMATIC RESPONSE STYLES

There is evidence to suggest that a person's visceral or somatic responses are related to and consistent with certain emotional states. For example, Malmo and others,[27] found that headache-prone patients were not only more tense people, but also developed more tension in their neck muscles than other patients. In another study, he found that certain feelings may elicit corresponding tension in various muscle groups. For example, a divorced woman was being interviewed about her problems, while electrical action potentials were recorded from different muscle groups. When she was talking mainly about her anger and hostility to her ex-husband (and other people), the major electrical activity was in her arm muscles; when she was discussing her sexual problems, the major activity was localized in her leg muscles.[28] In other words, as she experienced different feelings about different situations and people, she also experienced different muscle tensions related to the feelings she was having.

GRAPHIC RESPONSE STYLES

Each person's style of handwriting is unique. Proponents argue that handwriting is not merely handwriting, but "brainwriting," influenced by a complex circuitry of neural impulses which gives an individual flavor to how one writes. Critics who claim that there is "nothing to graphology" are probably as wrong as graphology enthusiasts who claim too much. Studies have indicated that graphologists are in fact able to relate handwriting to an individual's personality characteristics significantly more often than one might expect by chance.[29, 30] It is not only the professionals who have the skill to detect consistencies between handwriting and personality characteristics. We may all have this ability to some extent. For example, it has been found that a randomly selected group of people can tell the sex of writers correctly from script alone in about 70 percent of the cases.[31] In another experiment, college students, faculty members, and graphologists were given samples of handwriting from ten subjects. By chance alone, the judges would be expected to be correct one out of ten times. The college students averaged 1.77; the faculty group 1.80; and the graphologists, 2.41. The fact that all groups exceeded chance, even to this small degree, suggests that personality is at least to some extent revealed in handwriting.[32]

In an effort to be more precise in the measurement of relationships between graphic responses and personality, Mira[33] developed a standardized series of graphic tasks which he calls "myokinetic psychodiagnosis." For example, a subject starts to copy a simple design like, say, a staircase. As soon as he gets under way a shield is placed in front of his eyes so he can no longer see what he is doing, but he continues copying. In this way the coping behavior is reduced and the expressive component becomes more prominent. Mira believes he can identify certain deep tendencies in the personality by observing his expressive graphic behavior. For instance, a marked drift *away* from the body, in the case of lines drawn to and from the body, was related to aggressive attitudes towards others, while an *inward* drift was related to self-directed aggression. In addition, he found that elated people exaggerate upward movements, while depressed people tend to overdue movements toward the body.

Although it is only a matter of degree, there does seem to be a relationship between a person's graphic response style and his personality. Consider, for example, the musical scores in Figure 3.3 on the following page. One is by Beethoven, another by Mozart, and a third by Bach. If you know anything about the music of these three men, which score do you think was written by whom? Most people quickly see the unities: the tempestuousness of Beethoven (No. I), the spritely fastidiousness of Mozart (No. II), and the ordered and steady flow of Bach (No. III). These qualities were reflected not only in their music and graphic style, but in their personal lives as well.

VOICE AND SPEECH RESPONSE STYLES

A person's voice is a highly expressive aspect of his personality. Voice inflection, intonation, rhythm, accent, and pitch vary widely among individuals and research has shown that there are relationships between voice and personality. For example, using a matching method where the unanalyzed voice is compared with known expressions and facts about the person doing the speaking, the following tendencies have been discovered:[34]

1. Untrained voices are more expressive (more often correctly matched than trained voices).
2. Age can usually be told within ten years.
3. Deeper traits—whether the speaker is dominant, extroverted, esthetic, or religious in his interests, and so on—are judged with fair success.
4. Complete sketches of personality are matched with voice with still greater success. (This finding is important. It suggests that voice-as-an-expressive-pattern is consistent with personality-as-a-whole, which further suggests that too fine an analysis may lose the diagnostic revelation of the voice as an expressive response.)

There is also evidence to suggest that there are relationships between speech and personality. For instance, Doob[35] found that people who used many adjective and adverb modifiers also used more active verbs. Furthermore, they were able to give more "field-independent" judgments such as being able to pick out hidden or embedded figures in a complex visual field. This particular study shows well the consistency of different

I

II

III

Figure 3.3 Musical manuscript of Bach, Beethoven, and Mozart. (From W. Wolff, *The Expression of Personality*. New York: Harper, 1943, pp. 20ff., by permission.)

expressions. That is, people who are active, analytic, and discriminating in handling their environment show this same tendency in their speech habits. They are neither passive in relating to their environment nor passive in their use of speech. In a sense, their active lives are reflected in their active use of the language.

INTERRELATEDNESS OF MULTIPLE RESPONSE STYLES

In order to find out whether people expressed themselves in similar ways across many different kinds of activities, Allport and Vernon[36] conducted an extensive study on a group of subjects who were required to carry out several dozen different tasks and then measured for their performance. The response styles they measured included such things as reading and counting aloud, walking indoors and outdoors, appraisals of distances, drawing of circles to estimate the size of certain objects, estimates of angles and weights, and so on. The investigators found a marked tendency for each person to perform the same task in the same manner on two different occasions. They also found a strong consistency of expressive movement when the same task was performed with different muscle groups. For example, there were strong similarities and consistencies between a person's footwriting style and his handwriting style.

When the experimenters examined all their measures for the presence of general expressive traits, they found that there were indeed tendencies for the individual's expressive movements to be similar across many different kinds of activities. They reported, for instance, that there were significant intercorrelations among variables such as the following: voice intensity ratings; ratings on movement during speech; writing pressure; tapping pressure; overestimation of weights; underestimation of distance between hands; verbal slowness; pressure of resting hand, and others.

The investigators considered this group of interrelated measures and ratings as constituting an expressive factor of *emphasis*. For example, the confident, take-charge, aggressive individual is likely to express these characteristics across many tasks. In addition, we are apt to find this sort of person having a louder voice than most, exhibiting heavier (more aggressive) writing and tapping pressure, showing more restlessness during his talking periods, and probably more inclined to overestimate (like he may "over" do many other things?) the weight of various objects. On the other hand, a shyer, more withdrawn person might be expected to have a quieter (more passive) voice, exhibit lighter (less aggressive) writing and tapping pressure, show less body movement during his talking periods, and probably more inclined to underestimate the weight of various objects. Along this same line, Bills[37] found that people who have low acceptance of themselves underestimate their performances more than people with higher acceptance of themselves. As another indication to show the consistencies between feelings and behavior, there is also evidence to suggest that people who have low acceptance of themselves report on the average, twice as many physical complaints as people who are high in their acceptance of themselves.[38]

Maslow[39] found that high-dominance women (strong, self-confident, self-assertive characters) reflect their dominant, assertive characters in many different ways. For example, they choose foods that are saltier, stronger tasting, sharper, and more bitter, e.g., strong cheeses rather than milder ones; foods that taste good even though ugly and unattractive, e.g., clams; foods that are novel and different, e.g., snails, or fried squirrel. They are less picky, less easily nauseated, less fussy about unattractive or sloppily prepared food, and yet more sensuous and lusty about good food than low-dominance (passive, shy, retreating) women. These same qualities are apparent in other areas too. For example, the language of high-dominance women is tougher, stronger, harder; the men they choose are tougher, stronger, harder, and their reactions to people who try to take advantage of them is tougher, stronger, and harder. In still other research, Maslow[40] found that the high-dominance woman is more apt to be pagan, permissive, and accepting in all sexual realms. She is less apt to be a virgin, more apt to have masturbated, and more apt to have done more sexual experimentation. In other words, her sexual behavior is consistent with what seems to be a general personality characteristic, for here, too, she is apt to be dominant in terms of being more forward and less inhibited.

This, then, is some of the evidence which supports the idea of the personality having a unitary organization. In its simplest terms it suggests that an individual's "personality style" reflects a degree of unity across many different expressive behaviors. We must, however, be cautious in our judgments for two reasons: (1) behavioral consistency is never perfect; (2) we can too easily misinterpret the inner state underlying a person's mask if we are insensitive to that person's primary motives, or if the person tries to conceal his real feelings with masquerading behavior. For example, people frequently misinterpret shyness for snobbishness, and self-confidence for conceit. A ready smile and a firm handshake do not provide valid indicators of honesty and integrity; indeed, the confidence man and shyster are adept at providing such cues. It is only through remaining sensitive and alert to the total complex of perceptual, bodily, and graphic response styles that we can begin to see their overall interrelatedness in behavior.

OCCUPATIONAL CHOICE AS RELATED
TO PERSONALITY

If an individual relates to others in a characteristic way in a variety of life situations, we might expect that this type of relationship will be reflected in his occupational values and occupational choices as well. Every occupation has some interpersonal quality about it—the chance to enjoy interaction with other people, or to dominate them, or to get away from them. Although personality alone can rarely determine a *specific* choice, it may represent a channeling factor determining a broad *area* of choices.

Rosenberg[41] explored the idea that if a student selects those values which are consistent with his "self-other orientation," he would also tend to choose an occupation in which those values could most likely be satisfied. Rosenberg was able to identify three "pure" types and found that there were, indeed, relationships between personality types (styles) and broad occupational categories.

One style was reflected in the "detached type," who was characterized by a deep-seated resistance to coercion or domination of any sort. This type was highly conscious of his individuality and stressed independence and "freedom from supervision" among his top dominant values. Occupational fields such as art, architecture, journalism, drama, and natural science were most frequently chosen by detached personalities.

Another style was reflected in the "aggressive type," concerned primarily with "extrinsic-reward" values. He is motivated mostly by his need for domination and mastery. Two ways of getting ahead in the world and thereby establishing one's superiority are to earn "a good deal of money" and to gain a high degree of "status and prestige." It is these values, as it turns out, that aggressive people rank as highly important. Consistent with these values, they were likely to choose fields such as real estate, finance, hotel management, sales-promotion, law, advertising, and different kinds of business, all of which emphasize the extrinsic rewards of work and the promise of fame and fortune if one "makes it."

Still another style was the "compliant type," who wants to be liked, accepted, and to do things for others. This individual, anxious to please and be helpful, stresses values such as "wanting to work with people rather than things," and "wanting an opportunity to help others." As we might expect, the compliant's people-oriented values were reflected in occupational fields such as social work, teaching, medicine, social science, personnel work, and psychology.

We must keep in mind that these are pure types and the likelihood of a person being totally an aggressive, or a detached, or a compliant type are remote. A bit of each of these three types resides in each of us, but in different degrees and in different orders. The fact that a compliant type chooses, say, medicine more than the other two types does not mean that only compliant types become doctors. Not at all. Some choose to become doctors or teachers not because they are compliant, but because they are aggressive and see these choices as being their quickest routes to domination and mastery. Or the compliant type could choose journalism, let's say, because he saw it as a way of working closely with people's lives. These "type" categories are merely guidelines and not one-to-one relationships between personality and occupational choice. Research does show, however, that there are general relationships between personality types and occupational choices. An individual who is compliant and who wants to be helping and caring will be guided toward occupational fields in which friendly, frequent contacts with others is inherent in the structure of the occupation. Similarly, an aggressive person who needs to express control, mastery, or domination will move toward that general area of occupations in which this desire can find expression. Finally, the detached individual who wants as little as possible to do with others and who wishes to keep a certain emotional distance from people, tends to avoid occupations in which others are likely to make demands on him.

Cognitive Dissonance and the Need for Consistency

In a musical sense, dissonance is the result of a mingling of discordant sounds, while in a psychological sense it is the result of a mingling of discordant ideas and behaviors. As we have seen in our discussion to this point, inconsistent ideas and behaviors are a source of conflict and tension that a person is usually motivated to resolve in one way or another. We either choose one of the alternatives that face us or we try to avoid or ignore the conflict, which amounts to finding a third alternative in a two-choice conflict. Once the choice has been made, however, interesting changes in behavior are usually apparent. If Joan decides to ride the rollercoaster in spite of her fears, she may later deny or even forget that she thought of it as frightening. Or, if she decides not to ride, she may make a considerable fuss about how pale or shaken her friends look at the end of their ride. Choosing either alternative forces her to "do something" about the choice she did not make. Changing one's behavior (which includes feelings and attitudes) to make it consistent with what one has already done is the route most people take to solve their dissonant mental states.

Festinger's[42] model of cognitive dissonance is a good case in point, inasmuch as the entire theory rests on the premise that a person continuously strives for consistency among his thoughts. The kind of inconsistency or disagreement with which Festinger is chiefly concerned is that which occurs after a decision has been made so that there is an inconsistency between what one does and what one believes. In other words, if a person has two ideas or views which are "dissonant" or mutually inconsistent, he will take steps to reduce the conflict. For example, if a regular smoker happens to come across some startling new evidence linking smoking to lung cancer, his smoking and his new information will be dissonant. If he continues to smoke as much as ever, the only way he can reduce the dissonance is to: (1) act as if the medical report isn't really as serious as it sounds, or (2) disbelieve the report. On the other hand, if the decision is made to either give up smoking or drastically cut it down, the information linking lung cancer and smoking can be stoutly defended.

Take another example. Let's say an English teacher who has very firm, negative views about *Playboy* magazine finds himself in a circumstance where he has to wait for an extended period, with nothing to do, no one to talk to, and nothing to read except several *Playboy* magazines which happen to be on a table. A short while later, an acquaintance walks by and catches him looking at a *Playboy*. There he is, indulging in an activity which allegedly is against his principles. The friend says, "Do my eyes deceive me? Do I see you reading *Playboy*?" How does the teacher handle the dissonance? He may reply: "Thought I'd find out why men are attracted to these things." (In other words, "I'm not really reading them, I'm doing research.") Or, "In desperation, I'd even read *Sunshine and Health*." (In other words, "This is an emergency and it doesn't really count.")

Cognitive dissonance and the need for consistency between what one believes and what is actually happening was nicely illustrated by Festinger and his coworkers[43] when they studied a religious group who predicted the earth's destruction. This group believed that they were receiving communications from the gods stating that a castastrophic flood would overwhelm the world and that only members of this particular group would be saved when flying saucers would come to whisk them off to safety. On the day of the predicted flood, the chosen few were waiting at the proper places for the saucers to rescue them. When the saucers did not arrive at the time first predicted, this development naturally enough produced dissonance. What they believed and what was happening were inconsistent events and, in order to reduce this, the development was interpreted as a test set up by the gods to see if true believers could withstand uncertainty. Subsequent word was received that flying saucers would come at a later time. Then, when they did not come as predicted and when several other predictions about their arrival were also proved wrong, and when grave doubt began to surface concerning the coming of the catastrophic flood, the really true believers had a problem. Indeed, they were in a state of dejected puzzlement until they came by the happy construction, conveyed to them as if it were a message from the gods, that because of the faith and steadfastness of the followers, the gods had decided to spare the world, and to rearrange the divine plan for the true believers. Thus the dissonance was relieved and the events as they were happening were consistent with a new belief or idea. However, to keep it effective in relieving the dissonance, it had to be built up to more credible proportions. Consequently, the true believers exerted strong efforts, through new releases and missionary work, to publicize the great turn of events that had occurred and to win more converts to the cause. Through investing additional efforts in support of the interpretation of what had happened they made the new interpretation seem even more believable.

The steps people take to reduce dissonance has also been demonstrated in experimental settings. For example, Buss and Brock[44] asked a number of men and women who had previously said they were opposed to the use of electric shock in scientific research to participate in an experiment in which they believed they were administering electric shock to induce learning. Just before the experiment began, they were asked to read a statement purporting to emanate from medical authorities. One version stated that electric shocks were extremely harmful and the other stated that they were, in fact, beneficial. After the experiment subjects were asked to recall the content of the communication. Consistent with cognitive dissonance theory, there was significantly less recall of the medical statement which said that shocks were harmful. In other words, forgetting the negative material made it easier to accept the fact that they had, in fact, administered an electric shock to other persons and thus enabled them to reduce the dissonance between what they believed and what they had done. It is also an excellent example of how people selectively remember experiences and events so as to protect their self-concepts.

The point should be clear. Dissonant ideas and behaviors produce conflict and tension. In the quest for an overall unity of personality, changing one's behavior to make it consistent with what he has already done is a course which most people seek to reduce the dissonance and insure some degree of "sameness" on a day-to-day basis.

Consistency of Behavior over Time

To what extent does an individual remain consistent and how much does he change in time? Although we would not expect to find perfect consistency of behavior between a person's childhood behavior and adult behavior, we might expect to find some resemblances. What does research have to say about this?

EARLY REFLECTIONS OF UNIQUE
PERSONALITY CHARACTERISTICS

In observations of twenty-five babies during the first two years of life, Shirley[45] found that the children showed a high degree of consistency in the general pattern of their behavior from month to month. Developmental characteristics (locomotor ability, manipulatory skills, and general development) evidence the greatest constancy at the various age levels. Each baby tended to maintain its relative position in the group with respect to these. Shirley noted that their behavior changed as they matured but there were always "identifying earmarks." A given expression of behavior "would lapse only to be supplemented by another that apparently was its consistent outgrowth." For example, one baby was distinctive at an early age for his "timorous crying." As time went on, the crying waned, but then he exhibited "apprehensive watching" and, at a later age, showed similar fearful behavior by hiding behind his mother and by his reluctance to play and talk in the presence of a stranger. As you can see, even though the specific responses are different (timorous crying, apprehensive watching, hiding behind his mother), each is motivated by a basic feeling of fear. If we try to compare specific responses, we miss the boat by failing to see that the underlying consistency can express itself in different ways and at different times.

Shirley goes a step further and suggests that certain aspects of personality are inborn and persist from age level to age level. For example, Shirley states that:

> Both constancy and change characterize the personality of the baby. Traits are constant enough to make it plausible that a nucleus of personality exists at birth and that this nucleus persists and grows and determines to a certain degree the relative importance of the various traits. Some change is doubtless wrought by environmental factors, but this change is limited by the limitations of the original personality nucleus.[46]

A study by Martin[47] revealed a high degree of constancy in social behavior patterns of nursery school children. On the basis of observational records, fifty-three middle-class children during each of four semesters of nursery school were scored in terms of seven response categories, which included, dependency, nurturance, aggression, control-dominance, antonomous achievement, avoidance-withdrawal, and friendship affiliation. The findings revealed profile instability over the two-year period in only nine of the fifty-three children. Martin concludes that:

> . . . during a period in the life span when instrumental behavior is demonstrably changing, in response to modifications in individual capabilities and social expectations, and—more specifically in the nursery school

setting—and programs, a pattern of individual social behavior that is strikingly unchanging emerged. It is as if each child has his own *behavioral economy* which persists through time.[48]

In other research, Escalona and Heider[49] made predictions based on observations of the behavior of thirty-one infants, then tested these predictions against behavioral data gathered about five years later. Predictions were made for many different aspects of behavior and the outcomes were similarly focused. For example:

Prediction, item 35: I expect Janice to understand and use language with perfectly good competence. I would be surprised if her verbal abilities as measured by tests exceeded average standards for her age. Outcome: Achieved superior scores on vocabulary and verbal comprehension items.[50]

This was, as you can see, a predictive failure. In fact, most of the predictions for Janice were failures. A successful prediction is illustrated by the following protocols for Terry:

Prediction, item 41: Have thought that he will be very vocal in the sense of talking with a great deal of eagerness and intensity. Outcome: He talked freely, usually with enjoyment and often with a sort of urgency.[51]

Predictions were, in general, more successful with certain children than with others. With one child they were 92 percent successful, while at the other extreme there was a child for whom only 33 percent of the outcomes agreed with the predictions. Some aspects of behavior were more accurately predicted than others, particularly those having to do with life style and adaptation to sex roles. Predictions which dealt with characteristics such as competiveness or shyness were less accurate.

Studies dealing with the consistency of personality traits beyond the preschool or early school periods are relatively few in number, the major reason being that it is difficult to keep track of the same individuals over a long period of time. But there are some, however, and we will now take a look at the major studies related to long-term behavioral consistency to see if we can assess the relationships between childhood and adulthood behaviors in the same individuals.

CONSISTENCY OF BEHAVIOR FROM CHILDHOOD TO ADULTHOOD

Cited often among studies of long-term consistency and change is the effort by Neilon,[52] who, after a fifteen-year interval, followed up the individuals who had been studied by Shirley from birth to age two. Neilon collected extensive autobiographical sketches of fifteen of the original nineteen children at the age of seventeen—ten boys and five girls. Descriptive sketches of the infant personality and of the adolescent personality were prepared independently, and presented to psychologists who knew none of the children. The judges were asked to match the infant sketch with what they believed to be the corresponding adolescent personality. (It should be noted here that although Neilon and her associates knew the names of the children who had participated in the original study, they did not know which child was represented in each of Shirley's published biographies because of the use of pseudonyms in publication.) After the psychologists finished matching, Shirley's original data were then consulted to find out the real names of the children associated with each infant sketch so that the accuracy of the matching could be measured. The judges succeeded in matching the girls so successfully that their results could be obtained by chance less than once in a million times. With the boys they were correct to an extent that could occur by chance only once in 4000 tries. Although great individual differences existed among individual children, one girl being matched correctly by all ten judges and another by none, it was evident that there was considerable consistency in personality over a period of time. In other words, *many characteristics which were evident in early childhood persisted into late adolescence.*

In another study related to long-term behavioral consistency, McKinnon[53] observed eight boys and eight girls over a five-year period beginning at an average age of around four years. A fourfold classification of types was employed: conformity, invasiveness, caution, and withdrawal, according to the child's dominant pattern. Five children were rated as predominately conformist types at the earliest age level, and three of these were similarly rated at the age of eight to nine years. Of five initially characterized as invasive (forcible use of materials, active approach, physical and/or verbal attack) two were also seen that way at the upper age level. Three characterized by withdrawal persisted in this trait throughout the period. Three were first rated as cautious and two of these were still perceived this way at the end of the period. Thus, although changes in characterization occurred in some cases, consistency predominated.

A high degree of persistence in "ascendance-submission" was found in an investigation by Stott,[54] who studied over a hundred youngsters during a period of about twelve years. The first assessment was made while children were in nursery school, and later the children were observed in the recreational clubs they attended. They were rated on a scale of ascendance-submission ranging from extreme bossiness to "dependent ineffective submissiveness." Stott found that "persistence of pattern was far more frequent than change during the period covered" and that 82 percent of the children ". . . showed no consistent direction of change." When changes did occur, they were temporary in most instances, with a subsequent return to the earlier pattern.

Even more impressive is the material from investigations tracing the same individuals from childhood to maturity. Birren,[55] for example, reported on thirty-eight children who were examined in a child guidance clinic and who later became psychotic. He found that their symptoms corresponded closely to the pattern of traits observed in childhood. "Personality characteristics of psychotic patients," he concludes, "are stable and evidence continuous development from childhood."

Arkin[56] used case-history material to compare the personality traits of individuals five to eight years of age with their personality traits when twenty-five to forty years old. Forty cases were studied altogether. It was reported that 100 percent of the men were equally "emotional" at both age levels, but only 67 percent of the women were judged to be as emotional between twenty-five and forty as between five and eight years. Intellect, special endowment, social attitude, and initiative were judged to be consistent in 67 to 100 percent of the cases.

These results are consistent with those of Tuddenham,[57] who, following up individuals studied as adolescents nineteen years earlier, observed a significant stability in more than one-third of the traits studied.

The most extensive recent study of consistency over time was undertaken by Kagan and Moss.[58] They studied the stability from infancy to adulthood of such aspects of behavior as passivity, aggression, striving for achievement, and sexuality. Assessments were made over four childhood periods and again when some of the subjects were from nineteen to twenty-nine years old. Infant ratings for the eighty-nine subjects were compared with self-ratings and scores on various personality tests, and the results of interviews in adulthood. One characteristic which proved to be relatively stable was passivity. This generally became evident during the second year and it was expressed in various ways during the school years, for example, timid behavior in social situations, avoidance of dangerous activities, and conformity to parents. The authors believe that they have reasonable grounds for the hypothesis that the foundations for "extreme degrees of passivity, or its derivatives, in late childhood, adolescence and adulthood are established during the first six years of life."[59] Males were more stable when it came to aggressive behavior and females more stable in terms of dependency. Both males and females reflected stability from the standpoint of achievement behavior and the evidence suggests that the period from six to ten years of age is important in establishing this form of motivation. Indeed, it is claimed that the first four or five years of school provide "critical situations and experiences" that are necessary to crystallize this and related forms of motivation. Regarding the overall study, Kagan and Moss concluded that:

Many of the behaviors exhibited by the child aged six to ten, and a few during the age period three to six, were moderately good predictors of theoretically related behaviors during early adulthood. Passive with-drawal from stressful situations, dependency on family, ease-of-anger arousal, involvement in intellectual mastery, social interaction anxiety, sex-role identification, and pattern of sexual behavior in adulthood were each related to reasonably analogous behavioral dispositions during the early school years. . . . These results offer strong support for the gen-eralization that aspects of adult personality begin to take form during early childhood.[60]

In general, research strongly suggests that certain basic personality char-acteristics are fairly well established by the age of six. Indeed, after review-ing much of the research literature, one noted educational psychologist, Benjamin Bloom,[61] concluded that the "half-developed" age—when 50 percent of the individual difference variance is stabilized—occurs by about the age of three for aggression in males, age four for dependency in females, and about age four for intellectuality in both sexes.

A NOTE OF CAUTION REGARDING STABILITY OF BEHAVIOR OVER TIME

Impressive as the evidence for the early determination of personality and stability of behavior over time may seem, there are also reasons for believing that personality ordinarily remains open to change over extended periods. In the first place, the findings do *not* indicate that personality char-acteristics are *completely* formed during early childhood. Also, even though a general personality trend may be established quite early, the manner in which it is expressed, indeed whether it is expressed directly at all, may continue to be quite susceptible to change. Clinical and psychotherapeutic literature, for example, abounds with evidence suggesting that adults can change not only their general life styles, but specific behaviors as well.[62]

One of the most striking—and gratifying—features of studies of consist-ency and change in personality development is the evidence that has been unearthed regarding the tremendous adaptability of human beings. For example, MacFarlane[63] speaks of the ". . . almost incredible capacity" of the individual to process the ". . . welter of inner-outer stimulation." Many of the most outstandingly mature adults in the group MacFarlane and her associates studied had by-passed or overcome difficult situations, even though ". . . their characteristic responses during childhood or adolescence seemed to us to compound their problems."[64] MacFarlane went on to note that she and her associates had failed to appreciate the maturing utility of many painful, strain-producing and confusing experiences. On the other hand, many subjects who ". . . early had had easy and confidence-inducing lives," and who had been free from severe strains and had exhibited very promising abilities and talents were ". . . brittle, discontented, and puzzled adults."[65]

MacFarlane's observations are well taken. The fact that a person has certain personality characteristics in childhood is no guarantee that he will have those same characteristics in adulthood. There is little question but that a child's personality "style" begins in infancy. However, psychologists are pretty much in agreement that although the influence of the preschool years are important, the experiences of childhood and later years are also important in either reinforcing or changing the character structure tentatively formed during the early years. For example, after a thorough review of the empirical literature, one psychologist concluded that ". . . events subsequent to the first year or two of life have the power to "confirm or deny" the personality of the growing infant, to perpetuate or remake it, depending upon whether the circumstances of later childhood perpetuate or alter the situation in which the child was reared."[66]

On the whole, a child's personality continues to develop in the direction it started. Whether it be a shy, withdrawn four-year-old girl or an aggressive, demanding seven-year-old boy, these characteristics are likely to persist into adulthood if the primary people and basic life experiences remain essentially the same.

In Perspective

A person cannot help but be himself. Each of us behaves more or less consistently with the sort of person we conceive ourselves to be. If we are poor at sports we are not likely to participate in activities which call for physical coordination; if good at orally expressing ourselves, we may seek out public speaking opportunities. We behave in ways that are congruent with our self-concept: the beautiful woman, upon entering a new room, gazes into the mirror; the homely one studies pictures on the wall. Maltz[67] has suggested that just as the "success-type personality" finds some way to succeed, so, too, does the "failure-type personality" find some way to fail, in spite of his good intentions *not* to fail. The unity in one's behavior is related to his concept of self and to that cluster of primary motives and dominant values upon which his self-concept is built. The closer we come to truly understanding another person's primary motives and dominant values (not to mention our own), the better able we are to see the consistency in his behavior and the unity of his personality. Expressions of consistency can change with time, even though the primary motives may remain the same. For example, the fearful child at age one screams a great deal; at age five he is less vocal but runs away from threatening situations; at age fifteen he is quiet and somewhat of a loner; at age twenty-five he is shy, introverted and perhaps busy at some job where people contact is minimal. The consistency of behavior is not always in the overt action, but in the perception. Once we understand, for example, that the boy's primary motive is to avoid the threat he feels when too close to people, then we can see that there is much unity in his behavior over time even though its expression has been modified.

Practically everything one does is related to that central core which marks him as an unique individual unlike none other. Our perpetual style, in terms of how we "see" things, is related to how we view ourselves and our own particular personality "style." No matter how we respond, whether it be with our handwriting, our viscera, our voice, or our choice of an occupation, we reflect something of the nature of our feelings about ourselves and others in a more or less unified and predictable way.

Probably no individual can be counted on to behave in a completely consistent manner day in and day out. Indeed, what a bore such a person would be. Nonetheless, the evidence does suggest that people do strive for and exhibit some measure of personal consistency and unity in their everyday lives. If we work hard at being sensitive, patient observers of what is going on below the surface of behavior, we can see many outer signs of inner consistencies both within ourselves and others.

The purpose for understanding something about the nature and expressions of self-consistency and stability of behavior over time is not merely an academic one. The evidence suggests that basic personality styles begin early in life, which means that whether we are teachers or other professional people or parents we can be alert to early signs indicating the possible direction of a child's growth. Too often we wait for a child to "grow out of" his shyness, or aggressiveness, or lack of motivation, or speech problem, or whatever without realizing that we are confusing the symptom of a possible personality defect for what is frequently called "just a stage he's going through." Behavior which is established early and reinforced while the child is young is likely to remain stable over time and serve as the seedbed in which one's primary motives and dominant values are nurtured. The fact that a child's basic personality structure is established early and tends to remain stable over time would suggest that, if we are to modify and induce positive change in warped values and distorted primary motives, then we must do this while children are going through their formative years. Sensitive parents and psychologically tuned elementary level teachers working in conjunction with extended guidance and counseling programs in elementary schools would be a sound step in the right direction.

[1] K. J. Gergen, "Personal Consistency and the Presentation of Self," in G. Gordon and K. J. Gergen (Eds.), *The Self in Social Interaction*. New York: John Wiley & Sons, Inc., 1968, p. 300.

[2] K. J. Gergen and E. E. Jones, "Mental Illness, Predictability, and Affective Consequences as Stimulus Factors in Person Perception," *Journal of Abnormal and Social Psychology*. 1963, 67: 95–104.

[3] E. S. Gollin, "Forming Impressions of Personality," *Journal of Personality*. 1954, 23: 65–76.

[4] William James, *The Varieties of Religious Experiences*. New York: The Modern Library, 1929, pp. 77–162.

[5] Prescott Lecky, *Self-Consistency: A Theory of Personality*. New York: Island Press, 1945, p. 135.

[6] Carl R. Rogers, "Some Observations on the Organizations of Personality," *American Psychologist*. 1947, 2: 358–368.

[7] Carl R. Rogers, *Client-Centered Therapy; Its Current Practice, Implications, and Theory*. Boston: Houghton Mifflin Company, 1951, p. 503.

[8] E. H. Erikson, *Identity and the Life Cycle: Selected Papers*. New York: International University Press, 1959, p. 89.

[9] G. W. Allport, *Pattern and Growth in Personality*. New York: Holt, Rinehart and Winston, Inc., 1961, p. 384.

[10] H. Cantril, *Gauging Public Opinion*. Princeton, N.J.: Princeton University Press, 1943, Chapter 5.

[11] H. Hartshorne and M. A. May, *I: Studies in Deceit*. New York: The Macmillan Company, 1928.

[12] Allport, p. 385.

[13] Allport, p. 365.

[14] K. Lewin, *Field Theory in Social Science*. D. Cartwright, Ed. New York: Harper & Row, Publishers, 1951.

[15] Allport, pp. 364–365.

[16] Allport, pp. 462–464.

[17] Allport, p. 369.

[18] M. A. Wallach and R. C. Gahm, "Personality Functions of Graphic Constriction and Expansiveness," *Journal of Personality*. 1960, 28: 73–88.

[19] George Klein, "The Personal World through Perception," in R. R. Blake and G. V. Ramsey (Eds.), *Perception: An Approach to Personality*. New York: The Ronald Press Company, 1951, pp. 328–335.

[20] Philip S. Holzman and G. S. Klein, "Motive and Style in Reality Contact," *Bulletin of the Menninger Clinic*. 1956, 20: 181–191.

[21] H. A. Witkin, H. B. Lewis, K. Machover, P. B. Messiner, and S. Wapner, *Personality through Perception*. New York: Harper & Row, Publishers, 1954.

[22] R. Elliot, "Interrelationships among Measures of Field Dependence, Ability, and Personality Traits," *Journal of Abnormal and Social Psychology*. 1961, 63: 27–36.

[23] Else Frenkel-Brunswik, "Intolerance of Ambiguity as an Emotional and Perceptual Personality Variable," *Journal of Personality*. 1949, 18: 108–143.

[24] G. W. Allport, *The Nature of Prejudice*. Boston, Addison-Wesley Publishing Company, Inc., 1954, Chap. 25.

[25] J. Shaffer, S. Mednick, and J. Seder, "Some Developmental Factors Related to Field-Independence in Children," *American Psychologist*. 1957, 12: 399.

[26] Frank Barron, "Personality Style and Perceptual Choice," *Journal of Personality*. 1952, 20: 385–401.

[27] R. B. Malmo and C. Shagass, "Headache Proneness and Mechanisms of Motor Conflict in Psychiatric Patients," *Journal of Personality*. 1953, 22: 163–187.

[28] R. B. Malmo, A. A. Smith, and W. A. Kohlmeyer, "Motor Manifestations of Conflict in Interview: A Case Study," *Journal of Abnormal and Social Psychology*. 1956, 52: 268–271.

[29] H. J. Eysenck, "Graphological Analysis and Psychiatry: An Experimental Study," *British Journal of Psychology*. 1945, 35: 70–81.

[30] H. Cantril, G. W. Allport, and H. A. Rand, "The Determination of Personal Interests by Psychological and Graphological Methods," *Character and Personality*. 1933, 2: 134–151.

[31] P. Eisenberg, "Judging Expressive Movement: I. Judgments of Sex and Dominance—Feeling from Handwriting Samples of Dominant and Non-Dominant Men and Women," *Journal of Applied Psychology*. 1938, 22: 480–486.

[32] E. Powers, *Graphic Factors in Relation to Personality*. Hanover, N.H.: Dartmouth College Library, 1930.

[33] E. Mira, *M.K.P.—Myokinetic Diagnosis*. New York: Logos, 1958.

[34] H. Cantril and G. W. Allport, *The Psychology of Radio*. New York: Harper & Row, Publishers, 1935.

[35] L. W. Doob, "Behavior and Grammatical Style," *Journal of Abnormal and Social Psychology*. 1958, 56: 398–401.

[36] G. W. Allport and P. E. Vernon, *Studies in Expressive Movement*. New York: The Macmillan Company, 1933.

[37] R. E. Bills, "A Comparison of Scores on the Index of Adjustment and Values with Behavior in Level of Aspiration Tasks," *Journal of Consulting Psychology*. 1953, 17: 206–212.

[38] R. E. Bills, "About People and Teaching," *Bulletin of the Bureau of School Service*, Lexington: University of Kentucky Press, December 1955.

[39] A. H. Maslow, "Dominance-Feeling, Personality and Social Behavior in Women," *Journal of Social Psychology*. 1942, 16: 259–294.

[40] A. H. Maslow, "Self-Esteem (dominance-feeling) and Sexuality in Women," *Journal of Social Psychology*. 1942, 16: 259–294.

[41] Morris Rosenberg, *Occupations and Values*. New York: The Free Press, 1957, Chap. 4, pp. 36–37.

[42] L. Festinger, *A Theory of Cognitive Dissonance*. Evanston, Ill.: Row, Peterson & Company, 1957.

[43] L. Festinger, H. W. Riecken, and S. Schachter, *When Prophecy Fails: A Social and Psychological Study of a Modern Group That Predicted the Destruction of the World*. New York: Harper & Row, Publishers, 1956.

[44] A. H. Buss and T. C. Brock, "Repression and Guilt in Relation to Aggression," *Journal of Abnormal and Social Psychology*. 1963, 66: 345–350.

[45] M. M. Shirley, *The First Two Years: A Study of Twenty-Five Babies, Vol. III Personality Manifestations*. Institute of Child Welfare Monograph Series, No. 8, Minneapolis: University of Minnesota Press, 1933.

[46] Shirley, p. 56.

[47] W. E. Martin, "Singularity and Stability of Profiles of Social Behavior," in C. B. Stendler (Ed.), *Readings in Child Behavior and Development*. New York: Harcourt, Brace & World, Inc., 1964, pp. 448–466.

[48] Martin, p. 465.

[49] S. Escalona and G. M. Heider, *Prediction and Outcome: A Study in Child Development*. New York: Basic Books, 1959.

[50] Escalona and Heider, p. 175.

[51] Escalona and Heider, pp. 205–206.

[52] P. Neilon, "Shirley's Babies after Fifteen Years: A Personality Study," *Journal of Genetic Psychology.* 1948, 73: 175–186.

[53] Kathern M. McKinnon, "Consistency and Change in Behavior Manifestation," *Child Development Monographs.* 1942, No. 30. New York: Teachers College Press, Columbia University.

[54] L. H. Stott, "Persisting Effects of Early Family Experiences Upon Personality Development," *Merrill-Palmer School Quarterly.* 1957, Spring: 3 (Special Issue, Seminar on Child Development).

[55] J. E. Birren, "Psychological Examinations of Children Who Later Became Psychotic," *Journal of Abnormal and Social Psychology.* 1944, 39: 84–95.

[56] E. Arkin, "The Problem of the Stability of the Human Organism," *Journal of Genetic Psychology.* 1933, 42: 228–236.

[57] R. D. Tuddenham, "The Constancy of Personality Ratings over Two Decades," *Genetic Psychology Monographs.* 1958, 60: 3–29.

[58] J. Kagan and H. A. Moss, *From Birth to Maternity: A Study in Psychological Development.* New York: John Wiley & Sons, Inc., 1962.

[59] Kagan and Moss, p. 83.

[60] Kagan and Moss, pp. 266–268.

[61] Benjamin S. Bloom, *Stability and Change in Human Characteristics.* New York: John Wiley & Sons, Inc., 1964.

[62] Raymond J. Corsin, "Counseling and Psychotherapy," in E. F. Borgatta and W. W. Lambert (Eds.), *Handbook of Personality Theory and Research.* Skokie, Ill.: Rand McNally & Company, 1965, pp. 1105–1129.

[63] J. L. MacFarlane, "Perspectives on Personality Consistency and Change from the Guidance Study," *Vita Humana.* 1964, 7: 115–126.

[64] MacFarlane, p. 121.

[65] MacFarlane, p. 122.

[66] H. Orlansky, "Infant Care and Personality," *Psychological Bulletin.* 1949, 46: 35.

[67] Maxwell Maltz, *Psycho-Cybernetics.* Englewood Cliffs, N.J.: Prentice-Hall, Inc., 1960.

References of Related Interest

Bronfenbrenner, U., "Toward an Integrated Theory of Personality," in R. R. Blake and G. V. Ramsey (Eds.), *Perception: An Approach to Personality.* New York: The Ronald Press Company, 1951.

Chapanis, M. P., and A. Chapanis, "Cognitive Dissonance: Five Years Later," *Psychological Bulletin.* 1964, 61: 1–22.

Emmerich, W., "Stability and Change in Early Personality Development," in W. W. Hartup and N. L. Smothergill (Eds.), *The Young Child.* Washington, D.C., National Association for the Education of Young Children, 1967, pp. 248–261.

Glass, D. C., "Theories of Consistency and The Study of Personality," in E. F. Borgatta and W. W. Lambert (Eds.), *Handbook of Personality Theory and Research*. Skokie, Ill.: Rand McNally & Company, 1968, pp. 788–854.

Goffman, E., *The Presentation of Self in Everyday Life*. New York: Doubleday and Company, 1959.

Hamilton, D. L., "Responses to Cognitive Inconsistencies: Personality, Discrepancy Level and Response Stability," *Journal of Personality and Social Psychology*. 1969, 11: 351–362.

LaBarre, W., "The Cultural Basis of Emotions and Gestures," *Journal of Personality*. 1947, 16: 49–68.

Mussen, P. H., "Long-Term Consequents of Masculinity of Interests in Adolescence," *Journal of Consulting Psychology*. 1962, 26: 435–440.

Rokeach, M., *The Open and Closed Mind*. New York: Basic Books, 1960.

Rosenberg, M., "Psychological Selectivity in Self-Esteem Formation," in C. W. Sherif and M. Sherif (Eds.), *Attitude, Ego-Involvement and Change*. New York: John Wiley & Sons, Inc., 1967, pp. 26–50.

Secord, P. F., and C. W. Blackman, "Personality Theory and the Problem of Stability and Change in Individual Behavior," *Psychological Review*. 1961, 68: 21–32.

Stagner, R., "Homeostasis as a Unifying Concept in Personality Theory," *Psychological Review*. 1951, 58: 5–17.

Wylie, R. C., *The Self Concept*. Lincoln, Neb.: University of Nebraska Press, 1961, Chap. 5.

chapter four

Self-Concept as Related to Physical Growth and Developmental Outcomes

How a person feels about himself is related to how he feels about his body. The self-image is first and above all a body image. In fact, it is very likely that a child's first distinction between "me" and "you," between "I am running" and "he is running," is formed on the basis of his sensitivity to his own muscular reactions, his own viscera, his own bumps and falls. These internal sensory imputs may provide the nucleus for an emerging self.

A person's height, weight, girth, eye color, hair color, complexion, and general body proportions are very much related to his feelings of personal adequacy. The pace of a boy's total growth in relation to other boys in his class, or the extent of a girl's overall development in comparison to other girls her age play an important part in how they feel about themselves. In this chapter our attention turns to an examination of the relationships between self-concept variables and physical growth and developmental outcomes.

Physical Typologies and Personality

For thousands of years, philosophers and physicians and, more recently, anthropologists and developmental psychologists have speculated about and researched the relationships between physical factors and personality. Efforts to classify body types date back as early as 400 B.C. when Hippocrates wrote about the "humors" of the body and the effect of these "humors" on personality. In their review of the literature dealing with physical factors and personality, Sheldon and others state: "It is a curious and perhaps significant fact that 2500 years ago Hippocrates said that there are two roots of human beings. The long thins and the short thicks. Almost all simple classifications of type since that time have nearly the same basis, despite variety of nomenclature and detail of description."[1] Kretschmer[2] used a somewhat similar classification of body type in his controversial but influential hypotheses about the relations of body build to temperament and mental illness. For example, he said that any given body can be typed as *asthenic* (thin and frail), *pyknik* (short, soft, rounded), *athletic* (muscular), or *dysplastic* (one type in one segment and another type somewhere else). He asserted that if the asthentic type becomes mentally ill, he tends to develop schizophrenic symptoms. The normal version of these symptoms, such as idealism, introversion and withdrawal, were supposed to be found in normal people with asthenic bodies. Normal people with pyknik bodies, he said, tend to exhibit traits such as fluctuating moodiness, extroversion, joviality, and realism; mentally ill persons of this type were said to develop manic-depressive symptoms.

Among the more recent attempts to develop a method of classifying personality on the basis of physical characteristics, the efforts of Sheldon[3] has attracted the most attention from contemporary psychologists. He rejected the idea that individuals can be divided into distinct physical types and so he devised a method of classifying them according to three basic components. The terms used to describe the components are analogous to the names of the cell layers in the embryo from which different body tissues originate. The first or *endomorphic* component refers to the prominence of the intestines and other visceral organs. Obese individuals typically fit this category. The second or *mesomorphic* component refers to bone and muscle. The wide-shouldered, narrow-hipped, muscular athlete fits this category. The third or *ectomorphic* component is based on delicacy of skin, fine hair, and sensitive nervous system. Tall thin, stoop-shouldered individuals fit this category.

In rating a person's physical characteristics, Sheldon's system assigns one digit between 1 and 7 for each component in the order endomorph, mesomorph, and ectomorph with high numbers indicating more of a component. For example, a football fullback might be rated 3-6-2, which would suggest that he was low in respect to endomorphy, athletically powerful (with a 6 in mesomorphy), and low in the more delicate features of ectomorphy. A rating of 5-4-2 would describe a rounded but relatively muscular and sturdy individual and so on. Figures 4.1 and 4.2 will give you

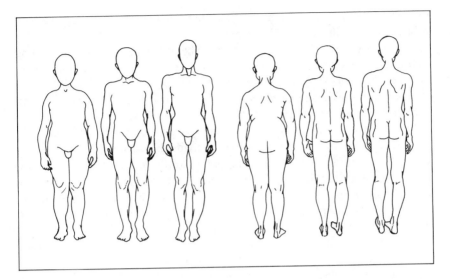

Figure 4.1 Front and rear views, reading from the left, of an endomorph, a mesomorph, and an ectomorph boy, aged about 11½ years. (From F. K. Shuttleworth. "The Adolescent Period: A Pictorial Atlas." *Monographs of the Society for Research in Child Development,* 1949, *14* (Ser. No. 50). By permission of The Society for Research in Child Development, Inc.

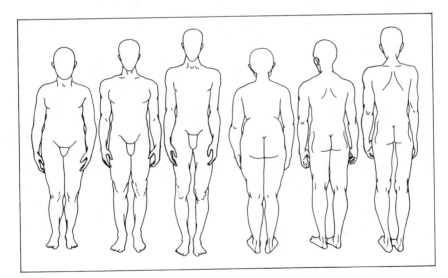

Figure 4.2 The three boys shown in Fig. 4.1, in the same order from left to right, at 15 years of age. (From F. K. Shuttleworth. "The Adolescent Period: A Pictorial Atlas." *Monographs of the Society for Research in Child Development,* 1949, *14* (Ser. No. 50). By permission of The Society for Research in Child Development, Inc.

an idea of the differences among these three components as they are seen in boys at two different age levels.

To each of these physical components Sheldon assigned a corresponding syndrome of psychological characteristics. For example, the predominately endomorphic person is classified as one who loves to eat, seeks bodily comforts, is sociable and outgoing. The predominately mesomorphic person is energetic, likes exercise, and is direct in manner. The ectomorph is classified as sensitive, given to worrying, fears groups, and needs solitude.

Sheldon's system for "somatotizing" individuals has not been universally accepted among developmental psychologists and, in fact, his technique of classifying and describing body build has been strongly criticized.[4, 5] The fact is, endomorphs (obese, heavy) are *not all* large eaters, outgoing, and sociable. Mesomorphs (athletic, muscular) are *not all* energetic and athletically inclined. Ectomorphs (tall, thin) are *not all* sensitive, introverted, and fearful. (Indeed, some ectomorphs are aggressive, fearless basketball players whose sensitivity, if that's what you could call it, is apparent only by the pained expression on their faces when caught on the tailend of an opposing team's fast break.) As we shall see, there *are* relationships between physical factors and personality, although it is doubtful that these relationships can be packaged as easily as suggested by Sheldon's numerical somatotizing system.

In considering the notion that certain personality characteristics are related to dimensions of physique, we are, of course, going beyond the mere description of what behaviors are associated with what body builds and are touching upon explanatory matters. The association between physical dimensions and behavioral characteristics at least suggests that the enduring attributes we see here are due to basic physiological processes, the same physiological processes that produce the structure of the body. If such a relationship could be demonstrated, we would be making heady progress toward an explanation of the unique organization of an individual's personality make-up. At the moment, however, the best we can do is speculate that the properties of the inherited physique help determine not only what a person can do, *but what he and those who are close to him expect that he should be able to do.*

Let us turn our attention now to what research says about the relationships between body structure and personality.

Body Build and Personality Correlates

Most of us don't have to go any further than our own personal experiences to know that different body proportions in men and women elicit different feelings, attitudes, and stereotypes in us. When we meet someone for the first time part of our response to that person is influenced by his physical features and proportions. An ingenious study by Brodsky[6] has demonstrated very nicely that there are indeed different social reactions to different body builds. He prepared five 15-inch silhouettes of males, representing: (1) endomorph (obese); (2) endomesomorph (muscular, but short and heavy); (3) mesomorph (athletic, muscular); (4) ectomesomorph (muscular, but tall and thin); (5) ectomorph (thin and tall). He also constructed a questionnaire containing such questions as the following: Which one of this group of five men is most aggressive? Which one is least aggressive?

Brodsky's research population consisted of seventy-five male college students from Howard University, all or almost all of whom would be expected to be Negro; and fifty white male college students from George Washington University. One of the things which Brodsky discovered was that there were no important differences in the way the two groups responded, which lends weight to the idea of a "cultural stereotype," or characteristic way of regarding body build.

Personality characteristics were usually assigned by the respondents in Brodsky's study to the "pure" silhouettes: the endomorph, mesomorph, and ectomorph. Those characteristics assigned to a given silhouette by a third or more of the respondents are discussed in the extracts following.

> More than one third of the respondents labeled the endomorph silhouette as representing the man who probably eats the most, would make the worst soldier, the poorest athlete, would be the poorest professor of philosophy, can endure pain the least well, would make the least successful military leader, would be least likely to be chosen leader, would make the poorest university president, would be the least aggressive, would drink the most, be least preferred as a personal friend (but, ironically, would have many friends), would make the poorest doctor, and would probably put his own interests before those of others.[7]

As you can see, the picture which emerged was an almost consistently negative one. If there is any truth to the idea that a person behaves as he is expected to behave, a dismal picture of the direction of personality growth of the endomorph is presented by this study.

> The *mesomorph* fared as favorably as the endomorph did unfavorably. The respondents said that he would make the best athlete, the most successful military leader, and the best soldier. They chose him as the man who would assume leadership, as well as the man who would be elected as leader. He was judged to be nonsmoker, and to be self-sufficient, in the sense of needing friends the least. However, he was most preferred as a friend, and was judged to have many friends. Respondents also said that

he would be the most aggressive, would endure pain the best, would be least likely to have a nervous breakdown, and would probably drink the least.

The stereotype of the *ectomorph* is far less socially desirable than that of the mesomorph, but in general more favorable than that of the endomorph. The ectomorph was judged to be the most likely to have a nervous breakdown before the age of thirty, to eat the least and the least often, to be a heavy smoker, to be least self-sufficient, in the sense of needing friends the most (but, unfortunately, was judged to have the fewest friends), to hold his liquor the worst, to make a poor father, and, as a military leader, to be likely to sacrifice his men with the greatest emotional distress.[8]

This study suggests that there may be characteristic stereotyped ways of reacting to different types of male physique, and that the trend of this reaction is such as to favor the mesomorph. Other studies support these findings. For example, in a study of high school senior boys and a sample of college girls, Cortés and Gatti[9] found that endomorphs rated themselves significantly more often as kind, relaxed, warm, soft-hearted; mesomorphs were also found to demonstrate a higher need for achievement than the other two body types.[10]

In an extensive study linking body build and behavior, Walker[11] had 125 preschool children rated by their teachers on sixty-four behavior items. He somatotyped the children using Sheldon's classification system. With regard to the relations between behavioral and physique data, more of the predictions were confirmed for the boys than for the girls, which suggests that physical factors may be more important in affecting the behavior of boys. Despite the popular concern about female measurements, our cultural stereotypes and expectations concerning physique and behavior do seem to be more firmly established for males. Consistent with the studies already cited, the mesomorphic body build, even among preschoolers, showed the strongest relationship to the behavioral ratings, especially for boys. Walker concluded:

Characteristic of both boys and girls high in mesomorphy is dominative assertiveness (leader in play, competitive, self-assertive, easily angered, attacks others, etc.), high energy output, openness of expression, and fearlessness. The girls combine this assertiveness with socialness, cheerfulness, and warmth, the boys' items give more suggestion of hostility (quarrelsome, revengeful, inconsiderate) and of an impulsive, headlong quality to their activity (daring, noisy, quick, accident-prone, self-confident, etc.).[12]

In regard to the ectomorphic physique, Walker made the following observations:

> In common for both sexes are items suggesting a certain aloofness. . . .
> For boys, the items in general define a cautious, quiet child, not self-assertive, hesitant to give offense, looking to adults rather than to children for approval, sensitive, slow to recover from upsets. He appears lacking in energy reserves. . . . For girls, the composite picture is similar but tends more to indicate a somberness of outlook—unfriendly, tense . . . irritable.[13]

Additional support for the relationships cited above between personality and body type was obtained from mothers' ratings of these same children.[14]

The stereotypes of the jolly, plump individual, the thin bookworm, and the aggressive mesomorph may not be very scientific descriptions, but they do establish certain expectations of behavior for both young and old with these body types. For example, a father is probably less apt to encourage a thin ectomorphic son than a muscular mesomorphic son to participate in athletics. These cultural stereotypes are adopted early by children. A case in point is the research of Staffieri,[15] who found that boys as young as six or ten years of age are already in close agreement when it comes to assigning certain personality characteristics to particular body types. For example, he found a remarkably similar tendency for the endomorphic silhouettes to be described as socially offensive and delinquent, the mesomorphic silhouettes as aggressive, outgoing, active, having leadership skills, and the ectomorphic silhouettes as retiring, nervous, shy, and introverted. He also found that ectomorphs and mesomorphs were chosen as the most popular by their peers, leading to the tentative conclusion that endomorphs are less popular, know that they are unpopular, and are inclined to reject their body image.

Body build and personality do seem to be related. These relationships are more definite for boys probably because we are clearer about what the physical criteria are for what a male should look like than we are for females. When it comes to being judged on the basis of physical appearance, the latitude allowed girls is apparently wider than is the case for boys. Be that as it may, the evidence does suggest that the broad-shouldered, muscular, narrow-hipped boy and the well-proportioned girl are more likely to win social approval and acceptance on the basis of pure physique than boys or men and girls or women who are either too heavy or too thin, too tall or too short. High self-confidence and self-esteem are personality correlates frequently associated with mesomorphic physiques in males and females. Although things like, say, leadership qualities, social approval, or high self-esteem are not *caused* by having a nice build or a well-proportioned figure, they may, in fact, be among the positive gains which *result from* a more mesomorphic appearance. Considering the feedback that a person both gives and receives on the basis of purely physical appearances, it is not difficult to see how an individual's physical proportions can influence his feelings about himself simply by affecting how other people react toward him. The overweight person who grows up in the face of assorted descriptive monikers like "Tubby," "Chubby," "Fatso," or "Lard," or the thin individual who is variously addressed as "Bony Ben," "Skinny Al," "Beanpole Sally," or "Hey, don't stand sideways—can't see ya" is hardly encouraged to develop self-confidence and self-esteem in the same way as is a person who is not markedly overweight, or underweight, or tall, or short. If used for a long enough period of time, the names that were originally meant to describe a person's physique can also have the effect of describing and defining, to some extent, his personality. Thus, the ectomorphic little boy who frequently hears adjectives like "delicate" and "fragile" ascribed to him may in fact grow up to be that kind of person—delicate and fragile with a low threshold for pain, stress, or frustration.

In short, one's physical appearance has a powerful potential for eliciting specific social responses. These can be positive or negative. How a person feels about himself depends, to some degree, on how he feels about the physical part of himself. How he feels about that depends, in large measure, on how others around him make him feel. Which brings us to our next topic for discussion.

Body Image as Related to Self-Concept

William James[16] was among the first psychologists to write specifically about the "physical self" as a way to underscore the fact that a person's physical features have an important place in his concept of self. The expressions "body image" or "body concept" have also been used to denote physical aspects of the self picture.

Like all other aspects of the self-concept, the image a person has of his body is subjective. A person may have a generally positive body image—he likes the way he looks, or he may have a negative body image—how he looks falls short of his expectations for himself.

The fact is, the most material and visible part of the self is our physical body. Like any other object in our physical environment, our bodies are perceived through the various senses. Occupying as it does a substantial portion of our visual and auditory fields, we see and hear a lot of ourselves. In a very important way our bodies come to occupy a central role in our perceptions.

Sometimes, however, there is a tendency to exaggerate the importance of the physical side of one's self.

The particular *way* a person perceives his physical body—whether distorted or not—may have important psychological consequences for him. For example, an adolescent boy may be overly concerned about his awkward coordination and refuse to attend dances; a girl may be overly sensitive to what she feels is inadequate breast development and be too embarrassed to date; a young man could have such a "narcissistic" love for his own body development that he neglects doing anything about his social or intellectual growth. Perception of the body relates intimately to perceptions of larger aspects of the self.

Body perception is so firmly established that even drastic changes in the body may not at once result in corresponding changes in body percept. A dramatic illustration of this is what psychologists have called the "phantom limb" phenomenon, which is an almost universal experience among amputation cases. For example, after a person has experienced the amputation of an arm or leg, he typically continues to feel that the limb is still there. In fact, he may feel itching in it, or feel that he can still move it, or even momentarily forget that it is gone and try to use it. Sometimes these feelings are of brief duration and sometimes they endure throughout a person's life. More often, however, they undergo gradual change in their perceived character. For example, Katz[17] has reported that a phantom hand may gradually shrink and move up into the stump so that it is eventually experienced or "felt" as a small hand embedded there. He also noted that sometimes an amputee can walk up to a wall and his hand (the amputated one) seems to go right through it.

Ordinarily, the body is experienced as a part or aspect of the self, often constituting its outer boundary. But there are some instances in which the body and self are not mutually inclusive. For example, we have probably all had the feeling of waking up in the morning after lying on our arm in such a way as to place it sound asleep so that it seemed as if it were not even a part of us. Even amputations of parts of the body may not be perceived as resections of the self, although there are instances in which the loss of a highly valued part may really be experienced as a partial destruction of self. For example, some years ago a psychology professor friend of mine had an unfortunate power saw accident in which he lost a portion of two fingers on his left hand. He viewed it as a dumb, careless mistake on his part, but persisted in going about the business of maintaining and enhancing his self-esteem and self-regard through being a professor of psychology. Another acquaintance of mine had a similar accident not long ago involving the loss of a portion of his left forefinger and its effect on him was great depression. The difference was that he was a skilled guitarist who earned part of his livelihood by being an entertainer. My psychology friend lost but a finger; my guitar-player friend lost not only part of a finger, but also one means of self-expression and self-support. When we look at it from that point of view, it is easier to see why the loss of part of his finger should be experienced more as a partial loss of self.

If you were to ask a person to specify *where* he feels the center of self to be, he almost always locates it somewhere inside his body. Most often he points it out as somewhere "in the head" or "in back of the eyes." This is not surprising, particularly in light of the fact that we are basically "visually oriented," having our most important commerce with the world around us through our eyes.

There is also evidence to suggest that different people assume different perspectives for the self in relation to the body. In connection to this, consider the following experiment reported by Krech and Crutchfield:

> In one demonstration the experimenter traced a script capital E on the subject's forehead. This symbol was deliberately chosen because its mirror image is a 3. Logically, then, it can be identified as an E or a 3. If he "viewed" the symbol as though he were "looking out" at it from inside his head, he would have perceived it as a 3. If he "viewed" the symbol as though he were looking at his own forehead from the outside, as the experimenter was, he would have reported it to be an E. . . . there are

pronounced individual differences in readiness to perceive from the "inside" or the "outside" when no prior set is given. For example, in one demonstration 76 percent of a group of 202 student subjects reported the symbol as a 3 (i.e., in accord with an "inside" perspective), whereas 24 percent reported it as an E. Moreover, the tendency to see the symbol in the latter way (that is, according to an "outside" perspective) was clearly more pronounced in the male than in the female students. Perhaps here is confirmation of the common notion that females (at least in our culture) tend to be more "subjective" in their outlook than do males![18]

The Body and Self-Esteem

There is a considerable amount of evidence to suggest that one's *appearance* is an important determiner of self-esteem, both among men and women. For example, in a study by Secord and Jourard,[19] it was found that the feelings an individual had about his body were commensurate with the feelings that he had about himself as a person. That is, the person who had negative feelings about his body was also likely to feel negatively about themselves as total persons and vice versa. In a series of studies by the same investigators,[20, 21] college students were asked to indicate the dimensions of different parts of their bodies, and to rate their feelings of satisfaction with these dimensions. In general, those who were satisfied with their bodies were also apt to be fairly secure and self-confident. In other words, persons who accepted their bodies were more likely to manifest high self-esteem than persons who disliked their bodies.

One possible reason for this relationship between self-acceptance and body-acceptance may be in the fact that the self-ideal includes attitudes related to the appearance of the body, or the so-called body-ideal. Each individual has a more or less clear idea of how he would *like* to look. If his actual body proportions come close to conforming to the dimensions and appearance of his ideal body image, he is more likely to think better of both his physical and nonphysical self. If, on the other hand, his body deviates too far from his body-ideal, then he is more likely to have lower self-esteem. It is not uncommon for a person with a poor body-image to compensate for this deficit by becoming proficient in other ways, such as, for example, developing his intellectual skill, or musical aptitude, or some other special talent or ability. In this way, the emphasis on the body-image is reduced or at least made less important through his ability to "know more" or "perform better" in specific areas than most other people. Of course another, but certainly a less healthy way of handling a poor body-image is by denying the idea that appearance or body-image is important in the first place. "Looks and appearance aren't important—how one behaves is what really counts." This is a praiseworthy attitude—one that most of us probably share to some extent. However, some persons proclaim this attitude as if it were some kind of Magna Charta releasing them from any sort of personal responsibility to themselves and use it to satisfy their needs to avoid the self-discipline involved in, say, eating less, or drinking less, or, in some instances, bathing more.

Usually, a person's body-ideal conforms more or less to the prevailing cultural standards of what a pleasant appearance is and what it is not. Margaret Mead,[22] in her studies of various cultures, has observed that each society has its own idiosyncratic attitudes and standards of personal beauty. The Kalihari desert Bushman, for example, places a high premium on having oversized hips and buttocks, while in America the desired hip-buttock measurements are much smaller. The American glamor queens of days gone by were considerably heftier than our contemporary *Playmate* foldouts. The cultural concept of an ideal body has consequences for personality hygiene, since the cultural ideal helps shape one's personal body-ideal which, in turn, influences for better or for worse an individual's overall self-esteem.

In a study of college women,[23] if was found that the ideal body proportions were five feet five inches in height, about 120 pounds in weight, and 35 inches, 24 inches and 35 inches for bust, waist, and hips respectively. As you might suspect, the girls liked their dimensions if they coincided with these ideals, but disliked them increasingly as they deviated from these ideals. Actually, the true measurements of the girls were slightly larger than their ideals, except for bust dimensions, where the average size was slightly smaller.

In a study of college males,[24] the acceptance of the body was more related to *large size*. While the women wanted to be slightly smaller in dimensions than they actually were, the men wanted to be larger, particularly in terms of being taller, with broader shoulders and chests.

Physical appearance is important to one's development of self-esteem because it plays a part in determining the nature of the responses a person receives from other people. However, we should keep in mind that it is only one of *many* determiners of self-esteem. A healthy, balanced person will build his feelings of self-regard on a variety of grounds, among which would include achievement, creativeness, social status, moral and ethical behavior, interpersonal relationships, and the like. While a certain degree of concern about one's total body-image is compatible with developing a healthy personality, too much concern may be a signal that the individual's self-esteem is standing on *too limited a foundation*. For example, the woman whose entire self is wrapped up in being beautiful or sexy is left with very little once the beauty and sex appeal are gone. The body-builder whose entire self rests on having large biceps and photographic muscle differentiation runs the risk of emotional bankruptcy when he gets older and discovers that there is more to life than bulging muscles and high protein diets. Body image and appearance are only one part of a person's total feelings about himself. When body-image and/or physical concerns begin to dominate one's self-perception, this may be symptomatic of deeper personality disturbances, a possibility to which we now turn our attention.

Physical Expressions of Body-Image Insecurity

We are using the term body image in its broadest sense to include one's perceptions of his total physical being. When a person has a secure body image, he is relatively free from anxiety growing from physical concerns. Insecurity, as related to body image at least, typically manifests itself as worry and anxiety about expected pains and catastrophes. Indeed, some people seem to delight in expressing a kind of morbid preoccupation with their physical conditions and general body states. Hypochondriasis and neurasthenia are two common, but neurotic, expressions of unhealthy preoccupation with physical concerns.[25] Let's look at the hypochondriac first.

© *1963 United Feature Syndicate, Inc.*

Physical pain (real or imagined) doesn't cure emotional problems, it only makes it easier to temporarily forget them.

HYPOCHONDRIASIS

In the first place, "hypochondria" has several meanings. It is used to refer to intense fear or anxiety regarding the state of one's health, and to a nonanxious but intense *preoccupation* with illness and symptoms. The term is usually used in the latter sense. The hypochondriac, like most neurotics, exhibits distinct personality characteristics. In the first place, his flight to illness is usually for purposes of protection. He typically is an individual continually preoccupied with his health, who complains about all manner of vague or specific aches and pains, and who may make frequent trips to the doctor's office, dose himself regularly with pills, sedatives, and other medicines. The primary symptoms are, of course, expressions of discomfort, illness, or suffering, which, when read for their psychological meaning, are usually pleas for attention, sympathy, affection, or help.

It is generally found that hypochondriacal anxiety with respect to physical health is a substitute for, or displacement of, anxiety that springs from other sources, as, for example, repressed hostility, sexual difficulties, or achievement problems. At other times, a hypochrondriac's "illness" may also be an expression of self-aggression or self-punishment for strong guilt feelings or hostility toward others.

Not infrequently, the hypochondriac is a product of an overprotecting home in which the parents repeatedly overreacted to pain and illness. Several things can happen as a consequence of overreacting parents. One, the child grows up with the uneasy feeling that his physical discomforts, no matter what they are, may be worse than he thinks. And two, he learns that one quick way to get attention, sympathy, or help is to complain about or exaggerate his physical symptoms. As he grows older, he may also discover that being "ill" is a convenient way to avoid responsibilities. Unfortunately, the hypochondriac launches himself into a perpetually self-defeating cycle. Since a lack of sufficient self-esteem is usually one of the major reasons for seeking a temporary respite in some form of illness in the face of a new responsibility or challenge, he is seldom in a position to assume the very challenge which might contribute to his having greater self-esteem if he assumed it and was successful. On the whole, the hypochondriac finds it less threatening to think about other problems. Health preoccupation takes his mind off more basic problems, as it were. A hypochondriac is tough to change because he gets so much satisfaction out of his assorted aches and pains and illnesses. And even if his family and friends won't give him attention and sympathy, he can at least call on doctors. Yes, tough to change indeed: you may recall the tale of the deceased, but formerly dedicated, hypochondriac whose tombstone bore the epitaph admonishing all who read it:

"See, I told you I was sick."

NEURASTHENIA

Neurasthenia is another neurotic disorder that reflects anxiety and undue body-image insecurity. Its primary symptom and characteristic is chronic fatigue, but other psychosomatic disturbances are usually present, including headaches, insomnia, digestive ailments, constipation, and assorted aches and pains. The dominant emotional characteristic of neurasthenia is anxiety, and the physical symptoms are expressions of the continuous emotional tension that anxiety causes. Like the hypochondriac, the neurasthenic needs to be wanted and cared for, and the flight into illness is his expression of those needs. Feelings of inferiority and insecurity, along with the characteristic sense of helplessness in stress situations, are factors that are found in the backgrounds of many neurasthenic persons. Also like the hypochondriac, the history of this sort of individual is likely to include favorable, albeit unfortunate, experiences with illness which led him to be coddled and overprotected as he was growing up.

A person doesn't have to be a hypochondriac or a neurasthenic in order for his anxieties and insecurities to seek some physical expression. For example, how many times have you had the feeling of suddenly feeling very tired and rundown when faced with a very important assignment like a paper due or an exam the next hour? This is a typical, normal neurasthenic reaction and usually represents a feeble effort to avoid an unpleasant task. How many mothers hear something like "Mom, my stomach aches. I just *can't* go to school today." (Of course, it just "happens" to be report card day.) College and university health services are typically jammed with students suddenly concerned with their physical well-being during finals week. One coed explained her trip to the health service during finals week this way:

"I went over there, you see, but I didn't know if there was really anything wrong. Actually it was that time of the month and I had cramps and I thought I'd better see if that's all it was. You never know about these things. It could've been intestinal flu or something." I questioned her further about her motivation for going and after some probing she finally said, "Actually, I really knew there was nothing wrong, but I think I hoped there would be, so I could have a good excuse for postponing some of my finals. But (a big sigh here), there wasn't."

Not unlike the true hypochondriac, she was looking for something to be sick about to avoid the responsibility of taking exams and thereby reduce the anxiety she was feeling. Persons who reduce their insecurities and anxieties by converting their shaky feelings into physical symptoms may find temporary relief, but by responding only to the physical symptoms the cause of the basic anxiety is likely to remain the same. In the case of the girl described above, even if she had found something to be ill about, the exams which were causing her anxiety would *still* be there upon her recovery.

In sum, body image, appearance, and self-esteem do seem to be related, although it is perfectly possible to establish one's self-esteem on other grounds if one's body image falls short of what he would like. Indeed, research has shown that how one feels about himself is related not only to his total appearance, but also to the rate and pace of his growth as he was moving through his developmental years. Whether a person experienced accelerated or slow growth *can* make a difference—a consideration to which we now turn our attention.

Variations in Physical Growth: Social and Psychological Effects

It is a well-documented fact that the timing of puberty and the marked physical changes which herald its onset are subject to wide individual differences. Figure 4.3 will give you a quick overview of percentage of boys and girls who can be expected to reach puberty and physical maturity between nine-and-a-half and seventeen-and-a-half years of age.

Individual differences in physical growth have been found to affect personal and social adjustment not only during the developmental years, but beyond that time as well. Since the effects of early or late growth are different for boys than for girls, perhaps we can more clearly see these differences, if we separate the sexes and examine them one at a time. Let's take the boys first.

EFFECT OF EARLY VERSUS LATE
PHYSICAL MATURITY ON BOYS

Highly significant and classical growth studies have emerged from the Institute of Human Development at the University of California. One of these studies, directed by Jones and Bayley,[26] focused on physical maturing among boys as related to behavior. From a group of ninety boys who were studied for an average of four-and-a-half years, the sixteen most consistently accelerated and the sixteen most consistently slow in growing were studied intensively by means of observations and ratings both by professional researchers and the boys' buddies. Figure 4.4 will give you an idea of the typical growth differences which exist between an early- and late-maturing boy over a five-year period.

Between twelve and seventeen years of age thirty-two boys were compared with regard to expressive traits, social behavior, and reputation

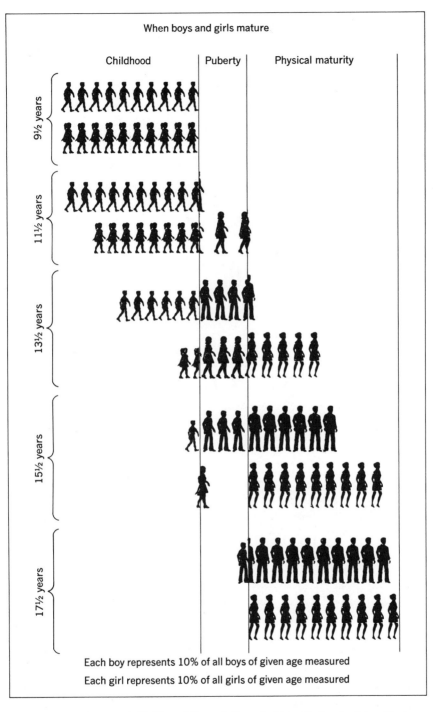

Figure 4.3 (From A. V. Keliher, *Life and Growth*. New York: Appleton-Century-Crofts, 1941, by permission.)

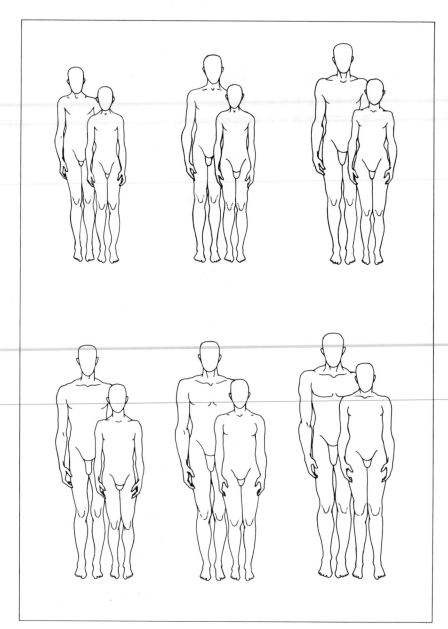

Figure 4.4 Differential growth of an early-maturing and a late-maturing boy. Drawings represent the boys' statuses at yearly intervals from 11½ to 16½ years of age. (From F. K. Shuttleworth, "The Adolescent Period: A Pictorial Atlas." *Monographs of the Society for Research in Child Development,* 1949, *14* (Ser. No. 50). By permission of The Society for Research in Child Development, Inc.

among classmates. Many significant differences between the two groups were found. For example, when rated by adults, the slower growing boys were judged as lower in physical attractiveness, less masculine, less well groomed, more animated, more affected, and more tense. They did not, however, differ from the more advanced boys in ratings of popularity, leadership, prestige, or social affect on the group. They were considered to be less mature in heterosexual social situations.

When rated by their buddies, the slower growers were judged to be more restless, talkative, and bossy. In addition, their peers regarded them as less popular, less likely to be leaders, more attention-seeking, and less inclined to be confident in class. Significantly, perhaps, they were also rated by their buddies as being shorter on a sense of humor about themselves.

In contrast, boys who were physically accelerated were usually more accepted and treated by adults and peers as more mature. They were more matter-of-fact about themselves, and had less need to strive for status and recognition, although from their ranks came the outstanding student body leaders in senior high school. The authors concluded by stating that "The findings give clear evidence of the effect of physical maturing on behavior. Perhaps of greater importance however, is the *repeated demonstration of the multiplicity of factors, psychological and cultural as well as physical, which contribute to the formation of basic personality patterns.*"[27]

In another investigation, Mussen and Jones[28] sought to find whether there were differences between the self-conceptions, motivations, and interpersonal attitudes of late- and early-maturing boys. They derived their data from the *Thematic Apperception Test* (TAT) which was given to seventeen late maturers when they were seventeen years of age. In this test, the subject is shown a series of pictures and is asked to tell a story about each one: who the characters are, what has happened, and how it comes out. It is assumed that the subject projects his own needs and ideas into the central character of the story he tells, which are then assumed to be those that the storyteller sees as reasonable and desirable for himself. In other words, the subject unconsciously "projects" himself into the story and psychologists then interpret and infer what those projections mean.

The faster growing boys more often than the slower growing boys told stories in which the hero was socially and physically aggressive. They also were more inclined to say that the picture elicited in them no thoughts or feelings of any kind. This is, perhaps, an indication of self-confidence (cockiness?)—the assurance that they could get away with aggressive behavior if they felt that way; and a tendency to be rather matter-of-fact, or detached, as was observed by the raters of the accelerated growers in the Jones-Bayley study mentioned above.

On the other hand, more of the slow-growers than the fast-growers made up TAT stories in which the hero (with whom each boy presumedly identified) was described in somewhat negative terms. For example, the hero was seen as being an imbecile, weakling, or fanatic, or he was rejected, scorned, or disapproved of, or he left home and/or defied his parents, or he was helped, encouraged, or given something by someone other than his parents. Taken all together, this would suggest that boys who mature late reflect social drives which are rated as feelings of insecurity and dependence and are often reflected in childish, affected, attention-getting social techniques.

These findings are consistent with those in another study reported by Mussen and Jones[29] in which they investigated the motivations of late- and early-maturing boys. In general, they discovered that high drives for social acceptance and for aggression are more characteristic of the slower growing than the faster growing boys. This may suggest that a late-maturer's high needs for social visibility may stem from feelings of insecurity and dependence, which conceivably serve as the basic motivators for recognition in order to compensate for underlying feelings of inadequacy and rejection. These findings are also similiar to those of Tyron,[30] who found that classmates regarded the late-maturing boys as more attention-getting, more bossy, more restless, and less grown-up than those who were physically accelerated. It is as if these boys were in many different ways saying, "Hey, lookit me!"

In line with the evidence thus far, Weatherly, in a study related to physical maturation and personality in late adolescence, concluded:

> . . . the late-maturing boy of college age is less likely than his earlier-maturing peers to have satisfactorily resolved the conflicts normally attending the transition from childhood to adulthood. He is more inclined to seek attention and affection from others and less inclined to assume a position of dominance and leadership over others. Yet he is not ready to accept the dictates of authority gracefully; he is inclined, rather, to deny authority and assert unconventional behavior in a rebellious vein. In view of the evidence of these potentially competing forces within him (it is not) surprising that he tends to see himself different from his peers and parents.[31]

As far as sexual seasoning is concerned, Kinsey[32] has pointed out that early-maturing boys not only precede late-maturers in regard to initial sexual experiences but they are engaged in a regular pattern for sexual satisfaction much earlier. This pattern may be a source of conflict for early-maturers during adolescence, but its net effects might be expected to be fairly positive, including as they do an important and enduring source of satisfaction and a contribution to the self-concept of sexual adequacy and virility. Such a self-concept should also encourage a favorable and appropriate sex-role identification in terms of knowing and appreciating what is masculine and what is not.

Taken together, these findings make it clear that the rate of physical maturing may affect self-concept development specifically and personality development generally in crucially important ways. We can reasonably infer that adult and peer attitudes toward the adolescent, as well as their treatment and acceptance of him are related to some extent to his perceived physical status. This suggests that the sociopsychological environment in which a late-maturer grows may be significantly different and less positive from that of their early-maturing peers. As a consequence, according to the studies we have examined above, they are likely to acquire different patterns of overt social behavior.

The findings in this series of studies follow logically from our cultural expectations for what the so-called "desired" male is supposed to look like and the consistent picture which emerges makes good theoretical sense. A large, strong stature fits nicely the mesomorphic body-image we have for the ideal masculine model in our society. Thus, it does not seem unreasonable to assume that the early development of the physical qualities associated with maturity serves as a kind of social stimulus which elicits from both peers and adults a reaction of acceptance, respect, and the general expectation that the individual concerned is capable of relatively mature behavior. Responses of this sort from others cannot help but reinforce and encourage adaptive "grown-up" behaviors and contribute to feelings of adequacy, confidence, and security in early-maturing boys. The slow-growing, later-maturing boy, on the other hand, is usually confronted with a quite different kind of feedback. His relatively small, immature body stature is likely to elicit in others at least mild reactions of derogation, along with the expectation that he is capable of only ineffectual, immature behavior. Feedback of this nature over a long period of time cannot help but breed feelings of inadequacy, insecurity, and defensive, "small-boy" behavior. Once these kinds of feelings are stated, they may well be self-sustaining as the slow-growing boy gets involved in a circular psychosocial process in which reactions of others and his own feelings interact with unhappy consequences for his personal and social adjustment.

Let us not forget to note that in any particular case the effects of early- or late-maturing may be significantly modified by the individual's psychological history and present circumstances. As was mentioned earlier, some very late-maturing boys are so talented in some specific area (music, math "whiz," athletics, etc.) that their stature is hardly noticed. On the other hand, being a fast grower is no guarantee of instant social status and popularity. Some boys' physical growth spurts ahead of their coordination, and they end up stumbling all over themselves. Other fast-growing boys may be unmotivated, or unimaginative, or simply lack the social finesse to be popular or accepted at *any* height or weight. Being an average or fast grower may give a boy the initial edge, but unless he has other personal qualities to accompany his bulk he is as likely as anyone else to flounder around in his interpersonal relationships.

THE LONG TERM EFFECT ON BOYS OF EARLY OR LATE MATURITY

It is clear that early- or late-maturing may have a considerable bearing upon the social life and personal adjustment of some individuals during the middle years of their adolescence. The next question is, how lasting is the impact of early or late maturity?

In an effort to answer this question, Jones[33] studied boys who had been classified as physically accelerated or retarded in terms of skeletal age during adolescence and compared them again when they were thirty-three-year-old young adults. One of the things that Jones found was that the marked physical differences noted for these boys at adolescence tended to disappear in adulthood. In other words, the late-maturers eventually "caught up" with their early-maturing peers as far as physical development was concerned, although the early-maturing boys remained, on the average, slightly taller, heavier, and more mesomorphic than the late-maturing. The physical differences that did remain were not, however, as striking as they were during adolescence. Personality characteristics, however, as appraised by the *California Personality Inventory* (CPI) and the *Edwards Personal Preference Schedule* showed some continuing differences. On the CPI, the early-maturing tended to achieve higher scores on such scales as "*socialization, self-control, responsibility*," and "*good impression*" (interest in, and capacity for creating a good impression on others). On the Edwards test, the early-maturing group scored high on the dominance scale: ("to be a leader, persuade, argue for a point of view"), while the late-maturing scored high on the succorance scale: ("to seek encouragement, to be helped by others, to have a fuss made over one when hurt"). These findings are certainly consistent with the descriptions of the early-maturing group when they were seventeen years old and noted as being more confident, more aggressive and more socially poised. They are also consistent with the descriptions of the late-maturing group when they were seventeen years old and noted as being less aggressive, more affected, and more tense. On the whole, *when personality differences were found, they tended to describe the young adults much as they had been described in adolescence.*

No differences were found between the two groups in terms of marital status, family size, or educational level. A few of the early-maturing had made exceptionally rapid professional progress and a few of the late-maturing were still searching for their vocational "niche." Again, we should remind ourselves that there are vast individual differences within each group which result from the complex interplay of many factors. With regard to the overall impact of early and late maturity on boys and its lastingness over time, Dr. Jones has expressed it best:

> During the adolescent period late-maturing is a handicap for many boys and can rarely be found to offer special advantages. Early-maturing carries both advantages and disadvantges. In our culture it frequently gives competitive status, but sometimes also involves handicaps in the necessity for rapid readjustments and in requiring the adolescent to meet adult expectations which are more appropriate to size and appearance than to other aspects of maturing. The adolescent handicaps and advantages associated with late- or early-maturing appears to carry over into adulthood to some extent, and perhaps to a greater extent in psychological than in physical characteristics.[34]

EFFECT OF EARLY VERSUS LATE PHYSICAL MATURITY ON GIRLS

What is perhaps most noteworthy in the research dealing with the relationships between developmental maturity and personality variables in girls is the fact that they are much less dramatic than those for boys. Among boys, for example, ascendence in size and musculature is an asset because of our cultural values and the functional advantages of such a build for athletic prowess. For girls, however, early maturing provides no obvious prestige-gaining advantage. Indeed, at the peak of their growth, early-maturing girls are not only taller than their girl classmates, but are actually taller than most of the boys in their class. In addition, there is evidence to suggest that many girls consider tallness to be a physical stigma, which interferes with their opportunity for wider social experiences.[35] Whereas research indicates that early-maturing boys are rated as more mature and more poised than late-maturing boys, studies related to early maturation among girls presents a different picture. For example, both classmates[36] and adult observers[37] rated the early-maturing girls as relatively listless, submissive, or indifferent in social situations and lacking poise. Such girls have also been judged to have little influence on their peers and seldom attain a high degree of popularity, prestige, or leadership.[38] Although early-maturing boys have physical advantages over other boys and are more likely to be socially in step with girls, the girl who "grows up" faster than her peers may be temporarily isolated. H. E. Jones has expressed this idea as follows:

> The early-maturing girl quite naturally has interests in boys and in social usages and activities more mature than those of her chronological age group. But the males of her age are unreceptive, for while she is physiologically a year or two out of step with the girls in her class, she

is three or four years out of step with the boys—a vast . . . developmental difference.[39]

The evidence favoring a positive self-concept and healthy personality development is hardly on the side of the early-maturing girl. If anything, the evidence seems to suggest that girls who mature at a slower rate enjoy more social advantages, mostly because they are inclined to be less stocky and less apt to tower over so many of their age-mates. On the other hand, we have to bear in mind that when we are talking about early-maturing girls, we are considering girls who are experiencing their peak growth years somewhere between eleven and fourteen years of age, which is during their junior high and early high school years. You may recall from your own junior high and early high school days the vast individual differences among both girls *and* boys when it came to height, weight, and assorted measurements. Considering that junior high is, for the most part, full of little boys and young women, it is no wonder that the buxom seventh-grade girl feels a degree of social isolation and receives feedback to reinforce the "out of it" feeling. It is not uncommon for early-maturing girls to date boys and seek social outlets with other older adolescents, which probably does a great deal to counteract feeling *too* out of it. Figure 4.5 may assist in giving you a clearer mental picture of the anatomical differences which exist between early- and late-maturing girls.

As you can see from Figure 4.5, the early-maturing girl is inclined to acquire a stocky, broader physique, while the late maturer tends toward a slim, slight build, more in keeping with the feminine ideal in our society.

In an effort to determine whether the psychological impact on girls of early or large growth persisted into later adolescence, Jones and Mussen[40] studied the self-conceptions, motivations, and interpersonal attitudes of thirty-four seventeen-year-old girls—sixteen who had been consistently fast growers and eighteen who had been consistently slow growers. They assumed that since the early-maturing girl had a harder time of it during her peak growing years, that she might be expected to reveal negative self-feelings and poor interpersonal attitudes as a late teenager. However, when the *Thematic Apperception Test* scores of early- and late-maturing girls were compared it was found that early-maturing girls had significantly lower scores on the category, *negative characteristics*, indicating more favorable self-concepts. From the picture we have to this point, we would have expected early-maturing girls to have lower self-concepts. Although this was not true, the fact that early-maturing girls did have a higher self-concept in later adolescence is consistent with the conclusion of Faust,[41] who found that, for girls, precocious physical development tends to become a decided asset as the girl moves through junior high and into the high school years. On the other hand, Weatherly's[42] effort to find whether late

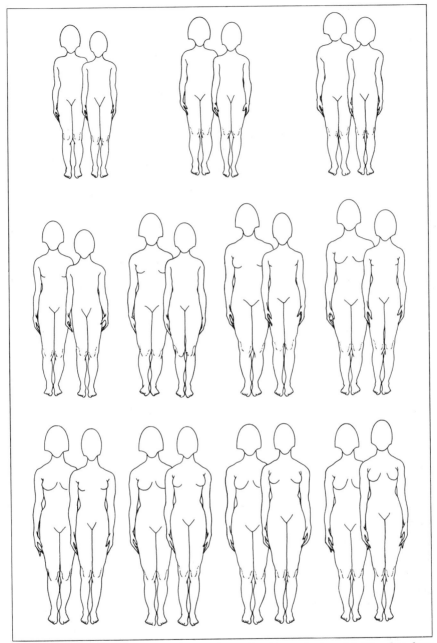

Figure 4.5 Differential growth of an early- and a late-maturing girl. The first four pairings are drawn at yearly birthdays from 8 through 11 years. Other pairings are at half-year intervals from 11½ years through 14½ years of age. (From F. K. Shuttleworth, "The Adolescent Period: A Pictorial Atlas." *Monographs of the Society for Research in Child Development,* 1949, *14* (Ser. No. 50). By permission of The Society for Research in Child Development, Inc.

physical maturation was a liability or asset to the personality development of girls did not result in a definite answer to the question. He did, however, observe that late physical maturation had adverse affects on personal adjustment in *both* sexes in late adolescence. This is quite consistent with the conclusion reached by Jones and Mussen:

> When the differences between early- and late-maturing girls are compared with the differences between early- and late-maturing boys, they are found to be in the same direction more often than in the opposite. These findings are interpreted to indicate that late-maturing adolescents of both sexes are characterized by less adequate self-concepts, slightly poorer parent-child relationships, and some tendency for stronger dependency needs.[43]

It seems apparent that the relationship between physical maturation and personality variables is much less definite for girls than boys. A logical conclusion is that rate of physical maturation is a less influential variable influencing personality development in girls than for boys. This is not surprising. The cultural sex-role prescription for males in our society is relatively clear and is one which places a high value upon factors such as physical strength, coordination, and athletic deftness, especially in the adolescent and young adulthood years. For girls, however, the feminine sex-role prescription is less definite and stereotyped and is, therefore, not as likely to be connected to any specific pattern of physical attributes. In addition, whereas people seem to respond more to a boy's or a man's total physical make-up, the response to a girl's physical make-up is apt to be more specific. That is, the physical qualities of a girl capable of eliciting a favorable response include her face, bosom, hips, legs, and total proportions (although not necessarily in that order). For example, one girl might have a pretty face and very little else, but this could be sufficient to win her many signs of approval. Another girl may have an extremely attractive figure and only very plain facial features, but her nice legs or substantial bosom may be quite enough to win her some feeling of social approval. In other words, it may be more possible for a girl than for a boy to elicit different responses to different parts of her body so that even though she may fall short in one area, she can make it up in another. Girls are expected to do little else with their bodies except adorn them and make them as attractive as possible. Boys, on the other hand, are expected to *do* something with their bodies and are judged more on that basis. Another way of stating it, I suppose, would be to suggest that when it comes to the physical side of the self girls are judged more in terms of how they *look* and boys more in terms of how they *perform*. If this is true, then a tentative speculation about why it is that the rate of physical maturation has less dramatic effect on girls than

Although it's not quite as simple as this, Lucy does have a point.

boys is that girls have greater flexibility for altering or changing their looks than boys do for altering or changing their performances. Even a very plain looking girl can look attractive with the aid of proper dress, padding, and cosmetics.

In Perspective

The evidence we have looked at in this chapter suggests that how we feel about ourselves is related to how we feel about our bodies. Although having a nice figure or a well-proportioned body does not guarantee a healthy, balanced, self-concept, research evidence does suggest that the nature of the feedback one receives from the world around is determined, at least in part, by the physical appearance one offers. More than that, people have certain stereotyped images which are conveniently attached to certain physiques or body "types." In a real sense of the word, people can have each other "pegged" merely by connecting the stereotype to the perceived body image.

Not only is appearance important in eliciting either positive or negative feedback, but so, too, is the rate at which a person grows. Attaining physical maturity at an early age is a distinct advantage for boys and research suggests that the advantages that a fast growing boy enjoys during his adolescent years are likely to persist into his adult years as well. True enough, his slower growing peers eventually catch up with him physically, but not necessarily as far as certain psychological gains are concerned. The outcomes of early or late maturation for girls are more difficult to predict, although the general weight of the evidence tenuously suggests that early-maturing girls, like early-maturing boys, have more advantages and are somewhat better off than their later-maturing counterparts.

In sum, body image is an important aspect of one's self-image. A person's physical self is the outer shell which houses all of his inner feelings and as such it deserves to be recognized and understood for whatever its potential is for eliciting social responses which contribute to an individual's overall concept of himself.

[1] W. H. Sheldon, S. S. Stevens, and W. B. Tucker, *The Varieties of Human Physique.* New York: Harper & Row, Publishers, 1940, p. 419.

[2] E. Kretschmer, *Physique and Characters* (2nd ed.). W. J. H. Sprott, trans. New York: Harcourt, Brace & World, Inc., 1925.

[3] W. H. Sheldon, *Atlas of Men: A Guide for Somatotyping the Adult Male at All Ages.* New York: Harper & Row, Publishers, 1954.

[4] W. H. Hammond, "The Status of Physical Types," *Human Biology.* 1957, 29: 223–241.

[5] L. G. Humphreys, "Characteristics of Type Concepts with Special Reference to Sheldon's Typology," *Psychological Bulletin.* 1957, 54: 218–228.

[6] C. M. Brodsky, *A Study of Norms for Body Form-Behavior Relationships.* Washington, D.C.: Catholic University of America Press, 1954.

[7] Brodsky, pp. 15–21.

[8] Brodsky, pp. 15–21.

[9] J. Cortés and F. M. Gatti, "Physique and Self-description of Temperament," *Journal of Consulting Psychology.* 1965, 29: 432–439.

[10] J. Cortés and F. M. Gatti, "Physique and Motivation," *Journal of Consulting Psychology.* 1966, 30: 408–414.

[11] R. N. Walker, "Body Build and Behavior in Young Children: I. Body Build and Nursery School Teachers' Ratings," *Monographs of the Society for Research in Child Development.* 1962, 27: No. 3.

[12] Walker, p. 78.

[13] Walker, p. 78.

[14] R. N. Walker, "Body Build and Behavior in Young Children: II. Body Build and Parents' Ratings," *Child Development.* 1963, 34: 1–23.

[15] J. Staffieri, "A Study of Social Stereotype of Body Image in Children," *Journal of Personality and Social Psychology.* 1957, 7: 101–104.

[16] William James, *Psychology: The Briefer Course.* G. Allport, Ed. New York: Harper & Row, Publishers, 1961, Chap. 3.

[17] D. Katz, *Gestalt Psychology.* New York: The Ronald Press Company, 1950.

[18] D. Krech and R. S. Crutchfield, *Elements of Psychology.* New York: Alfred A. Knopf, 1959, p. 203.

[19] P. F. Secord and S. M. Jourard, "The Appraisal of Body-Cathexis: Body-Cathexis and the Self," *Journal of Consulting Psychology.* 1953, 17: 343–347.

[20] S. M. Jourard and P. F. Secord, "Body-Cathexis and Personality," *British Journal of Psychology*. 1955a, 46: 130–138.

[21] S. M. Jourard and P. F. Secord, "Body-Cathexis and the Ideal Female Figure," *Journal of Abnormal and Social Psychology*. 1955b, 50: 243–246.

[22] Margaret Mead, *Male and Female*. New York: William Morrow & Company, Inc., 1949, pp. 138–142.

[23] Jourard and Secord, 1955b.

[24] S. M. Jourard and P. F. Secord, "Body-Size and Body-Cathexis," *Journal of Consulting Psychology*. 1954, 18: 184.

[25] Alexander A. Schneiders, *Personality Dynamics, and Mental Health* (rev. ed.). New York: Holt, Rinehart and Winston, Inc., 1965, pp. 335–336.

[26] M. C. Jones and N. Bayley, "Physical Maturing among Boys as Related to Behavior," *Journal of Educational Psychology*. 1950, 41: 129–148.

[27] Jones and Bayley, p. 146.

[28] P. H. Mussen and M. C. Jones, "Self-Conceptions, Motivations and Interpersonal Attitudes of Late- and Early-Maturing Boys," *Child Development*. 1957, 28: 243–256.

[29] P. H. Mussen and M. C. Jones, "The Behavior-Inferred Motivations of Late- and Early-Maturing Boys," *Child Development*. 1958, 29: 61–67.

[30] Caroline M. Tyron, "Evaluation of Adolescent Personality by Adolescents," *Monographs of the Society for Research in Child Development*. 1939, 4, No. 4.

[31] Donald Weatherly, "Self-Perceived Rate of Physical Motivation and Personality in Late Adolescence," *Child Development*. 1964, 35: 1197–1210.

[32] A. C. Kinsey, W. B. Pomeroy, and C. E. Martin, *Sexual Behavior in the Human Male*. Philadelphia: W. B. Saunders Company, 1948.

[33] M. C. Jones, "The Later Careers of Boys Who Were Early- or Late-Maturing," *Child Development*, 1957, 28: 113, 128.

[34] Jones, p. 127.

[35] H. R. Stolz and L. M. Stolz, "Adolescent Problems Related to Somatic Variations," *Yearbook of the National Society for the Study of Education*. 1944, 43: Part I, 80–99.

[36] Tyron, 1939.

[37] F. B. Newman, "The Adolescent in Social Groups," *Applied Psychological Monographs*. 1946, 9.

[38] M. C. Jones, "A Study of Socialization at the High School Level," *Journal of Genetic Psychology*. 1958, 93: 87–111.

[39] H. E. Jones, "Adolescence in Our Society," Anniversary Papers of the Community Service Society of New York in the *Family is a Democratic Society*. New York: Columbia University Press, 1949, pp. 70–82.

[40] M. C. Jones and P. H. Mussen, "Self-Conceptions, Motivations and Interpersonal Attitudes of Early- and Late-Maturing Girls," *Child Development*. 1958, 29: 491–501.

[41] Silerf Faust, "Developmental Maturity as a Determiner in Prestige of Adolescent Girls," *Child Development*. 1960, 31: 173–184.

[42] Weatherly, p. 1209.

[43] Jones and Mussen, p. 500.

References of Related Interest

Ausubel, D. P., *Theory and Problems of Child Development*. New York: Grune & Stratton, Inc., 1958, Chap. 5.

Berelson, B., and G. A. Steiner, *Human Behavior: An Inventory of Scientific Findings*. New York: Harcourt, Brace & World, Inc., 1964, Chap. 3.

Bower, P. A., "The Relation of Physical, Mental, and Personality Factors to Popularity in Adolescent Boys" (Unpublished doctoral dissertation). University of California, Berkeley, 1941.

Calden, G., R. M. Lundy, and R. J. Schlafer, "Sex Differences in Body Concepts," *Journal of Consulting Psychology*. 1959, 23: 378.

Eichorn, D. H., and H. E. Jones, "Maturation and Behavior," in G. H. Seward and J. P. Seward (Eds.), *Current Psychological Issues*. New York: Holt, Rinehart and Winston, Inc., 1958, pp. 211–248.

Garn, S. M., "Body Size and Its Implications," in L. W. Hoffman and M. L. Hoffman (Eds.), *Review of Child Development Research*, Vol. II. New York: Russell Sage Foundation, 1966, pp. 529–562.

Hamachek, Don E., "A Study of the Relationship between Certain Measures of Growth and the Self-Images of Elementary School Children" (Unpublished doctoral dissertation). University of Michigan, 1960.

Johnson, R. C., and C. R. Medinnus, *Child Psychology: Behavior and Development* (2nd ed.). New York: John Wiley & Sons, Inc., 1969, Chap. 3.

Kagan, J., "Body-Build and Conceptual Impulsivity in Children," *Journal of Personality*. 1966, 34: 118–128.

McCandless, B. R., *Children: Behavior and Development*. New York: Holt, Rinehart and Winston, Inc., 1967, Chap. 9.

Shuttleworth, F. K., "The Physical and Mental Growth of Girls and Boys Age Six to Nineteen in Relation to Age at Maximum Growth," *Monograph of the Society for Research in Child Development*. 1939, 46: No. 210.

Thompson, W. R., "Development and the Biophysical Bases of Personality," in E. F. Borgatta and W. W. Lambert (Eds.), *Handbook of Personality Theory and Research*. Skokie, Ill.: Rand McNally & Company, 1968, pp. 149–214.

Williams, R. J., *Biochemical Individuality*. New York: John Wiley & Sons, Inc., 1956.

chapter five

Self-Concept as Related to Child-Rearing Practices

In all societies, the nuclear family is the initial unit within which a child's personality is rooted and nourished. It is within the context of some kind of family unit that he feels either loved or unloved, wanted or unwanted, capable or incapable, worthy or unworthy. It is probably safe to say that no parents who consciously choose to have children deliberately set out to make their children more unhappy than happy, more fearful than adventurous, more closed-minded than open-minded, or more neurotic than adjusted. Most parents, in a word, want to give their children the best they can give them.

In spite of good intentions, however, children do not always turn out for the best. Some turn out to be hostile, hateful, and suspicious. Others are chronic complainers, still others are fearful and anxious, and some turn out to be unhappy, shy adults wondering who they are and what they stand for. Although all human relationships are unique, the one existing between a child and his parents is an enormously important one. A child is influenced, formed, and eventually shaped through a slow process of witnessing and participating in the day-to-day interactions of the people in his life who are important to him. The intimacy and intensity of contact and the everyday interaction and interchange exist in an emotionally charged atmosphere. Whether a child gets no attention at all or too much, whether he is punished too often or too little, he is forming attitudes about himself.

How a child is raised, whether by his natural parents or someone else, *does* make a difference in terms of how he feels about himself and other people. In this chapter we will take a look at what research is teaching us about the relationships which exist between the way a child is raised and his behavior and his feelings about himself. How a child is reared depends partly on current trends in child-rearing and these have a tendency to vary with each new generation, a phenomenon to which we turn our attention first.

Changing Trends in Child-Rearing Practices

As a general rule, each new generation's attitude toward child-rearing is influenced by two primary considerations, (1) personal standards of child-rearing as influenced by each parent's life history and, (2) the current social standards and expectancies, which, if powerful enough, can change one's personal child-rearing preferences in the direction of the prevailing standards. The major emphasis during the 1800s, for example, grew out of certain assumptions about the nature of man and his innate depravity. Calvinists believed the newborn to be damned as a result of "original sin" and, as a consequence, both evil and rebellious. The child's will had to be broken so that he would submit to parents and to God's will. Religious orientations were very strong in nineteenth-century America and had a significant impact on child-rearing practices. Consider, for example, the following episodes reported by Sunley:

> . . . One mother, writing in the *Mother's Magazine* in 1834, described how her sixteen-month-old girl refused to say "dear mama" upon the father's order. She was led into a room alone, where she screamed wildly for ten minutes; then she was commanded again, and again refused. She was then whipped, and asked again. This kept up for four hours until the child finally obeyed. Parents commonly reported that after one such trial the child became permanently submissive. But not all parents resorted to beatings to gain this end. One mother spoke of "constant thorough gentle drilling," which consisted partly of refusing to give the child an object just out of its reach, however much it cried. Another mother taught submission and self-denial at one and the same time by taking objects away from the child. Strictness in diet and daily routine was apparently frequently an accompaniment to obedience training.[1]

(You will recall that, in Chapter Two, we discussed how and why it is that people behave in terms of what they "believe" to be true. The above excerpt is a striking example of how a belief—in this instance, in a child's innate depravity—served as the rationale for behaving toward a child in a sadistic manner because it was "what the child needed.")

The attitude about the "evilness of the child" was around for a long time and in fact was still apparent during the early 1900s. Wolfenstein, for example, analyzed the advice given to parents in a 1914 edition of the U. S. Children's Bureau pamphlet, *Infant Care* and on the basis of that analysis made the following observations:

> . . . The infant appeared to be endowed with strong and dangerous impulses. These were notably autoerotic, masturbatory, and thumb-sucking. The impulses "easily grow beyond control" and . . . "children are sometimes wrecked for life." The mother was warned that the baby may achieve the dangerous pleasures to which his nature disposes him by his own movements or he may be seduced into them by being given pacifiers to suck or having his genitals stroked by the nurse. The mother . . . is further told that masturbation "must be eradicated . . . and that the child should have his feet tied to opposite sides of the crib so that he cannot rub his thighs together." Similarly for thumb-sucking "the sleeve may be pinned or sewed down over the fingers of the offending hand for several days and nights. . . ."[2]

From this point in time we may stand back and incredulously wonder how thumb-sucking and thigh-rubbing could be viewed as so much fun, but when seen in terms of impulses which "easily grow beyond control," then the incredible restraints placed on infants can at least be understood, if not accepted. Of course, not all parents raised their children as the 1914 pamphlet suggested, but there was, nonetheless, a general attitude about how to raise children which made the whole process of child-rearing a bit more impersonal than is the case today. This impersonalness is probably reflected best in a 1928 book authored by the famous behavioristic psychologist, John B. Watson, titled, *Psychological Care of Infant and Child*. Consider, if you will, some typical passages from the book which eager parents, anxiously looking for guidance in how to raise their children, read back in the late 1920s:

> The behaviorists believe that there is nothing from within to develop. If you start with a healthy body . . . you do not need anything else in the way of raw material to make a man, be that man a genius, a cultural gentleman, a rowdy or a thug. . . .

> There is a sensible way of treating children. Treating them as though they were young adults. Dress them, bathe them with care to circumspection. Let your behavior always be objective and kindly firm. Never hug and kiss them. Never let them sit in your lap. If you must, kiss them once on the forehead when you say goodnite. Shake hands with them in the morning. Give them a pat on the head if they have made an extraordinarily good job of a difficult task. Try it out. In a week's time

you will find how easy it is to be perfectly objective with your child and at the same time kindly. You will be utterly ashamed of the mawkish, sentimental way you have been handling it.[3]

As you can see, the Watsonian parent was relatively free of the usual emotional expressions and ties which have come to be accepted as a normal part of our contemporary child-rearing ethic. Although parents of the early twentieth century were encouraged to care for their children, they had to be constantly watchful as to how the caring was expressed. Apparently, caring was all right so long as the child was not too overtly aware of it.

In contrast to this coldly mechanistic view of child-rearing, the ideal home or school in the forties and early fifties was organized around unlimited acceptance of the child's needs for gratification in order for him to experience maximum freedom of choice and self-expression. The first complete turn-about of the Watsonian trend was by Margaret Ribble in her book, *The Rights of Infants*.[4] She maintained that depriving a child of such basic human interactions as fondling, hugging, kissing, and other forms of body contact was as serious as denying him nourishment or sunshine. She further asserted that some of these interactions, often lumped together as "tender loving care" were necessary for the physical, intellectual, and emotional growth and well-being of any child. Support for Ribble's position came fast. A new "softer," warmer approach grew more popular. Granting the child maximum freedom of choice and self-expression became the thing to do. Indeed, Dr. Spock's very influential 1946 edition of *Baby and Child Care*[5] not only advocated the above practices during infancy, but encouraged their extension into the child's developmental years as well.

However, by the mid-fifties the pendulum was beginning to swing back again. For example, comparing the changes in child-rearing practices from 1940 to 1955 in his 1957 edition of *Baby and Child Care*,[6] Spock stated that "Since then a great change in attitude has occurred, and nowadays there seems to be more chance of a conscientious parent's getting into trouble with permissiveness than with strictness."

Oddly enough, each generation of parents seems to reflect a kind of reaction-formation behavior to its own parents' child-rearing standards. Although the intensity of the reaction no doubt varies from parent to parent, one hunch may be that the child raised under a firm, unbending, authoritarian hand is likely to modify that position in his own parental behavior because he may not want his own children to be as constricted or inhibited as he was. On the other hand, the parent raised in a very permissive home is likely to modify that position for the same reasons as cited above, i.e., he may see a greater need for direction in his own children's lives precisely because he felt a greater need for direction in his *own* life.

Current trends in child rearing do not suggest that we have returned to firm, heavy-handed discipline, but there are indications that parents are less easy-going than was the case in the forties and early fifties. If anything, the current emphasis is on *understanding* the child rather than being too restricting or too laissez-faire. If, for example, a three-year-old is frightened by thunder, rather than saying, "There's nothing to be scared of, it's just a loud noise," or "It can't hurt you, it's just clouds banging together," a parent is encouraged to understand the *meaning* of it to the child and respond with something like "I know sounds are very scary to children—come sit in my lap," or "Almost all kids your age get frightened of thunder —it's a kind of angry sound, isn't it? But I promise it won't hurt you." Or, as another example, let's say that a five-year-old is afraid to fight back when a bully keeps attacking him on the street or playground (even though they may be matched in physical size). Rather than a parent saying "You're acting like a sissy—all you have to do is let him know you're not afraid of him," or "You're as big as he is, so learn to fight back. Here, I'll show you how," a parent is encouraged to respond with comments which recognize the child's feelings—like "I guess the best thing to do is to try to play somewhere else—I know he's a bully," or "Sometimes you do have to let a mean boy know he can't push you around, but for a person like you that can be very hard. You're a strong boy, but you're also a nice boy."

What this current psychological approach does is to remind us that, whether a child is five or fifteen, he tends to see everything as either black or white, with no shades of gray in between. He sees things as either good or bad, cowardly or courageous, nice or naughty, lovable or awful. It also reminds us that to be human is to have all kinds of feelings—love and hate, compassion and competitiveness, courage and cowardice—and that children wrestle daily with this profound fact of life, trying to reconcile themselves to accepting all of it.

The fact is, what a child becomes depends to a large extent on how he is raised. What we have looked at so far are some of the more significant social trends which have influenced child-rearing practices and how these shift over time. Let's turn now to a more personal question.

What Influences a Parent To Become as He Is?

We somehow assume that all parents instinctively know "how to be a parent," which is in the face of a large body of evidence suggesting that this is not true. A human mother or father cannot rely on innate, "built-in" mechanisms to guide their parental behaviors. To what sources, then, may we attribute parental behavior and attitudes? We have already seen how current fads and fashions in child-rearing infleunce parental behavior; now we will turn to two additional parent variables, generational continuity and parent personality.

INFLUENCE OF GENERATIONAL CONTINUITY

When you think about it, an individual's own parents (or parent substitutes) are probably the only persons he has had an opportunity to observe intimately in the parental role. Whether he likes his parents or not, they nonetheless serve as models for his own parental behavior, not to mention wielding an enormous influence on his personality development and adult behavior.

Researchers have studied the similarity between parent and offspring in their management of the parental role and have also looked into the influence of a person's own childhood and early attitudes towards his parents and the impact this has on his own behavior as a parent. In other words, does the way one is raised influence his behavior toward his *own* children? Research suggests that it does. Let's take some examples of this.

In a study of four groups of parents—accepting, rejecting, dominating, and submissive—Symonds[7] observed that accepting parents were more likely than not to have had parents who were themselves adjusted and accepting. He also found that dominating parents were likely to have been dominated by their parents and that submissive parents experienced considerable leeway for personal expression in their own childhood. What this suggests is that a parent is inclined to behave like his own parents and in so doing establish similar relations with his own children. Symonds also observed that parents were likely to adopt an attitude toward their children that resembled the attitude taken toward them by the parent of the same sex. It should be noted here that copying the behavior of one's own parents is not necessarily a conscious process, but more usually represents one of the consequences of having identified with one's parents' "parenting style" over a long span of time.

When it comes to discipline, Radke[8] found that there was a tendency for parents to use disciplinary techniques similar to those remembered from their own childhood. Along this same time, Bronson, Kalten and Livson's[9] investigation of the patterns of authority and affection over two generations discovered that mothers were likely to wield strong authority in their homes if they remembered their own mothers as having been strong authority figures. A similar pattern was noted among fathers in the study. That is, they were apt to copy their fathers, but more so in the area of affectional relationships than of authority. Why this should be more so in one area than another is open to speculation, but one reason may be that, in our culture at least, giving or receiving affection by a man is not well-defined, certainly less specifically defined than is the case for girls. We are more certain about how the American male should demonstrate his strength and stability, but somewhat more hazy about how he should show his caring and affection. Since the rules for what constitute appropriate or inappropriate expressions of affection for a man are more diffuse, he may rely more heavily on his father for cues in this area.

In a study of the backgrounds of a group of normal children, Harris[10] observed that what had happened to the mothers as children was also happening to their own children, and that what had happened to their parents was also happening to them as parents. Four considerations influenced this continuity from one generation to the next. One was the degree to which the mothers were consciously aware of the similarities between their own childhood behavior and that of their children: "Joan is just like I was at that age—sort of flighty and unconcerned." The second was the extent that they wished to see repeated the experiences of their own childhood: "I want Debbie to enjoy the kind of summer outings I enjoyed as a child." The third was the degree to which the mothers wanted to have the same kind of role as adults that they had in childhood: "I really need my mother's advice about what is the best thing to do." (A dependency role in this case.) The fourth consideration was in the extent that some mothers reflected about their own unfulfilled childhood expectations: "I want to be a much better mother to my children than my mother was to me."

Harris found that the kind of connection the mother made to her own childhood affected the way she adjusted to her maternal role. For example, mothers who adhered too rigidly to the past or who had too much unresolved conflict associated with it were likely to have more problems with their own children. Three general mother "types" were described: traditional, rebellious, and dependent mothers. Each type carried over into her own maternal role attitudes which had a direct bearing on how she related to her children. The *traditional* mother was reasonably satisfied with her own mother's child-rearing practices and attitudes and used them as a frame of reference in raising her own children. The *rebellious* mother, on the other hand, made a conscious effort to be less controlling than her own mother, toward whom she had negative feelings because of excessive control, strictness, and interference. Indeed, there was some evidence to suggest that mothers of this kind sought to work out their rebellious feelings toward their own parents through their children, which usually meant going in the direction of having too few rules and being too lenient. As you might suspect, the children of rebellious mothers were inclined to fuss more about rules and boundaries which interfered with having things their way. The third type, the *dependent* mother, was disenchanted with her own mother because she felt deprived of sufficient attention, love, and interest as she was growing up. Children of such mothers seemed to search for interpersonal warmth. Not having received a great deal of warmth as they were growing up, these mothers were less able to show warmth to their own children.

These continuity considerations are not necessarily conscious, nor do they work directly on the child. The point is, an individual's child-rearing practices and attitudes are related to the practices and attitudes of his own parents. To some extent at least, a parent passes on to his children those fundamental child-rearing attitudes transmitted to him by his own parents. What happens between a child and his parents during his developmental years will greatly influence—for better or for worse—that child's own behavior as a parent later on.

A parent's personality can make a difference. The question is, how much?

Influence of Parent Personality on Children's Behavior

Inasmuch as personality is the sum of an individual's character traits, attitudes, and values, we might reasonably expect that the personality of a parent can have considerable influence on the personality and self-concept development of a child. In a review of psychological studies of whole families, Handel[11] noted that each family tends to evolve its own unique culture —its norms, values and role definitions. Family interaction frequently comes to be centered around "themes," which are given form and expression through the personalities of individuals within the family unit. Whether a family's theme or "personality" is active and outgoing or passive and quiet, the ultimate impact of a parent's personality on a child lies more in how a parent *feels* than in what a parent *does*. The fact that a family is active and *does* many things together is no guarantee that the children within the family will develop healthy, positive self-images unless there is also a positive *valuing* and *feeling* for each other. One nineteen-year-old male client of mine put it to me this way:

> Sure my dad did a lot of things with me—even bought me most of the things I wanted—but I never had the feeling that he really *cared* for me. I think he really enjoyed hunting, fishing, and various kinds of sports activities, but I think the only reason he sometimes included me was because he felt he had to—sort of like it was his obligation as a father or something. Sometimes he'd tell me he liked the way I steered the boat, or liked the fact I made the team, or liked the fact I got good grades, but he never told me he liked *me*.

Interestingly, the father referred to above turned out to be an extremely self-centered, narcissistic personality so busy loving himself that he had barely any energy left over to care for others. It was precisely because the boy *did* enjoy doing things with his father that the absence of any kind of *caring* or feeling from his father was so painful. Like many young people who end up angry or disillusioned about their parents, this boy had to accept the idea that his father would probably never change and that if he wanted a relationship with his father to exist at all he would have to cease fretting about what his father *could* be and accept him for what he *was*. No simple task, this, because it demands that the boy be more mature, more understanding, and certainly more giving than his own father.

One way of assessing the impact of parental personality on children's overall psychological growth is through an examination of the general morale pattern which exists in a family. One of the best attempts to measure family morale and relate it to specific personality characteristics was done by Stott,[12, 13] who administered to some 1800 adolescents a personality inventory and a parent-child relationships questionnaire. Three family personality or "morale" patterns emerged from his data: a group of families characterized by mutual confidence, affection, and compatibility between parents and children (good morale), a "family-discord" pattern, and a "nervous-tension" pattern. Special analysis was made of the first two factors and it demonstrated that children coming from the "good morale" homes were better adjusted, more independent, and more satisfactorily related to their parents than were the average of the group. Those coming from the "family discord" pattern were, in general, poorly adjusted, particularly in social relationships. In every respect, the conclusions favored the idea that "good" (positive, high) family morale is productive of desirable personality characteristics.

There is evidence to suggest that a parent's total personality style can influence a child's self-feeling for better or for worse. For example, Behrens[14] assessed the adjustment of a group of twenty-five preschool children with clinical problems and related their feelings to the feeding, weaning, and toilet-training methods of their mothers. Also, she rated each mother as a "total mother person," which signified the woman's character structure as reflected in how she fulfilled the maternal role. Although there was little consistency among the three child-rearing practices and no tie between the ratings of children's behavior and their mothers' procedures, there was a close connection between child adjustment and "total mother ratings." Again, evidence to suggest that what a mother *is* bears more on child adjustments that what she *does*.

While studying maternal attitudes and characteristics of maternal personality, Zuckerman and Oltean[15] found a relationship between the scores of mothers on a hostility-rejection scale and three measures of personality. Mothers who tended to be hostile and rejecting as parents had a low need for being nurturant. The study also indicated that hostility and rejection were related to psychopathological symptoms of the mother. Apparently, expressions of hostility and rejection are connected to deeper personality problems which can be detrimental to positive mother-child relationships.

Fromm[16] and Horney,[17] among others, have observed that a lack of self-love is frequently accompanied by an inability to love others. On the other hand, ability to accept one's self is usually accompanied by the capacity to accept others. A study by Medinnus and Curtis[18] of fifty-six mothers of children in a parent-participating cooperative nursery school found this to be true. That is, their findings strongly supported the hypothesis that mothers who had high self-acceptance reflected higher acceptance of their children than mothers with low self-acceptance. This conclusion is consistent with those reached by Coopersmith[19] in his investigation of the antecedents of self-esteem among over 1748 fifth- and sixth-grade children. He found that mothers of children with high self-esteem tended to be high in their own self-esteem. At the same time, mothers of children with low self-esteem were themselves low in self-esteem. In addition, they were fairly apt to be emotionally unstable. Apparently high self-esteem mothers (and fathers, as noted later) convey a certain confidence, poise, and liking for themselves which is mirrored in their general personality style, which their children, in all likelihood, eventually identify as part of themselves.

Bayley and Schaefer[20] have indicated in their research on maternal behavior and personality development that mothers who have social, outgoing personalities are likely to have daughters who are rated as popular, out-going, and adjusted. On the other hand, girls who were maladjusted, (i.e., rated as gloomy, unhappy, sulky, and hostile) more often have mothers whose personalities were more hostilely controlling (i.e., punitive, irritable, isolating, and exhibiting excessive contact with their daughters).

Overall, the influence of a parent's personality on a growing child's ideas and attitudes about himself are considerable. Although the research devoted to assessing the impact of parents' personality on children has concentrated mainly on mothers (for the simple reason that moms are home more often and therefore more available to study), there is no reason to suspect that a father's personality has any less influence, particularly as children in the family grow older. In fact, there is increasing evidence to suggest that the father plays a vitally important role in the total family complex.[21] For example, Coopersmith[22] found that fathers of children with high self-esteem take a more active and supportive position in the rearing of their children than fathers with low self-esteem children.

Erich Fromm has described a father's influence on a child in the following manner:

(A child's) . . . relationship to father is quite different. Mother is the home we come from, she is nature, soil, the ocean; father does not represent any such natural home. . . . But while father does not represent the natural world, he represents the other pole of human existence: the world of thought, of man-made things, of law and order, of discipline, of travel and adventure. Father is the one who teaches the child, who shows him the road to the world. . . . Fatherly love is conditional love. Its principle is "I love you *because* you fulfill my expectations, because you do your duty, because you are like me. . . . Mother has the function of making him secure in life; father has the function of teaching him, guiding him to cope with those problems with which the particular society the child has been born into confronts him. . . . Eventually the mature person has come to the point where he is his own mother and his own father.[23]

The Role of Identification in Parent-Child Relationships

In its simplest terms, identification is a process whereby one individual takes on the behavior of another significant individual and behaves as if he were that individual. Indeed, one's self-concept is built on the foundation of his earliest and most primary identification with people (or a person) most meaningful to him. The identification process begins early in a child's

It's nice to be able to remember back to positive early life experiences.

life and is preceded by what is commonly referred to as *sex-typing*, which can be most easily distinguished from identification by saying that it is *imitative* or *modeling* behavior. Sex-typing is a more conscious process of copying specific behaviors. Examples would include such behavior as the three-year-old boy mimicking his dad shaving in the morning by lathering up and going through all the same shaving motions dad uses, or the little four-year-old girl with her own gob of dough going through all the motions that her mom does as she bakes bread. Sex-typing is the manner in which a child acquires the psychological and social behavior appropriate to his/ her own biological sex and covers all of the processes by which men become different from women (and women from men). We can say that a person has incorporated his sex-role identification into his concept of self when masculine or feminine behavior is no longer conscious or deliberate, but rather automatic and generalized to all areas of the self, ranging all the way from style of walking and talking to the expression of sexual behavior.

At what age does sex-typing and identification begin? Since sex-typing and identification occur without any direct teaching, it is difficult to say, exactly. Usually, however, a child at about age two or so begins to develop interests and attitudes similar to his parents. Many subtle, as well as obvious pressures are placed on children to behave in ways appropriate for their sex. By the time most boys and girls reach kindergarten, they're usually pretty certain what sex they are and what is expected of them in that sex role. You are not likely, for example, to find a five-year-old boy assuming the "mother" role or a six-year-old girl taking the "daddy" role as they play house. This is not to suggest that the crossing of sex-roles cannot happen after the preschool years, but it does occur with less frequency, particularly if the identification is normal and going according to schedule. Which brings us to our next consideration.

A PARENT'S ROLE IN SEX-TYPING
AND IDENTIFICATION

Parents are enormously important in determining a child's sex-role preference. The most fortunate child is the one who has so adequate a father (male model) and mother (female model) that he comes early to prefer the sex-role dictated by his physiology, moves naturally and easily into its rehearsal, and eventually identifies thoroughly with it. Unfortunately, identification does not always work out so neatly, as anyone who has known a very effeminate man or a very masculine woman knows.

The boy who has made a male identification is the boy who has happily and willingly adopted maleness as his way of life. He thinks of himself as a male, he accepts and likes his biological status, its advantages and disadvantages, and he assumes the responsibility and challenge that being male demands. In order for this to happen, he must be *identified with* (love, respect, and, in many ways, imitate) his father or father-figure in order to be consistently and genuinely *male-identified*.

With respect to the girl, identification is very much as it is for the boy, except, of course, that she identifies with the mother or mother-figure.

There are certain types of parent-child relationships that are more apt to encourage correct sex-role identification. For example, Sears[24] noted that five-year-old boys of fathers who were warm, permissive, and easygoing, in other words, *rewarding*, tended to behave in a manner appropriate to their sex. On the other hand, boys who preferred the mother role as judged from their behavior in doll-play situations, were likely to come from homes in which the mother, but not the father, was high in warmth. The mothers presented themselves as the major source of authority and influence and were critical in their evaluation of their husbands. A study by Moulton and others[25] has provided additional data to support this point. In an earlier study, Sears[26] observed that little boys whose fathers were not living at home showed less aggressive fantasy play than those whose fathers were living with them, that is, they were more like girls. This result may be due either to lack of opportunity to imitate the father or to less frustration at his hands. Why should frustration be a factor? Consider it this way: fathers ordinarily share part of the disciplinary role in the family and usually discipline their sons more severely than they do their daughters. Fathers also take some of the mother's time that the boy would like to have. If little boys are particularly close to their mothers, then having to share her might be somewhat frustrating to them. Then if, as seems likely, frustration instigates aggression, boys growing up with their fathers around will be more aggressive (directly or in fantasy-play) than boys whose fathers are away. Lynn's[27] summary of research related to sex-role identification also lends weight to this point.

There are definite indications that appropriate sex-role identification for boys, in particular, results in better adjustment to the day-to-day demands of living. For example, Heilbrum,[28, 29] found that male college students identified with their fathers were better adjusted, had stronger sexual identity (more certain about their "maleness"), a higher development of conscience, and that identification is stronger when mother approves of father. In a similar vein, Helper[30] found that the degree of "likeness" or "identification with" the father was related to the popularity of high school boys. That is, popular boys were more identified with their fathers.

There is also evidence to suggest that low or insufficient identification with a male model can have detrimental effects on a boy's personality development. As an example of this, the results of a study by Sutton-Smith and Rosenberg[31] involving a group of upper elementary grade boys showed that boys who were "indecisive, dependent, affectionate, and more prepared to admit to anxiety of weakness" clearly reflected more signs of feminine identification than boys who were more decisive, independent, and less affectionate. Another study found that a group of homosexual men were clearly more identified with their mothers than their fathers.[32]

As far as boys are concerned, the existing evidence supports the notion that boys identify more completely with loving fathers and powerful fathers, particularly when this "power" (size, strength, total presence, ability to make decisions, etc.) is primarily benevolent than they do with rejecting and punishing fathers. A boy *may go through the motions of identifying with a powerful, but rejecting, punishing father while young* (I'll never beat him—I'd better join him), *but grow increasingly more alienated from his father as he is able to match him in size and strength.* One seventeen-year-old, six-foot, one-inch delinquent boy serving time in a boys' training school expressed it to me this way when asked about his feelings about his father:

> That bastard used to beat me when I was small, used to beat me all the time. And I'd take it. I even remember hanging around him when I could and hugging his leg so he would think I really liked him and maybe he wouldn't beat me. Didn't really work though. Still beat me. (Clenching his fist) I'd like to see him try to lay a hand on me today—just once—I'd show him.

In our complicated society, where masculine and feminine roles are often not clearly defined, a certain amount of cross-sex identification with the mother is also desirable. Common "feminine" qualities such as intuitiveness, sympathy, interest in people, willingness to compromise, and so on are usually more easily incorporated into one's total self-picture from the maternal rather than the paternal model. It does not seem unreasonable to suggest that if a boy has truly liked his mother and respected, even internalized, some of her basic characteristics, he will, as an adult, make a more sympathetic and understanding husband and father to daughters without necessarily sacrificing any of his male prowess.

The process of identification is a far more complicated thing for girls than is the case for boys. McCandless[33] has noted, for example, that girls who are strongly identified with their mothers do not seem to be superior in adjustment to girls who are less strongly identified. In fact, some cross-sex identification of girls with their fathers appears to be desirable. That is, girls *do* compete. There is a place in their lives for striving, for doing well, for achieving, for being aggressive. Indeed, most girls are encouraged to be aggressive and achieving as they grow up. Moreover, as a girl grows up there is less pressure on her to be "girl-like" in all of her behaviors than there is for a boy to be manly. For example, a girl can wear all sorts of male apparel, but what boy would be caught dead in a dress? Nor does tomboyishness in girls lead to ridicule. Girls may play with boys without censure, but boys are made fun of for playing with girls. Hence, girls grow up with many adult-sanctioned opportunities for participating in masculine-related activities. Modified incorporation of certain "masculine" traits is probably useful. Girls' marriages, and certainly their relationships to their sons, should be helped if they have a sympathetic understanding of and liking for the male characteristics they will encounter in their husbands (which they grew to like first in their fathers)—characteristics which, in quiet tones, they understand and respect as part of themselves.

In sum, let us say that in order to encourage maximum self-concept integration, boys need every opportunity possible to identify with a father figure during their developmental years and girls with a mother figure. A boy learns how to be a man *by being around a man he values and feels close to.* A girl learns how to be a woman *by being around a woman she values and feels close to.* Although boys who identify with their fathers are better adjusted than boys who have apparently failed to make this identification, the same cannot be said for girls in relation to their mothers. Both boys and girls seem to profit from a certain amount of "cross-identification" with the parent of the opposite sex and this is even truer for the girls. For example, Mussen and Rutherford,[34] in their study of parental personality

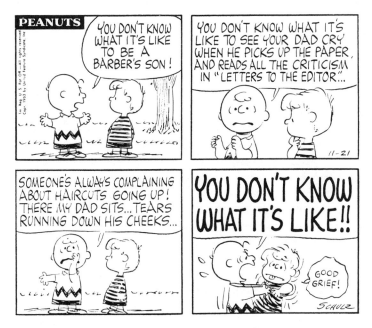

© *1963 United Feature Syndicate, Inc.*

A child's identification with his parents can have a strong influence on his behavior.

and children's sex-role preferences, found that fathers of highly feminine girls play a very important role in their daughter's feminization. Compared with fathers of girls *low* in femininity, these fathers tended to be more masculine and gave their daughters significantly more encouragement to participate in feminine activities.

Self-Concept Outcomes Related to Specific Child-Rearing Practices

There is little question but that personality expands in complexity and consistency as the years pass. It grows more complex because each person's range of experience increases, producing more intricate and overlapping interactions. It increases in consistency because, as one's physical growth terminates, body image becomes more stable and roles become clearer and more tightly incorporated into the self-concept.

Since child-rearing practices play such a critical part in shaping a person's ideas about himself and others, what we will do now is examine specifically those expressions of the self which have their origin in the experiences of early parent-child relationships. These are dependence-independence, aggressiveness, conscience development, and social development.

DEPENDENCE-INDEPENDENCE

Dependency is a condition of the human infant and since independence grows out of dependence, the two must not be considered distinct from each other. What are the earmarks of independent and dependent behavior? Beller[35] has suggested that symptoms of dependency in children are expressed in behaviors such as the following: seeking help, seeking physical contact, seeking attention and recognition and hanging around one or both parents. Independent behaviors included such things as taking initiative, working through problems by one's self, finishing things once they are started, and trying to do routine tasks by oneself. In general, the independent child or adult is relatively detached from outside sources of appraisal and relies heavily on himself in making judgments and appraisals. The dependent child is much more at the mercy of others and there are some sources, possibly as few as one, from whom he cannot dismiss himself and who have the capacity to raise, lower, threaten, or stabilize his self-esteem. For example, the mother-dependent little six-year-old boy may not care what his teacher, his brothers, or sisters, or the whole neighborhood thinks about his watercolor painting, but he does care about what his mother thinks. As we discuss the dependency-independency continuum of behavior, we should keep in mind that even though some children display generally more dependent behavior than others, some of both kinds of behavior can be seen in all children. The question is, to what *degree* does it exist? Another question is, when does it start?

CRITICAL PERIODS FOR DEPENDENCY DEVELOPMENT

Stendler[36] has made a case for the idea that there are two critical periods during the early years when overdependency may result. The first of these occurs toward the end of the first year when the infant becomes aware of his dependence on mother. Having made this discovery, Stendler asserts that the child shows his sudden recognition of the importance of his mother by his demands upon her and especially for wanting his mother around him. In effect, he tests his mother to see if he can really depend on her when he needs her and to see if he can control her. During this critical period from about nine to twenty-four months, it is imperative that the child have his dependency needs met in a manner to which he has grown accustomed. If, for some reason during this period, the child is denied the consistent attention of his mother during his waking hours (e.g., if the child is hospitalized, or mother becomes ill, or goes to work), Stendler reasons that the child will become increasingly anxious and will attempt to resolve this anxiety by making excessive demands on his mother when he does have her. Thus, it is through the mother's absence during a critical period, during a time that a child really needs her, that he becomes more *dependent* on her because of his *anxiety about losing her*. This is also consistent with a study by Gewirtz[37] who noted a high frequency of attention seeking in children when the primary adult was relatively unavailable. This would suggest that dependency behavior is likely to increase when the primary adults in a child's life are not readily available. *Perhaps one of the conditions of the growth of independence is that a child must first know for sure he can be dependent on at least one person.*

The second critical period for the formation of *overdependency* occurs during the two- to three-year-old period. In Stendler's words:

> . . . this is the time in our society when demands upon the child to change his old ways of doing things increase tremendously. Now the child must give up his control of his mother and come to accept his dependence upon her, yet at the same time learn to be independent in culturally approved ways. In normal socialization the anxiety generated (about having to be less dependent on the mother) produces the right amount of dependency. But where disturbances of a traumatic nature occur (e.g., death, separation, divorce, remarriage, both parents working, etc.) so that important habits must be suddenly and drastically changed, so much anxiety may be generated that overdependency will result.[38]

To support her critical periods idea, Stendler[39] has shown that a larger number of disturbances in personality adjustment turned up in *dependent* children than in others.

Why does dependent behavior persist? One obvious reason is that dependent behavior ("Help me"; "look at me"; "show me"; "tell me how") is encouraged and rewarded and competence or independence behavior ("I can do it"; "no, let me"; "I'm big enough now"; "don't help") is not. In fact, some parents seem fearful that their children will become *too* competent because *then their children would not need them as much.* (And some parents *do* need to be needed—so much so, that sometimes the children feel guilty if they venture too far away—even as adults.)

OVERCONCERN AND OVERPROTECTIVENESS

Although no single explanation accounts for why some children are overly dependent, several studies point strongly to the conclusion that dependent behavior is likely to grow from too much maternal overconcern and overprotectiveness. Heathers,[40] for example, noted that the homes of dependent youngsters rated higher on child-centered and babying counts. Coopersmith[41] observed that "One of the more striking expressions of dependency-inducing behavior is the mother's protectiveness of the child." Another study found that parental conflict and rejection of the child were prominent in the family backgrounds of extremely dependent boys.[42] From what we have seen so far, it is apparent that either rejection at an early age or too much protectiveness can result in overdependency. On a more positive note, how can we encourage greater autonomy and independence?

TOWARD ENCOURAGING INDEPENDENCE BEHAVIOR

Using college students as his subjects, Mueller[43] found that the *most* independent boys perceived their fathers as both *strong* and *passive*; that is, the father had plenty of power (psychologically) but kept quiet about it, thus leaving the boy free to develop his own independent ways, but all the time being sure his father could rescue him if necessary. A comforting feeling—to be free and protected at the same time. Another factor encouraging the growth of independence is the parent's willingness to permit independent and exploratory behavior without becoming unduly alarmed by a growing child's natural inclinations to expand the range of his activities and experimentations. (A natural human laboratory for observing the dynamics of parent-child interactions is in supermarkets and department stores. Observe for yourself the vast differences among parents when it comes to allowing their children freedom to explore—in this case, in store settings, which we might reasonably infer would be a good index of a parent's attitude toward exploratory behavior in other places as well. Some children, you'll find, are free, within limits, to explore, roam, and touch things while other children are admonished severely if they venture too far from mother's side. Who, in the long pull, do you think might develop a keener sense of independence?)

Another way parents can foster independence is by being careful of the duration and intensity of contact with their children. Sometimes parents fail to recognize that by monopolizing their child's time, they limit his possibilities of contact with other persons and thus make it more difficult for the child to test himself outside the protective tent of his parents' influence. For example, among preschool children a negative relationship has been shown to exist between dependence on adults and popularity among peers, which means that children depending most on adults participate least with peers.[44] Thus, dependence on adults apparently hinders a child's interaction with his peers and independence, even at the preschool level, is a valued trait.

In sum, dependent persons have learned, since the time they were children, to place heavy reliance on others to determine their opinions, courses of action, and sense of personal worthiness. The child who is protected and restricted, who is indulged, and constrained, is existing in an artificial environment. Like a plant growing within a house, he can survive within its shelter, but frequently is too fragile to survive the shifting elements of the real world. Parents who seriously restrict their child's freedom and constantly worry about his private enterprise and exploration ("Will he drive carefully?" "Will she behave herself?" "Will she come home on time?" "Oh dear, where is he now—I can't see him.") seriously hinder a child's need to discover his strengths and weaknesses for himself. They may raise a child carefully tuned to the needs of his parents, but they will also turn out an adult who may seek constant assurance about the significance of his own views about most anything, including himself. Unfortunately, dependency-producing parents are often self-indulgent, somewhat helpless souls who lack fulfillment in their own lives and seek to gain it vicariously through their children.

AGGRESSIVENESS

In our culture there is some ambivalence as to how aggressive behavior should be regarded. During childhood, aggression is discouraged and yet aggressiveness carries a certain premium in the adult world. Indeed, our society encourages and rewards such disguises of aggression as competitiveness, ambition, standing up for one's rights, and even getting downright angry or at least "righteously indignant" over certain personal or social issues. The whole thing must be pretty confusing for children. Consider it. We tell youngsters not to fight, but yet we persist in waging wars; we support "death rows," we produce television series in which three stooge-like characters bang each other around, coyotes fall off 200-foot cliffs, and in the interests of producing "successful" shows, literally hundreds of persons are shot, stabbed, beaten, maimed, or murdered during any given evening's prime time hours. In the midst of this "tranquil" setting, we try to teach children something about impulse control and regard for others.

Aggression in childhood seems to be almost universal. For example, of the 379 mothers studied by Sears, Maccoby, and Levin,[45] every mother at one time or another had been forced to cope with angry outbursts or quarreling on the part of her children and 95 percent reported instances of strong aggression directed by the child against his parents. Another study reported that some kind of conflict, ranging from fairly mild to violent, occurs during free play about every five minutes for boys to about every seven or eight minutes for girls.[46] As Sears and his co-workers have pointed out, the aggressive child is likely to be an angry child, and an angry child is not a happy child. Indeed, there is evidence to suggest that aggressive behavior is related to low self-esteem. For example, one study concluded that college students who had *low* self-esteem were more likely to react aggressively in aggression-provoking situations than students with *high* self-esteem.[47] Coopersmith's study of elementary school children, also reported the same phenomenon, namely, low self-esteem children are more destructive than high self-esteem children. He noted that low self-esteem children were more prone to vent their hostility against inanimate objects and remarked that:

> Destructiveness represents an externalized response but one without confrontation with a person or issue. It is the reaction of an individual who admits his weakness to himself, but is in no position to confront his adversary.[48]

HOW AGGRESSIVE BEHAVIOR IS ENCOURAGED

The parent serves as a model for the child and sets examples for his children. Logically, then, it would follow that the more aggressive the adult's behavior, the more aggressive the child's. This view is supported by the data from the study by Sears and others,[49] who observed that when parents punish—particularly when they use physical punishment—they are providing a living example of the use of aggression at the very moment they are trying to teach the child not to be aggressive. This "counter-attack" on the part of the parent, though it may work for a moment, appears to generate still more hostility, anger, and resentment in the child, which eventually gets expressed. An angry, resentful child may not attack his parents back directly, but what he frequently does is *displace* it, that is, he takes it out on someone else, his younger brother, or the boy across the street (when no one's looking), or kids on the playground. (I wonder how many bullies, who usually delight in terrorizing smaller, younger children are themselves physically abused by their bigger, stronger parents?)

Several studies[50, 51] have shown that a boy's expression of aggression is strongly related to the aggression they observe in a male model, which would suggest that a father interested in tempering his son's aggressive expressions would do well to watch his own.

Aggression is more likely to occur when it is permitted and it has been observed that highly aggressive children can also come from homes in which the parents are permissive of the child's outburst, whether or not the aggression is directed against them. It has been noted, for example, that mothers who are both permissive and physically punishing are most likely to produce highly aggressive children.[52]

Although the discussion here has focused on the parents as models, we know from our everyday observations that a child may also imitate siblings, peers, and other adults. In fact, one study with preschoolers showed that exposure to aggressive behavior in a peer model is highly effective in eliciting imitative aggressive behaviors.[53] In general, we are fairly safe in saying that the more a child is exposed to aggressive behavior in others, in real-life or on television, the more likely he is to manifest such behavior himself and to incorporate aggressive behavior as a part of his self-concept.

COPING WITH AGGRESSION

The literature concerned with aggression, as well as everyday social observation, clearly suggests that a child's aggression cannot be so thoroughly squelched that he becomes defenseless and passive. Indeed, from the natural aggression expressed in childhood is born the self-confidence it takes to express one's ideas and opinions in adulthood. On the other hand, rampant acting out of aggression through physical violence and verbal tirades can be socially and personally destructive and must be controlled.

The way for parents and teachers to cope with aggression is to make it abundantly clear that destructive, physical aggression is frowned upon and to stop this sort of aggression when it occurs with the use of some non-physical punishment technique. The best, or at least the most effective, ways of handling aggressive behavior are the use of diversion, appeal to non-hostile motives, such as friendship and rational explanations about *why* aggressive acting-out behavior is undesirable. Spanking a child for being aggressive only makes him more aggressive. However, we must also remember that children easily construe adult permissiveness about aggression as

Although a certain amount of aggressiveness in childhood is healthy, it can *be carried to extremes.*

approval and, when so handled, are likely to be more aggressive than the average. A growing child *wants* adults to help him control aggressive behavior and finds considerable security in growing up with someone who not only cares for him but helps him control his periodic impulse to slug someone.

Let us remember that a child, like anyone else, should have the right to have angry feelings. The fact that a person is angry is not so important as what he does with it. Constructive anger, i.e., finding out what is wrong, working harder to solve the problem, can lead to positive changes in one's self and others. Destructive anger, i.e., losing one's head, physical violence, is usually harmful to one's self, to others, and if there is a "cause" involved, to that as well. Honest recognition and acceptance of angry and aggressive feelings is one of the most important facets of good adjustment and a healthy self-concept.

CONSCIENCE DEVELOPMENT

Sooner or later, if all goes well, each child acquires a conscience, a system of ideas, attitudes, and inner controls that decree what is right and wrong and what are his duties and responsibilities. It is a significant aspect of a person's self-concept since it reflects one's acceptance of values concerning right and wrong behavior. Conscience is sometimes referred to tongue-in-cheek as "that which keeps us from doing what we shouldn't do when no one is looking." Jersild very aptly defines the conscience as follows:

> The conscience usually does not represent a unitary, internally consistent set of principles or sanctions. It has many facets. It may be the voice of experience (better not, someone might be looking). It may be rigorous in some matters, not in others. It may prevail over temptation. Or it may be sort of a gadfly, which does not prevent a person from doing what he thinks he ought not to do, but only prevents him from enjoying it.[54]

SIGNS OF HEALTHY CONSCIENCE DEVELOPMENT

Sears, Maccoby, and Levin[55] have observed that there are at least three signs of healthy conscience development which adults should be alerted to when assessing a child's ability to know the difference between "right" and "wrong" behavior. One sign is the extent to which a child can resist temptation, even when he knows he's not being watched by a potential punisher. If, for example, a parent can leave valuable possessions or tempting foods within reach of a child who has been asked "not to touch or get into things" and feel sure that the child will obey in the parent's absence, then this is one indication that the child is learning to control his impulses.

A second sign of healthy conscience development which usually means accepting his parents' standards as his own, is the child's efforts to teach these standards to his friends and siblings, i.e., to act the parental role. For example, a brother admonishing his sister with something like "You better get out of mom's jewelry, she wouldn't like it." or a little boy reminding his friend with "You shouldn't go to the bathroom outside—that's not nice." are each examples of assuming a kind of parental role in real-life interactions with siblings or friends.

A third sign of conscience development is the way a child acts *after* he has done something wrong. A child with a well-developed conscience is troubled not only by a fear of punishment, but also by a certain amount of self-blame. If, in fact, he disapproves of himself in the same way he thinks his parents will disapprove of him, he can only feel better after he has atoned for, or has been punished for the misdeed in some way and has been forgiven. In fact, he may act guilty and sheepish and even hang around his mother in such a way that she knows something is wrong. Sometimes a child will arrange things in such a way so his parents are bound to find out what he's done, even though he might not actually confess. (In my own case, as a young boy, I was always too anxious to do a lot of "extra" favors for my mother, a dead giveaway to her that I was wrong *and* guilty about something.)

In general, a child's capacity to admit that he did something "bad" and to apologize or make some kind of restitution, are important steps along the road to the development of a self-concept which is able to discriminate between right and wrong. It means that he is willing to risk outside punishment in order to recover his self-esteem and the esteem of his parents.

SIGNS OF UNHEALTHY CONSCIENCE DEVELOPMENT

Redl and Wineman[56] have described some ingenious rationalizations which a group of delinquent children used to justify, without guilt, a wide variety of immoral behaviors. Consider them carefully. These included:

1. *Repression of intent.* An inability to recall the original motive for performing the crime, though there was full recall of the details of the crime itself.
2. *"He did it first."* Though the action was wrong, the fact that another person had done such a thing evidently served as a precedent, and this precedent made the action "legal."
3. *"Everybody else does such things anyway."* If everybody does such things, then they can't be wrong, and so I need not feel any guilt for doing them.
4. *"We were all in on it."* Since it was a group activity, the responsibility, and hence the guilt, either belongs to the leader or else to no one person.
5. *"But somebody else did that same thing to me before."* Because I was once the victim of such an act before, I am entitled to do the same thing to some present innocent party without having to feel guilt for it.
6. *"He had it coming to him."* The wronged person was such a sinner himself that he deserved to be sinned against; ergo, I need not feel guilty.
7. *"I had to do it, or I would have lost face."* Justifying one's actions on the assumption that status in a group with deviant values is more important than conformity with society's morals.
8. *"I didn't use the proceeds anyway."* An appeal to the "Robin Hood" mechanism. If I used the proceeds of illegally gotten money, and so on, for charitable or highly moral purposes, there need be no guilt.
9. *"But I made up with him afterwards."* If I befriend the victim of

my immoral activity, I have thus undone the crime and need feel no guilt.

10. *"He is a no-good so-and-so himself."* Similar to No. 6.

11. *"They are all against me, nobody likes me, they are always picking on me."* Since the person is living as if he is in an enemy camp, then all activity is justifiable.

12. *"I couldn't have gotten it any other way."* Self-exculpation on the premise that what was gained immorally was somehow the person's inviolable right; he is entitled to get it by any means.

Although these rationalizations were gathered from a group of delinquent preadolescents, it is not difficult to see that they are also the prototypes of many adult rationalizations. These are unhealthy reactions and interfere with normal conscience development, because they represent efforts to run away from one's guilt or wrong-doing rather than facing it. When a person has repressed, projected, displaced, or rationalized the guilt he accumulates, his defenses usually have to become more drastic to keep the guilt from conscious awareness. Typically, reactions of this sort lead to increased alienation from the self, ease of being threatened ("What if someone finds out what I'm *really* like; I'd better be careful."), and a reduction in the capacity for free, open, honest communication with others—all unhealthy consequences. A person—no difference the age—with something to hide is a cautious, guarded, closed person.

TOWARD ENCOURAGING HEALTHY CONSCIENCE DEVELOPMENT

The concept used most frequently to explain a child's conscience development is that of *identification*, which we discussed earlier in this chapter. Conditions which favor strong positive identification with parents also tend to encourage conscience development. That is, as a child "becomes like" his parents, he also comes to adopt his parents' values about "right" and "wrong." For example, it has been found that kindergarten boys who were highly masculine, presumably because of identification with their fathers, were also high in conscience development.[57] There is also experimental evidence to show that in temptation situations children are inclined to imitate the adult model who yields to temptation,[58] which suggests that parents serve rather directly as models for their children with regard to moral behavior.

As you might suspect, the kind of discipline parents use is very much related to a child's conscience development. For example, Sears and his colleagues[59] observed that psychological or "love-oriented" techniques as reflected in the use of praise, isolation, and withdrawal of love produced relatively more children with high conscience than the use of more "thing-oriented" or physical methods such as those reflected in tangible rewards, deprivation, and physical punishment.

Basically there are at least three essential conditions for conscience development: (a) The child has to know what is right and wrong, what is acceptable and what isn't; (b) He has to be loved and know it; (c) He must know for sure that those who care for him do not indiscriminately accept everything he does. If a child has free reign to do pretty much what he wants, in the absence of expectations to live up to, then he seldom has to live with the guilt which usually follows from letting someone valued down. *Experiencing and working through guilt feelings is a primary prerequisite to healthy conscience development.* If a child violates an expectation and the parent tries to comfort him with either a subtle or obvious, "Well it really doesn't matter that much anyway." response, the effect of this on the child is two-fold: (a) It deprives him of an opportunity to modify his behavior and sharpen his sensitivity to the demands of the outside world and, (b) it makes the parent look not only inconsistent, but also like someone who doesn't really mean what he says anyway.

SOCIAL DEVELOPMENT

Whether a child is popular with his peers and has leadership potential, or whether he is a social isolate and is one of the followers depends on many things, not the least of which are the methods his parents use in raising him. Recent studies have attempted to sort through the antecedents responsible for producing different levels of social acceptance and some interesting trends have emerged. For example, in a study of family influences on adjustment to peers, Hoffman[60] observed that children from homes which were dominated by the mother experienced difficulties in their relations with the opposite sex. Another study found that boys who experienced social adjustment problems suffered a basic lack of affectional relationships within their families and were likely to have fathers who resorted to cold, harsh, and punitive child-rearing practices.[61] Assuming that these boys identify with their fathers' life-style, we can see how they might have social problems if they copied their fathers' behavior in treating their peers.

Research indicates that the child who is most effective in his social relations, and most popular, is likely to be the one who combines sensitivity to the desires of others with a confident reliance on his own resources. For example, in a series of studies by McCandless and his associates[62] and by Moore and Updegraff,[63] it was found that children who depend heavily on adults are not likely to be popular. Apparently, however, the *kind* of dependency a child shows makes a difference. A child who is dependent on adults for *emotional* support (seeking reassurance, clinging to the adult as a helpless child might lean on his mother) is less likely to be popular than a child who leans on an adult for "instrumental" support, that is, seeks out an adult for practical help in carrying out a specific project. In addition, it appears that the child who looks for help and support from his agemates is likely to be more popular than the one who continues, as he grows older, to depend on adults. From one point of view of children themselves it's apparently all right for one of them to seek adult help in doing something that is obviously beyond his ability to do (pound a big nail, ride a bike for the first time, lift a heavy object), but running home to momma as a general solution to problems is socially frowned upon in a child's peer culture. Indeed, "momma's boys" at any age seem to experience more social difficulties, unless, of course, they associate with other momma's boys.

SEX DIFFERENCE IN SOCIAL DEVELOPMENT

There is increasing evidence to suggest that expressions of affection and punishment, as two major factors in child-rearing, are used in somewhat different ways, for somewhat different purposes, and with somewhat different effects when applied to boys and to girls. For example, it has been shown that girls are more likely than boys to be subjected to "love oriented" techniques and evidence is accumulating that such techniques are effective in encouraging healthy social adjustment.[64, 65] In contrast, a rather different child-rearing style is used for boys. That is, parents are more likely to use physical punishment, to be permissive of and even encourage aggressiveness, to minimize the emphasis on conformity, and to stress the value of independence and achievement. With boys, socialization practices are focused more specifically on *directing him toward the environment*, while with girls the emphasis is more on *protecting her from the environment*.

These contrasting means and ends help to explain in part why it is that girls are usually found to be more obedient, cooperative, and in general, better socially adjusted than boys at comparable ages.[66] At the same time, research also indicates that girls tend to be more anxious, dependent, and sensitive to rejection. The characteristics of independence, self-confidence, initiative, and self-sufficiency, which are included among the top criteria of a boy's successful socialization in our culture, require for their development a different balance of authority and affection than is found in the more "love-oriented" strategies employed with girls. Although, as we have noted, parental affection is important for a boy's overall socialization and self-concept development, it must also be accompanied by and be compatible with a strong blend of parental discipline. Otherwise, the boy is likely to find himself in the same situation as the girl, who, having been the object of greater affection, is also more sensitive to its withdrawal. In other words, since a girl is likely to *receive* more affection than a boy, she is also likely to be *more responsive* to its loss, which is, in fact, why her socialization pattern is marked by predispositions to greater anxiety, dependency, and sensitivity to rejection. Along this same vein, Hoffman and others[67] have noted that ". . . It seems likely that assertiveness in girls is less valued by others," and that girls are more likely to "respond to the emotional rejection that coercion (being aggressive, getting others to do what she wants, etc.) implies." This is not the sort of behavior that is normally encouraged in boys and, as we have noted earlier, dependent boys have a more difficult time with their social adjustment than do more independent and more aggressive boys. Bronfenbrenner[68] has noted that "for boys, who tolerate and require higher levels of discipline on an affectional base, problems derive most commonly from the failure on the part of the parents to provide adequate emotional support and—especially—firm authority."

TOWARD ENCOURAGING POSITIVE SOCIAL DEVELOPMENT

In general, research is showing that the emergence of effective social development is a function of an optimal balance of affection and control,

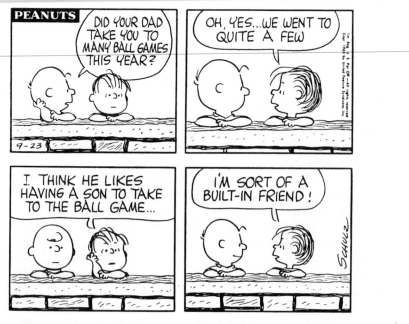

© *1963 United Feature Syndicate, Inc.*

Boys who have dads who feel like this are fortunate indeed.

which is different for boys and girls and involves different risks in the process of child-rearing. Specifically, the major obstacle to the development of appropriate social adjustment among boys, particularly as this adjustment is reflected in their sense of responsibility and leadership capacity, stems from too little parental support and authority. The affection existing between parent and child is especially critical for a child's acceptance by his peers. Optimal social development, as it is expressed in getting along with others, being accepted as a leader and assuming responsibility is most likely to be encouraged when sons and daughters *experience the parent of the same sex taking an active role in child-rearing.* Bronfenbrenner, notes that:

> Relative deprivation of affection from the parent of the same sex is especially deleterious. . . . Boys tend to be most responsible when the father is the principal agent of discipline; girls when the mother has relatively greater power. . . . In short, boys thrive in a patriarchal context, girls in a matriarchal.[67]

Birth Order: Influence on Child-Rearing Practices and Personality Outcomes

A child's place in the family by way of birth can have a powerful effect on his attitudes toward himself and others. Our everyday observations have taught most of us that whether a child is the only child, or the first-born, or the second-born, or the third-born, and so on, seems to make a difference in behavior. From his vantage point as a practicing psychoanalyst, Alfred Adler made the following observation:

> After a few years another child comes along and the situation of the older is not so pleasant. He is no longer the center of the scene. . . . He is always striving in a thousand ways to recapture his old situation of power and importance with his family. Feeling an obstacle in his way, he wants to overcome it by fighting. Unless he can overcome in the struggle for supremacy in his universe he is apt to become depressed, peevish, more or less hopeless, and will show his hopelessness later in life if confronted by problems. He is very likely to be conservative, to understand power and to agree with it. If he is strong enough he becomes a fighting child.

> As for the second child he is never alone, but is always confronted by the older child. This constant picture before him of an older and bigger child begets in him a sense of rivalry. He has a pacemaker in his older brother. . . . If successful, he is an excellent type, but if defeated, for instance, if he is not able to compete successfully with the older child in word and play, he loses hope, becomes depressed and has a bad time of it.

The third child has to fight for a place in the sun, but he has no successor, this gives him a great sense of power, and if he is capable overcomes the older child by his sense of importance. If he is not capable, he perhaps hides behind the fact of being spoiled, and becomes lazy, escaping from tasks, wasting time, and making excuses.[70]

It makes no difference to a baby—and to the roles he eventually plays—whether he comes first in a family or follows other children. Typically, the first child "breaks trail"—that is, the parents learn about child-rearing the hard way, by practicing on their first-born, who is on the receiving end not only of their fumblings, uncertainties, and downright mistakes, but who may also bear the brunt of excessive anxiety and overprotectiveness often expended on a first child. The research related to birth order and its effects on personal-social development is voluminous, to say the least, and what follows is a sampling of that research as it relates directly to child-rearing practices and personality outcomes.

One of the most consistent findings related to birth order is that first-born children achieve eminence in higher proportion than do subsequent children within the same family. For example, it has been noted that:

> . . . marked surpluses of first-borns have been reported in samples of prominent American men of letters, of Italian university professors, of the starred men in *American Men of Science,* of the biographies in Who's Who, of ex-Rhodes scholars and of eminent research biologists, physicists, and social scientists.[71]

This finding is similar to the conclusion of another study which found that first-borns were overrepresented in the college population.[72] Interestingly enough, there is also evidence to suggest that college attendance decreases regularly with each later birth-order position.[73] There are several plausible reasons for the excesses of first-borns among persons of eminence and scholastic achievement; one of them is related to the apparent fact that first-borns perform more effectively in the classroom than do later-borns.[74]

The superior academic performance of the first-born does not necessarily mean he has superior intelligence, but seems to be more related to his greater striving for academic achievement. Why should this be? Consider it: not only is the first-born likely to receive overdoses of parental anxiety and insecurity, but also overdoses of their love and attention, which is directed at him and him alone. As a consequence, first-borns tend to learn to speak earlier and more precisely and, as research has indicated, are also likely to receive a great deal more verbal stimulation from their parents than will later-born children, who must compete for their parents' attention.[75, 76] Since the first-born is likely to continue to be the child to whom the parents direct their commentaries on performance and the one at whose level conversation is pitched, he is seemingly more inclined toward greater acceptance of conventional or adult-approved activities and interactions—traits that frequently lead him to be variously labeled as *adult-oriented, conscientious, studious, serious,* and so on. And then, too, parents seem to expect more of their first child, almost as if he were a kind of trail-blazer responsible for establishing the standards and establishing guidelines for subsequent children. Indeed, some parents seem to feel that, if they do a good job raising their first-born, later children will just naturally follow in his footsteps and are shocked to find that subsequent children are not at all like either the first-born or each other. In any case, although the superior school performances of the first-born and their greater frequency among eminent scientists and men of letters is a fairly consistent finding, it is not at all clear that first-born children strive comparably or excel in other pursuits. For example, there is suggestive evidence that outstanding athletes are more likely to be *later-born* than first-born.[77] This is consistent with more recent evidence which indicates that first-borns respond with more fear to physical harm than do later-borns,[78] and also that their greater anxiety about the prospect of physical harm is likely to discourage them from participating actively in high-risk (injury-wise) sports such as football, baseball, or basketball.[79] Since new parents tend to overreact and to respond with greater fear and anxiety to anything physically wrong with their first-born, it is not difficult to see how this anxiety could influence a first-born child to adopt a cautious, conservative approach to physical activities.

It has also been suggested that the first-born, confronted by powerful adults, learns to repress his aggressive tendencies while the later-born, having an older sibling (or siblings) with whom to contend, can more readily express aggression.[80] Moreover, parents are more likely to constrain the older, stronger child who aggresses against a younger sibling, while at the same time encouraging the younger child to stand up for his rights.

A recent review of the literature by Clausen[81] indicated that first-born males are more readily influenced than are later-borns, more likely to yield to group pressures, and are more suggestible. First-born females, on the other hand, seem, if anything, less susceptible to influence than later-born females, more responsible, aggressive, and competitive. There is no clear explanation for this, but one reason may be that a mother is more inclined to overprotect and overreact to her first-born if it is a son than if it is a daughter partly because she knows less about "what makes little boys tick" and so is more cautious with him. It may also be due partly to the fact that she responds to "the son her husband always wanted" and so takes extra precautions to see that nothing happens to him.

In a study involving interviews with 3050 adolescents, Douvan and Adelson[82] produced a number of interesting findings. For example, they found that first-borns of both sexes were highly ambitious and achievement-oriented, while middle children tended to have lower aspirations. While the oldest child showed close identification with parents, the youngest was more closely identified with the peer group and relied less on the family. This difference may well reflect changes in parental needs and concerns. For example, it is conceivable that the younger child is given greater freedom of social interaction because the parents do not need to form the close emotional attachment with him that they had with the older child.

Let us remember that the general conclusions we have discussed in regard to birth order and behavior may hold statistically, but there are many, many individual exceptions. And let us also remember that a child's order in the family is far less important than are attitudes and interaction patterns of his parents toward him. There are apparent advantages and disadvantages associated to each birth-order position and an awareness of these can help us understand and perhaps modify certain child-rearing practices as we work toward encouraging positive self-concept outcomes.

So far, our discussion of the various facets and styles of child-rearing and their impact on personality and self-concept development has assumed that a child will experience the influence of *both* a male and female model as he grows up. What happens when this is *not* the case?

Self-Concept Development as Related to Broken Family Units

The 1960 census of population revealed that slightly more than one household in ten, among those containing children under eighteen, had only one parent present. Population surveys in urban centers suggest that by age eighteen between 30 and 40 percent of all children have experienced a broken home.

That the loss of a parent through divorce, separation, or death hampers a child's adjustment cannot be denied. On the other hand, the evidence does not allow us to assume that *because* only one parent lives at home the child or children in that home will be maladjusted or emotionally damaged. What seems to make a difference to a child is not so much that a separation, or divorce, or death has occurred, but rather *how it is handled by the adults involved*.

An intact family is no guarantee that the children within it will grow up to be happy, productive, high self-esteem adults. For example, in his investigation of family disorganization, Goode observed:

> . . . that a family in which there is continued marital conflict, or separation, is more likely to produce children with problems of personal adjustment than a family in which there is divorce or death. . . . (The) choice

usually has to be between a continuing conflict or divorce. And the evidence suggests that it is the *conflict of divorce,* not the divorce itself, that has an impact on the children.[84]

Consistent with this observation, Nye[85] found that adolescents from *broken homes* showed *less* psychosomatic illness, less delinquent behavior, and better adjustment to parents than those from *unhappy, unbroken* homes, which would suggest that in some cases separation and disruption of the home is desirable. Perhaps this might follow an additional finding of Nye's that indicated that the adjustment of parents individually and to their spouses were superior in broken homes than in unhappy homes that remained intact.

Burchinal,[86] in a study involving over one thousand adolescents, found that youth in homes broken by divorce do not fall into a class by themselves, with common characteristics that distinguish them from other children. In fact, they are as heterogeneous, with their share of good adjustment and poor adjustment, as young people who do *not* come from broken families. There are indications, however, that adolescents who formerly perceived their home as a happy place are more disturbed by divorce than youth who viewed their home as unhappily torn by dissension.[87]

Evidence related to the long-range impact of broken homes and rearing by a single parent is extremely meager. One of the most thorough studies of adult mental health—the Midtown Manhattan Project—found that people who had experienced a broken home in childhood had only slightly higher risk of psychological difficulties later in life than those from intact homes.[88] There was, however, a marked increase in the number of emotional problems among those whose remaining parent remarried, especially in those instances when the same sex parent remarried.

Since remarriage is a frequent sequence to divorce, many children must adapt themselves to stepparents. Studies of children reared by a remarried parent suggest that ambivalence toward the stepparent and interpersonal friction are extremely common, especially when the child is nearing or has entered adolescence. This point was apparent in a study by Bowerman and Irish[89] who compared information obtained from 2000 seventh- to twelfth-grade stepchildren with similar information drawn from several thousand children of unseparated parents. Children with stepparents reported more stress, ambivalence, and less cohesiveness in the home than children living with their natural parents. As a group, daughters reacted more strongly than sons to the presence of a stepparent.

Since in divorce or separation the mother is given legal custody of the children roughly nine times out of ten, the mother in these circumstances carries an enormous responsibility for the self-feeling and personality development of the children. This is particularly critical for boys raised in father-absent homes. Recent research literature in this area clearly indicates that lack of a masculine relationship during childhood has the effect of feminizing the young boy, creating eventual difficulties in his peer relationships, and producing initially blunted aggressiveness and greater maternal dependency. Overall, this can lead to difficulty adjusting to the masculine sex role.

Perhaps even more important than the absence of a male model for the boy reared by his mother will be her expressed attitudes about the boy's father and other men. Derogation of males by a mother could conceivably produce deep feelings of self-doubt in a son and plant the seeds of distrust of all males in the daughter. In general, the evidence suggests that boys suffer more than girls from the effects of divorce. However, let us remember that this is less likely to be so if the father persists in having a positive, active relationship with his children. Ceasing to be a wife or a husband through separation or divorce does not mean that one has to stop being a parent.

Tensions, insecurities, lack of proper and available models for identification, hostilities, guilt feelings—all of these can follow in the wake of broken family units. To understand and identify the precise impact of death, separation, or divorce on any child, one needs to know how much love and understanding will continue after the action and how much real concern and affection remains for the youngster. In other words, does the child see the "brokenness" of the home as punishment and rejection or has the situation been handled with the sort of maturity and understanding that allows the child to retain his love and confidence in the parents? A basic condition for healthy self-concept development for a child from a broken home lies in the fact that he is loved and *knows* it—not the overindulging, overprotecting love of guilty parents trying to undo what they've done, but rather a love which allows him to grow up without feeling responsible for something he had no control over in the first place.

Toward Raising Children with High Self-Esteem

When we talk about self-esteem, we are referring to an individual's *personal* judgment of worthiness or unworthiness, approval or disapproval that are expressed in the attitudes he holds toward himself. In his monumental investigation of the antecedents of self-esteem among 1700 fifth- and sixth-grade children, Coopersmith found that high self-esteem persons view themselves somewhat along the following general lines*:

> I consider myself a valuable and important person, and am at least as good as others of my age and training. I am regarded as someone worthy

* Quotation pp. 164–165 from *The Antecedents of Self-Esteem* by Stanley Coopersmith, p. 47. W. H. Freeman and Company. Copyright © 1967.

of respect and consideration. . . . I'm able to exert an influence upon people and events, partly because my views are sought and respected, and partly because I'm able and willing to present and defend those views. I have a pretty definite idea of what I think is right . . . and have a fairly good understanding of the kind of person I am. I enjoy new and challenging tasks and don't get upset when things don't go well right off the bat.

At the same time, a similar monologue by an individual with negative self-esteem might proceed as follows:

I don't think I'm a very important or likeable person, and I don't see much reason for anyone else to like me. I can't do many of the things I'd like to do or do them the way I think they should be done. I'm not sure of my ideas and abilities, and there's a good likelihood that other people's ideas and work are better than my own. Other people don't pay much attention to me and given what I know about myself I can't say I blame them. I don't like new or unusual occurrences and prefer sticking to known and safe ground. . . . I don't have much control over what happens to me and I expect that things will get worse rather than better.

As you might suspect, the characterization of a person with medium self-esteem falls between these two descriptions, and is more moderate in its appraisals of competence, significance, and expectations. Specifically, then, how are children encouraged in the direction of high self-esteem?

Baumrind[90] has noted that a combination of parental warmth and firm discipline is likely to produce a self-reliant, buoyant, self-controlled child. Conclusions reached by Coopersmith[91] also support this observation. For example, he found that most notable antecedents of high self-esteem were directly related to parental behavior and the consequences of the rules and regulations that parents establish for their children. As an illustration, he noted that definite and consistently enforced limits on behavior were associated with high self-esteem; that families which maintained clear limits utilized less drastic forms of punishment; and that families producing high self-esteem children exerted greater demands for academic performance and excellence.

It should also be noted that parents of high self-esteem children had attitudes of total or near total *acceptance* of their children and also allowed considerable flexibility for individual behavior *within* the established limits.

Why firmness and clearly defined limits are associated with high self-esteem can be explained in several ways. One, establishing a limit: "Yes, you can ride your bike up to Tom's, but stay off the street," or "Yes, you can go out tonight, but remember to be home by 10 o'clock," is an expression of *caring*, particularly if the parent is viewed as warm, understanding, and autonomy-granting. If, on the other hand, the parent is cold, distant, inconsistent, rejecting or some combination of these behaviors, his limits are more likely to be seen as unfair ("All the other kids are going."), or arbitrary ("Well, you let me do it yesterday."), or punitive ("You never let me do anything!") power assertions. Indeed, research shows that restrictiveness, when positively related to parental hostility, tends to be associated in the child with passivity, dependence, social withdrawal, and passively expressed hostility.[92] When a child is loved and accepted and knows it, he is much more likely to interpret the limits and discipline he is subjected to as expressions of caring. On the other hand, a child who is *not* accepted, usually interprets parental restrictions exactly for what they are, namely, expressions of rejection and hostility. This is significant, since high self-esteem is deeply rooted in the experience of *being* esteemed (valued, prized) by others.

Secondly, clearly defined limits not only provide the child with a basis for evaluating how well or how poorly he's doing, but they also serve to define a child's social world in terms of what is safe and what is hazardous, what he can and cannot do. For example, if a child is supposed to keep his room clean and does it, he *knows* he's successful. If he's supposed to stay off the street and does it, he *knows* he did right. If he's supposed to be in

© 1959 United Feature Syndicate, Inc.

Youngsters may not always like it, but firm, consistent expectations are best for them in the long run.

by ten o'clock and makes it, he *knows* he lived up successfully to an expectation. In other words, the existence of limits can leave the child with the feeling that a definition of his social environment *is* possible and that the world does impose restrictions and make demands that he can learn to handle in everyday living. Parents who are less certain and more permissive about their standards are likely to have children who are not only more dependent on their parents (not knowing exactly what's expected, they may linger around longer waiting to be told), but more compliant with their peers. Another consideration is that if a child has no limits to live up to, he is apt to be left with the feeling that everything he does is all right, which, in the long run, robs him of important practice opportunities in dealing with situations and circumstances when everything is *not* all right.

Coopersmith also found that parents who *expect* their children to live up to the standards they established were more likely to facilitate healthy growth than parents who do *not* have these expectancies. Expectations perform an important function. They not only represent a belief in a child's adequacy, but they also relay the message that he has the ability to do what is required of him. When set at reasonable levels, expectations represent the strongest vote of confidence possible. Self-esteem grows out of successfully doing those things we weren't too sure of being able to do in the first place, and if we have someone who believes in us, "expects that we can," then taking that first step is at least a bit easier.

Another important observation growing out of the Coopersmith study was that, although all parents wanted their children to be self-confident, some behaved as if they wanted this characteristic to exist only *after the children grew up and left home.* In the meantime they preferred to keep their children meek, submissive, and dependent. For example, how often have you heard parents make remarks such as these to their children: "Here, let me do that. You're so clumsy, you'll probably drop it." "No, no! Put the fork on the left side—can't you tell right from left?"

Such remarks reveal quite clearly a parent's desire, conscious or unconscious, to lower a child's self-esteem—at least for the present. Unfortunately, children who are thus belittled while they are small are all too likely to carry a crippling self-distrust with them into the outer world.

A reasonable question at this point is whether there is a *pattern* of conditions necessary to produce high self-esteem, or whether there is any single condition or set of conditions which plays a greater role than others. In answer to this question, Coopersmith observes*:

> First and foremost, we should note that there are virtually no parental patterns of behavior or parental attitudes that are common to all parents of children with high self-esteem. Examination of the major indices and

* Quotation pp. 167–168 from *The Antecedents of Self-Esteem* by Stanley Coopersmith, pp. 239–240 (emphasis added). W. H. Freeman and Company. Copyright © 1967.

scales of *acceptance, limit definition, respect, and parental self-esteem* provides explicit support for the view that not all of these conditions are essential for the formation of high self-esteem. . . . (The data) suggest that *combinations* of (these) conditions are required—more than one but less than the four established for this study. . . . In addition it is likely that a minimum of devaluating conditions—that is, rejection, ambiguity, and disrespect—is required if high self-esteem is to be attained.

In Perspective

How a child behaves and what he becomes depend, in large measure, on how he was reared and the nature of his relationship to the adults who were primarily responsible for raising him. Indeed, how any of us feel about ourselves and others is linked to the relationships we had with our own mothers and fathers. The influence that parents can have on the lives of their children over a period of fifteen to eighteen years is incredible. Through the subtle, but powerful process of identification we are like our parents in ways which are beyond conscious recognition. No single day, or hour, or experience with our parents made a difference in our lives. Rather, it is the total of many days, and hours, and experiences strung together over many years that has shaped and formed the essence of our self-other attitudes. Whether parents are aware of it or not, through their daily life styles and the *consistency* of their behavior they teach their children how to blend, for better or worse, the basic ingredients for living—how to deal with anxiety, failure, how to handle money, make friends, *be* a friend, how to resolve conflicts and make decisions, how to love and how to be loved.

Some parents—the wise ones—recognize that they begin to lose their children almost as soon as they get them. They have what you might call a "readiness to be forgotten" and are willing participants in their children's growth toward independence. They recognize that it is their task to help develop their children into the best kind of human beings they are capable of; they also know that this will be their whole reward. Wise parents know that a child, as he matures, must first of all fall *out* of love with his own parents—and feel free to do so—before he can fall *in* love with another person and become, of all things, a parent himself.

Some parents—the not-so-wise ones—assume that a child "belongs" to them, like a thing. But a child is not a thing and can never be a possession. A child treated like a possession you do things to is robbed of many experiences, not the least of which is the experience of being valued for his humanness, for his capacity to feel and have emotions. Children raised as possessions by cold, detached, uninvolved parents may learn to *think* feelings, but they may be hard-pressed to know what it is to *have* feelings.

Research is telling us that healthy, balanced children who value themselves and others are likely to come from homes in which the parents respect and care for the children, each other, and themselves; where there are firm rules which are consistently enforced; and where there are high standards for behavior and performance which children are *expected* to live up to.

Raising children is a delicate process, but fortunately children are resilient enough to survive many foolish adult mistakes. Child-rearing involves many things, among which include the proper blend of encouraging a child to do those things he *can* do and pushing him in the direction of doing those things he *should* do. And perhaps, as adults, who supposedly know about such things, we ought to remember to encourage a growing child to *be* something in whatever route he chooses to *accomplish* something.

[1] R. Sunley, "Early Nineteenth Century American Literature on Child Rearing," in M. Mead and M. Wolfenstein (Eds.), *Childhood in Contemporary Cultures.* Chicago: University of Chicago Press, 1955, pp. 150–167.

[2] M. Wolfenstein, "The Emergence of Fun Morality," *Journal of Social Issues.* 1951, 7: 15–25.

[3] John B. Watson, *Psychological Care of Infant and Child.* New York: W. W. Norton and Company, 1928, pp. 41, 81–82.

[4] Margaret A. Ribble, *The Rights of Infants.* New York: Columbia University Press, 1943.

[5] B. M. Spock, *Baby and Child Care,* New York: Pocket Books, 1947.

[6] B. M. Spock, *Baby and Child Care: Revised and Enlarged.* New York: Pocket Books, 1957, p. 2.

[7] P. M. Symonds, *The Psychology of Parent-Child Relationships.* New York: Appleton-Century-Crofts, 1939.

[8] M. J. Radke, *The Relation of Parental Authority to Children's Behavior and Attitudes.* Minneapolis: University of Minnesota Press, 1946.

[9] W. C. Bronson, E. S. Kelton, and N. Livson, "Patterns of Authority and Affection in Two Generations," *Journal of Abnormal and Social Psychology.* 1959, 58: 143–152.

[10] I. D. Harris, *Normal Children and Their Mothers.* New York: The Free Press, 1959.

[11] G. Handel, "Psychological Study of Whole Families," *Psychological Bulletin.* 1965, 63: 19–41.

[12] Leland H. Stott, "Some Family Life Patterns and Their Relation to Personality Development in Children," *Journal of Experimental Education.* 1939, 8: 148–160.

[13] Leland H. Stott, "Parent-Adolescent Adjustment: Its Measurement and Significance," *Character and Personality,* 1941, 10: 140–150.

[14] M. L. Behrens, "Child Rearing and the Character Structure of the Mother," *Child Development.* 1954, 25: 225–238.

[15] M. Zuckerman and M. Oltean, "Some Relationships Between Maternal Attitude Factors and Authoritarianism, Personality Needs, Psychopathology, and Self-Acceptance," *Child Development.* 1959, 30: 27–36.

[16] E. Fromm, "Selfishness and Self-Love," *Psychiatry.* 1939, 2: 507–523.

[17] Karen Horney, *Neurosis and Human Growth.* New York: W. W. Norton & Company, Inc., 1955.

[18] Gene R. Medinnus and E. J. Curtis, "The Relation Between Maternal Self-Acceptance and Child Acceptance," *Journal of Consulting Psychology.* 1963, 27: 542–544.

[19] Stanley Coopersmith, *The Antecedents of Self-Esteem.* San Francisco: W. H. Freeman and Company, 1967, Chap. 6, pp. 96–117.

[20] Nancy Bayley and E. S. Schaefer, "Maternal Behavior and Personality Development: Data from the Berkeley Growth Study," *Psychiatric Research Reports.* 1960, 13: 155–173.

[21] John Nash, "The Father in Contemporary Culture and Current Psychological Literature," *Child Development.* 1965, 36: 261–267.

[22] Coopersmith, Chap. 6.

[23] Erich Fromm, *The Art of Loving.* New York: Bantam Books, Inc., 1956, pp. 35–37.

[24] Pauline S. Sears, "Child-Rearing Factors Related to Playing of Sex-Typed Roles," *American Psychologist.* 1953, 8: 431 (abstract).

[25] R. W. Moulton, P. G. Liberty, Jr., E. Burnstein, and N. Altacher, "Patterning of Parental Affection and Disciplinary Dominance as a Determinant of Guilt and Sex-Typing," *Journal of Personality and Social Psychology.* 1966, 4: 356–363.

[26] Pauline S. Sears, "Doll-Play Aggression in Normal Young Children: Influence of Sex, Age, Sibling Status, Father's Absence," *Psychological Monographs.* 1951, 65: Whole No. 323, No. 6.

[27] David B. Lynn, "Sex-Role and Parental Identification," *Child Development.* 1962, 33: 555–564.

[28] A. B. Heilbrum, "An Empirical Test of the Modeling Theory of Sex-Role Learning," *Child Development.* 1965, 36: 789–799.

[29] A. B. Heilbrum, "The Measurement of Identification," *Child Development.* 1965, 36: 111–127.

[30] M. M. Helper, "Learning Theory and the Self-Concept," *Journal of Abnormal and Social Psychology.* 1955, 51: 184–194.

[31] B. Sutton-Smith and B. G. Rosenberg, "Development of Sex Differences in Play Choices During Preadolescence," *Child Development.* 1960, 31: 307–311.

[32] Judy Chang and J. Block, "A Study of Identification in Male Homosexuals," *Journal of Consulting Psychology.* 1960, 24: 307–310.

[33] B. R. McCandless, *Children: Behavior and Development* (2nd ed.). New York: Holt, Rinehart and Winston, Inc., 1967, p. 472.

[34] P. Mussen and E. Rutherford, "Parent-Child Relations and Parental Personality in Relation to Young Children's Sex-Role Preferences," *Child Development.* 1963, 34: 589–607.

[35] K. K. Beller, "Dependence and Independence in Young Children," *Journal of Genetic Psychology.* 1955, 87: 25–35.

[36] Celia B. Stendler, "Critical Periods in Socialization and Overdependency," *Child Development.* 1952, 23: 3–12.

[37] F. L. Gewirtz, "A Factor Analysis of Some Attention-Seeking Behavior of Young Children," *Child Development.* 1956, 27: 17–36.

[38] Stendler, p. 8.

[39] Celia B. Stendler, "Possible Causes of Overdependency in Young Children," *Child Development.* 1954, 25: 125–146.

[40] G. Heathers, Emotional Dependence and Independence in a Physical Threat Situation," *Child Development.* 1953, 24: 169–179.

[41] Coopersmith, p. 223.

[42] W. McCord, J. McCord, and P. Verden, "Familial and Behavioral Correlates of Dependency in Male Children," *Child Development.* 1962, 33: 313–326.

[43] W. J. Mueller, "Need Structure and the Projection of Traits Onto Parents," *Journal of Personality and Social Psychology.* 1966, 3: 63–72.

[44] B. R. McCandless, C. B. Bilous, and H. L. Bennett, "Peer Popularity and Dependence on Adults in Pre-School Age Socialization," *Child Development.* 1961, 32: 511–518.

[45] R. R. Sears, E. E. Maccoby, and H. Levin, *Patterns of Child Rearing.* Evanston, Ill.: Row, Peterson & Company, 1967.

[46] B. R. McCandless, C. Balsbaugh, and H. L. Bennett, "Pre-school Age Socialization and Maternal Control Techniques," *American Psychologist.* 1958, 13: 320 (abstract).

[47] M. E. Rosenbaum and R. F. Stamers, "Self-Esteem, Manifest Hostility, and Expression of Hostility," *Journal of Abnormal and Social Psychology.* 1961, 63: 646–649.

[48] Coopersmith, p. 137.

[49] Sears, Maccoby, and Levin, Chap. 7, pp. 218–269.

[50] C. L. Winder and L. Rau, "Parental Attitudes Associated with Social Deviance in Preadolescent Boys," *Journal of Abnormal and Social Psychology.* 1962, 64: 418–424.

[51] H. Levin and R. R. Sears, "Identification with Parents as a Determinant of Doll Play Aggression," *Child Development.* 1956, 27: 135–153.

[52] Sears, Maccoby, and Levin, Chap. 7, pp. 218–269.

[53] D. Hicks, "Imitation and Retention of Film-mediated Aggressive Peer and Adult Models," *Journal of Personality and Social Psychology.* 1965, 2: 97–100.

[54] Arthur T. Jersild, *Child Psychology* (6th ed.), Englewood Cliffs, N.J.: Prentice-Hall, Inc., 1968, p. 512.

[55] Sears, Maccoby, and Levin, Chap. 10, pp. 376–381.

[56] F. Redl and D. Wineman, *Children Who Hate.* New York: The Free Press, 1951, pp. 145–156.

[57] P. Mussen and L. Distler, "Child-Rearing Antecedents of Masculine Identification in Kindergarten Boys," *Child Development.* 1960, 31: 89–100.

[58] A. Stein, "Imitation of Resistance to Temptation," *Child Development.* 1967, 38: 157–169.

[59] Sears, Maccoby, and Levin, Chap. 10, pp. 376–381.

[60] L. W. Hoffman, "The Father's Role in the Family and the Child's Peer-Group Adjustment," *Merrill-Palmer Quarterly.* 1961, 7: 87–105.

[61] A. Bandura and R. H. Walters, *Adolescent Aggression: A Study of the Influence of Child-Training Practices and Family Interrelations.* New York: The Ronald Press Company, 1959.

[62] McCandless, Bilous, and Bennett, 1961.

[63] S. Moore and R. Updegraff, "Sociometric Status of Preschool Children Related to Age, Sex, Nurturance-Giving, and Dependency," *Child Development.* 1964, 35: 519–524.

[64] Sears, Maccoby, and Levin, Chap. 10, pp. 362–393.

[65] D. R. Miller and G. E. Swanson, *The Changing American Parent.* New York: John Wiley & Sons, Inc., 1958.

[66] L. M. Terman and L. E. Tyler, "Psychological Sex Differences," in L. Carmichael (Ed.), *Manual of Child Psychology.* New York: John Wiley & Sons, Inc., 1954, pp. 1064–1114.

[67] L. Hoffman, S. Rosen, and R. Lippin, "Parental Coerciveness, Child Autonomy,

and Peer Group Role at School." Paper presented at 66th Annual American Psychological Association Convention, Washington, D.C., September 1958, p. 5.

[68] Urie Bronfenbrenner, "Some Familial Antecedents of Responsibility and Leadership in Adolescents," in L. Petrullo and B. M. Bass (Eds.), *Leadership and Interpersonal Behavior*. New York: Holt, Rinehart and Winston, Inc., 1960, p. 260.

[69] Bronfenbrenner, pp. 267–269.

[70] Alfred Adler, "Characteristics of the First, Second, Third Child," *Children*. 1928, 3: 14.

[71] S. Schachter, "Birth-Order, Eminence and Higher Education," *American Sociological Review*. 1963, 28: 757–767.

[72] W. Altus, "Birth Order and Academic Primogeniture," *Journal of Personality and Social Psychology*. 1965, 2: 872–876.

[73] J. R. Warren, "Birth Order and Social Behavior," *Psychological Bulletin*. 1966, 65: 38–49.

[74] G. H. Elder, Jr. "Family Structure: The Effects of Size of Family, Sex Composition and Ordinal Position on Academic Motivation and Achievement," in *Adolescent Achievement and Mobility Aspirations*. Chapel Hill, N.C.: Institute for Social Research, 1962, pp. 59–72.

[75] H. L. Koch, "Sibling Influence on Children's Speech," *Journal of Speech Disorders*. 1956, 21: 322–328.

[76] J. K. Lasko, "Parent Behavior toward First and Second Children," *Genetic Psychology Monographs*. 1954, 49: 96–137.

[77] E. Chen and S. Cobb, "Family Structure in Relation to Health and Disease: A Review of the Literature," *Journal of Chronic Disease*. 1960, 12: 544–567.

[78] R. E. Nisbett and S. Schachter, "Cognitive Manipulation of Pain," *Journal of Experimental Social Psychology*. 1966, 2: 227–236.

[79] R. E. Nisbett, "Birth Order and Participation in Dangerous Sports," *Journal of Personality and Social Psychology*. 1968, 8: 351–353.

[80] P. Zimbardo and R. Formica, "Emotional Comparison and Self-Esteem as Determinants of Affiliation." *Journal of Personality*. 1963, 31: 141–162.

[81] John A. Clausen, "Family Structure, Socialization and Personality," in H. W. Hoffman and M. L. Hoffman (Eds.), *Review of Child Development Research,* Vol. 2. New York: Russell Sage Foundation, 1966, pp. 1–53.

[82] E. Douvan and J. Adelson, *The Adolescent Experience*. New York: John Wiley & Sons, Inc., 1966.

[83] T. S. Langner and S. T. Michael, *Life Stress and Mental Health*. New York: The Free Press, 1963.

[84] William J. Goode, "Family Disorganization," in R. K. Merton and R. A. Nisbet (Eds.), *Contemporary Social Problems*. Harcourt, Brace & World, Inc., 1966, pp. 425–426.

[85] F. I. Nye, "Child Adjustment in Broken and in Unhappy Unbroken Homes," *Marriage and Family Living*. 1957, 19: 356, 361.

[86] L. G. Burchinal and J. E. Rossman, "Relations among Maternal Employment Endices and Developmental Characteristics of Children," *Marriage and Family Living*. 1961, 23: 334–340.

[87] Landis, J. T., "The Trauma of Children when Parents Divorce," *Marriage and Family Living*. 1960, 22: 7–13.

[88] Langner and Michael, 1963.

[89] C. E. Bowerman and D. P. Irish, "Some Relationships of Stepchildren to Their Parents," *Marriage and Family Living*. 1962, 24: 113–121.

[90] Diana Baumrind, "Parental Control and Parental Love," *Children.* 1965, 12: 230–234.

[91] Coopersmith, pp. 236–242.

[92] W. C. Becker, D. R. Peterson, Z. Luvia, D. J. Shoemaker, and L. A. Hellmer, "Relations of Factors Derived from Parent-Interview Ratings to Behavior Problems of Five Year Olds," *Child Development,* 1962, 33: 631–648.

References of Related Interest

Borgatta, Edgar F., and W. W. Lambert (Eds.), *Handbook of Personality Theory and Research in Child Development.* Skokie, Ill.: Rand McNally & Company, 1968, Chap. 4, 5.

Breckenridge, M. E., and L. E. Vincent, *Child Development* (5th ed.), Philadelphia: W. B. Saunders Company, 1965, Chap. 12, 13, 14.

Evans, E. D. (Ed.), *Children: Readings in Behavior and Development.* New York: Holt, Rinehart and Winston, Inc., 1968, Chap. 1.

Ginott, Haim, *Between Parent and Child.* New York: Crowell-Collier and Macmillan, Inc., 1965.

Ginott, Haim, *Between Parent and Teenager.* New York: Crowell-Collier and Macmillan, Inc., 1969.

Grinder, Robert E. (Ed.), *Studies in Adolescence* (2nd ed.), New York: Crowell-Collier and Macmillan, Inc., 1969.

Hamachek, Don E. (Ed.), *Human Dynamics in Psychology and Education.* Boston: Allyn and Bacon, Inc., 1968, Chap. 8.

Jersild, Arthur, *Child Psychology* (6th ed.), Englewood Cliffs, N.J.: Prentice-Hall, Inc., 1968, Chap. 11, 12.

Johnson, R. C., and G. R. Medinnus, *Child Psychology: Behavior and Development* (2nd ed.), New York: John Wiley & Sons, Inc., 1969, part three.

McNeil, Elton B., *The Concept of Human Development.* Belmont, Calif.: Wadsworth, 1966. Chap. 5.

Medinnus, Gene R. (Ed.), *Readings in the Psychology of Parent-Child Relations.* New York: John Wiley & Sons, Inc., 1966.

Meyer, William J. (Ed.), *Readings in the Psychology of Childhood and Adolescence.* Waltham, Mass.: Blaisdell Publishing Company, 1967.

chapter six

Self-Concept, Academic Adjustment, and Implications for Teaching Practices

Psychologists and educators are becoming increasingly aware of the fact that a person's idea of himself, or self-concept, is closely connected to how he behaves and learns. Indeed, as we will see in this chapter, increasing evidence indicates that low performances in basic school subjects, as well as the misdirected motivation and lack of academic involvement characteristic of the under-achiever, the dropout, the culturally disadvantaged, and the failure, may be due in part to negative perceptions of the self. Many students for example, have difficulty in school, not because of low intelligence, or bad hearing, but because they have learned to consider themselves unable to do academic work. For example, if a student says, "I'll *never* pass that test, I just know it," he is expressing something not only about his potential behavior, but he is also reflecting something about how he feels about himself. All things being equal, chances are good that a student with this attitude probably *will not* do well on the test. Research is teaching us that how a student (or anyone else, for that matter) performs depends not only on how intelligent he actually is, but also on how intelligent he thinks he is. Indeed, classroom and clinical research evidence suggests that school or life success may depend less on those qualities a person has by way of genes or circumstances and more on how he *feels* about those qualities. Basically, the self has two aspects—concept and feeling. That is, each knows himself to have particular qualities and he feels certain ways about those qualities. For example, a student may "know" that his measured IQ is, say, 125, but unless he has the self-confidence and belief in himself to accompany his intelligence, his 125 IQ is a practically useless possession.

Can a person's feelings about himself influence his school performance? Is there a relationship between self-concept and academic achievement? How much of an influence do child-rearing practices have on a youngster's academic self-concept? What teaching practices are most conducive to healthy self-concept development? It is to these and related questions that we will address ourselves in this chapter.

Self-Consistency and School Behavior

As noted in earlier chapters, each person, whether conscious of it or not, carries about with him a mental blueprint or picture of himself. It may be vague and ill-defined, but it is there, complete down to the last detail. The blueprint is composed of a system of interrelated ideas, attitudes, values, and commitments which are influenced by our past experiences, our successes and failures, our humiliations, our triumphs, and the way other people reacted to us, especially during our formative years. Eventually, each person arrives at a more or less stable framework of beliefs about himself and proceeds to live in as consistent a manner as possible within that framework. In short, an individual "acts like" the sort of person he conceives himself to be. Indeed, it is extremely difficult to act otherwise, in spite of a strong conscious effort and exercise of will-power. The boy, for example, who conceives himself to be a "failure-type student" can find all sorts of excuses to avoid studying, doing homework, or participating in class. Frequently, he ends up with the low grade he predicted he would get in the first place. His report card bears him out. Now he has "proof" that he's less able! Or, as another example, the socially isolated boy who has an image of himself as the sort of person nobody likes may find that he is indeed avoided by others. What he does not understand is that he may behave in a style that literally invites rejection. His dour expression, his hangdog manner, his own overzestfulness to please, or perhaps his unconscious hostility towards those he anticipates will affront him may all act to drive away those who might otherwise be friendly.

Because of this objective "proof," it seldom occurs to a person that his trouble lies in his own evaluation of himself. If you tell a student that he only "thinks" he cannot grasp algebra, or English, or reading, or whatever, he may very well give you that "Who are you trying to kid?" look. In his own way, he may have tried again and again, but still his report card tells the story. A request (more often a demand or admonishment) destined to fall on deaf ears is the one parents and teachers frequently make of some students to "study harder." This is fine if the student already has a high self-concept and high need for achievement, because he is likely to respond to the challenge in order to produce at a level consistent with his self-image. However, for a student whose self-picture is that of being a poor student, the impact is lost. As a low-concept, low-achieving ninth-grade girl once told me, "Study? Ha! Why should I study to fail?"

Although we may not like this girl's flip answer, it is important to understand that from her point of view it was a perfectly logical conclusion. She saw herself as fairly dumb and of course dumb people don't do well. So why study? She was expressing a need that all of us have, namely, the need to maintain an intact self-structure so that the person we are today can be counted on as being pretty much the same person tomorrow. Again, we should remind ourselves that this consistency is not always voluntary or deliberate, but compulsive, and generally unconsciously motivated.

It is important to keep the self-consistency idea in mind because it will help us understand better the relationship between school performance and self-concept. Once a student "locks in" on a perception of what he is and is not able to do, it is difficult to shake him from it, particularly if the perception has time to root itself into a firmly established belief.

A pioneer in the area of relating self-consistency to school performance was Prescott Lecky,[1] who was one of the first to point out *that low academic achievement may be related to a student's conception of himself as being unable to learn academic material.* He observed, for example, that some children made the same number of errors in spelling per page no matter how difficult or easy the material. These children spelled as though they were responding to a built-in upper limit beyond which they could not go. It occurred to Lecky that they were responding more in terms of how they *thought* they could spell than in terms of their *actual* spelling abilities. He arranged to have a group of these children spend some time with the counselor who helped them explore their feelings about their spelling abilities. As a consequence of these discussions and despite the fact that these children had no additional work in spelling whatever, there was a notable improvement in their spelling! There was less improvement for some children than for others, but the general trend was in the direction of better spelling. One can only speculate about the dynamics at work here, but it does not seem unreasonable to suggest that as the childrens' spelling *confidence* increased, so, too, did their spelling *skills*. In other words, as they acquired new perceptions of their spelling abilities, they also acquired new consistencies, which is to say that as a child moves from believing he is a poor speller to believing he is at least a better speller than he thought he was, his performance changes in the direction of being consistent with his new perception.

Self-Concept Variables Related to School Adjustment and Academic Achievement

The role of the school in the development and change of self-concept is enormous. It dispenses praise and reproof, acceptance and rejection on a colossal scale. School provides not only the stage upon which much of the drama of a person's formative years is played, but it houses the most critical audience in the world—peers and teachers. And it is here, in the face of his severest critics, that a student, whether in kindergarten or graduate school, is likely to be reminded again and again of either his failings and shortcomings or of his strengths and possibilities.

EFFECTS OF A POOR SELF-CONCEPT BEGIN EARLY

There is evidence to suggest that a low or negative self-concept can have adverse affects on a child's school performance even at a very young age. For example, Wattenberg and Clifford[2] found that an unfavorable view of self and poor achievement is already established in many children before they enter first grade. The investigators studied the relationship of kindergarten children's self-attitudes to subsequent school achievement in elementary school. Their method was to study 128 kindergarten students in two schools, one serving lower-class, the other middle-class neighborhoods. They measured intelligence, self-concept, ego-strength, and reading ability of all the students when they were in kindergarten, and then measured these same variables again when these same students finished second grade. They found that measures of self-concept and ego-strength made at the beginning of kindergarten were more predictive of reading achievement two and one-half years later than were measures of intelligence. In other words, the self-attitudes of the kindergarten student were a more accurate indication of his potential reading skills than his intelligence test scores. We cannot, however, assume from this finding that there is no relationship between mental ability and reading achievement. All we can safely conclude is that a measure of a kindergarten student's self-concept and ego-strength is a better predictor of how he might fare in his reading skills by the third grade than is a measure of his intelligence. In addition, we should also keep in mind that a five-year-old's verbal skills are usually not sufficiently developed to be measured with great accuracy, which may be one reason why Wattenberg found a low relationship between intelligence and later reading achievement.

If a child starts with a negative self-image about his ability to do school work, we might expect that the signs of low or poor academic achievement will be apparent during the early elementary years. For example, Shaw and McCuen[3] reasoned that if it is true that academic underachievement is related to basic personality structure, then such behavior is likely to occur during the early school years. To check this out they took a group of eleventh- and twelfth-grade students who had been in the same school system since the first grade and who scored in the upper quarter of an intelligence test administered in the eighth grade and divided them into achiever and under-achiever groups, which were separated for males and females: thirty-six male achievers, thirty-six male under-achievers, forty-five female achievers, and seventeen female under-achievers. The mean grade point averages were computed for each group at each grade level. They found that there were significant differences between male achievers' and under-achievers' grade point average at the third grade, while nonsignificant differences were noted as early as the third grade. The grade point difference between the two groups increased at each grade level from grade three up to grade ten, where there was a slight decrease. There were no significant differences between female achievers and under-achievers before grade nine, although nonsignificant differences were apparent in grade six. These differences between the two groups of girls continued to increase through grade eleven. So, as you can see, under-achievement for boys can begin as early as the first grade, is definitely present by third grade, and becomes increasingly more serious into the high school years. For girls the problem may exist as early as grade six and is definitely present and of increasing importance from grades nine to eleven.

EFFECTS OF SELF-CONCEPT ON PERSONAL ADJUSTMENT IN SCHOOL

In an effort to determine some of the basic personality differences between elementary school achievers and under-achievers, Teigland[4] studied a group of fourth-grade male and female achievers and under-achievers. He found a significant difference between achievers, and under-achievers in terms of peer relationships, with achievers being chosen more often. Further, it was found that achievers scored higher, or toward better adjustment on all scales of the *California Test of Personality*, which includes dimensions such as self-reliance, sense of personal worth, feelings of belonging and so on. Teigland also observed that the peers of under-achievers reject them not only in school work situations, but in play and social situations as well. Lack of overall personality adjustment for under-achievers suggests that the personal-social difficulties commonly associated with under-achievement at the secondary and college levels are also present in the early elementary grades as well.

An investigation by Shaw[5] and his co-workers on bright under-achieving high school students found that male achievers feel relatively more positive about themselves than do male under-achievers. No simple generalization could be made for the female groups except to say that female under-achievers had clearly ambivalent feelings toward themselves. A later study by Shaw and Alves[6] found that not only did male achievers have a more positive self-concept than male under-achievers, but that there was a difference in the general perceptual mode between males and females. That is, the negative perceptual attitudes of male under-achievers appears to revolve primarily around themselves, while the negative attitudes of female under-achievers were centered more on the perceptions of themselves by others.

Combs[7] conducted a study with high-school boys to determine whether academically capable, under-achieving high-school boys tend to see themselves and their relationships with others in ways that differ from those students who make a happier and more successful adjustment to the scholastic situation. Each of the boys in the two groups of twenty-five eleventh graders had IQ's of 115 or better. Under-achievers were defined as those falling below the twenty-fifth percentile for eleventh grade in cumulative grade point average and achievers were defined as those with cumulative grade point averages above the fiftieth percentile. He found that under-achievers saw themselves as less adequate and less acceptable to others and they also saw peers and adults as less acceptable. This is consistent with other research which suggests that an individual is inclined to project his feelings about himself onto others. For example, Reese,[8] while working with fourth-, sixth-, and eighth-grade children, found that both boys and girls who "liked themselves" also liked others. Returning to Combs, he concluded that under-achieving academically capable high-school boys differ significantly from achievers in their perceptions of self, of others, and in general and emotional efficiency.

A recent investigation by Williams and Cole,[9] which related specifically to relationships between self-concept and school adjustment among eighty sixth-grade students found positive relationships between self-concept and emotional adjustment. In other words, students who viewed themselves positively were also likely to be emotionally well-adjusted. In addition, high self-concept students were more likely to enjoy high social status among their peers than was the case for low self-concept students.

From these and other studies it seems fairly clear that adjustment in school is indeed related to basic personality structure, particularly as this involves a student's concept of self. The personal, social, and academic difficulties commonly associated with a low self-concept apparently begin early in elementary school and affect not only a student's performance in the academic arena, but in his broader social world as well. There is also evidence to suggest that anxiety interacts with self-concept in such a way so as to affect how a student does in school—an idea to which we now turn.

SELF-CONCEPT AND ANXIETY

Anxiety is a chronic, complex emotional state with apprehension or fear as its most prominent component. The fear bringing on anxiety is usually generated by dread of the past or apprehension of the future rather than a specific fear-provoking situation in the present. For example, if a person is walking across a narrow board high over deep water and hears the board begin to crack and he starts to sweat—that's fear! If a person walks across a well-constructed reinforced bridge and worries about the whole thing crashing down—that's anxiety.

As any one of us who has ever panicked or "clutched" the moment an exam was put before him knows, anxiety, self-concept, and the ability to engage in deliberate thinking are closely interrelated. A student in school constantly faces situations whose demands he must compare with his own resources. And whenever a person's assessment of the situational demands leads him to conclude that they are greater than his own resources, he is ripe for the various consequences of anxiety. How much anxiety two given individuals feel when confronted with a similar situation depends partly on their overall concept of personal adequacy and self-esteem and partly on their specific feelings about being able to cope with the circumstances at hand. Experimental evidence, for example, shows that low self-esteem persons, when faced with anxiety-provoking situations, are inclined to make hasty, impulsive judgments—behavior not unlike that of a student who feels overwhelmed (either for real or imagined reasons) by an exam and answers questions without really knowing what he's doing just so he can hand the test in and relieve the anxiety. On the other hand, high self-esteem persons when faced with anxiety-provoking situations (at least as judged by an outside observer) are more deliberate and careful in making judgments.[10]

Studies involving both children and college students indicate a relation between self-rejection or negative self-concept and measures of anxiety. In one of these, Lipsitt[11] obtained an overall index of the "good-bad" dimension of the self-concepts of about three hundred fourth-, fifth- and sixth-grade boys and girls and related this to their scores on an anxiety test. Both boys and girls with poor self-concepts were found to be more anxious than were boys and girls with good self-concepts. Other research has shown that high-anxious children, when compared to low-anxious children, are less popular;[12] have greater difficulty with conceptually complex learning tasks;[13] and in at least some cases do less well in the more complicated school subjects.[14]

Coopersmith[15] measured the anxiety level of 102 fifth- and sixth-grade students and found that children who had high self-esteem were significantly less anxious than those with low self-esteem. In addition, high self-esteem youngsters were also more popular. In a later research report, Coopersmith[16] noted that fifth- and sixth-graders who had positive self-concepts were better able to recall (presumably so as to correct) their failures than are children with negative self-concepts, who apparently repress and deny their poor performances.

Such relations between self-concept and anxiety are not limited to children. For example, Mitchell[17] measured the self-concepts and anxiety levels of one hundred freshman and sophomore women students and found that the better the self-concept the less the anxiety.

Anxiety and self-concept do, indeed, seem to be related. How, then, does anxiety affect academic achievement?

EFFECTS OF ANXIETY ON ACADEMIC ACHIEVEMENT

According to conventional wisdom, things are either "good" or "bad" for a person, and since anxiety may have negative effects on behavior, it therefore must be "bad." Part of the difficulty here lies in the *degree* of anxiety that is desirable, particularly as it is related to school learning. In regard to this question of "degree," a number of research efforts suggest that some, but not too much, anxiety is helpful. For instance, Sarason and his co-workers[18] presented a group of high-anxious and low-anxious col-

All students seem to have a certain amount of anxiety about school.

lege students with a specific task and found that low-anxious students did better in general than high-anxious students, and that pressure to finish the task (from the experimenters) resulted in improved performances for low-anxious students, but not for high-anxious students. As another example of the effect of anxiety on performance, Cox[19] found that fifth-grade boys scoring in the *middle range* of two measures of anxiety tended to have better school marks than those scoring at the high or low ends of the scale.

What we call anxiety is actually a form of activation or tension. When a person is too relaxed and too free from anxiety, he is not likely to be very attentive to the kind of stimuli that might otherwise result in problem-solving activity and other forms of learning. On the other hand, when anxiety is too high, he is likewise unable to attend to stimuli that might lead to learning-related activity because of his overwhelming fear of failure. The optimum level of anxiety is thus somewhere between the two extremes. In general, research indicates that the differences in performance between high-, medium-, and low-anxious students are evidently due to tendencies of people to maintain anxiety at rather consistent levels. In other words, a student who is consistently relaxed and who has a relatively low level of anxiety tends to be somewhat unresponsive, and consequently a rather poor learner. Other students are characteristically over-tense and over-anxious and experience difficulty in coping with new learning situations.

The best classrooms, as far as learning is concerned, are probably those which combine a happy blend of tension and acceptance—not so tense that students are afraid to speak out and not so accepting that they never feel challenged.

Students' Perceptions of Self and School

A student not only learns about things and ideas in school, but also learns about himself. Indeed, one of the striking things we are currently discovering is that the most important ideas which affect a student's behavior are those ideas or conceptions he has about himself, which, in part, are a consequence of his school experiences. Unfortunately thousands upon thousands of students graduate from high school with the "I can't" rather than the "I can" feeling about themselves. During the 1960s for example, 7.5 million youngsters did not even finish high school—many because of the "I can't, so why try anyway?" attitude.

As we have seen earlier in this chapter, the negative effects of a poor self-image on academic performance begin their toll early in the elementary years. Even though a child's self-perceptions start out on a positive note, this is no guarantee that they will end up that way. For example, Morse[20] found that to a statement like "I feel pretty sure of myself," 12 percent of the third-graders say "unlike me," while 34 percent of the eleventh-graders make that response. Morse further reported that 84 percent of the third-graders were proud of their school work, while this was true for only 53 percent of the eleventh-graders. In the elementary grades, 93 percent feel they are doing the best they can, but only 37 percent of the seniors can say the same thing. Morse concluded with the observation that "the general impression one gets is that for the young child, school is a secure place with regard to mental health, but as they grow older this confidence diminishes."

Another study, designed to assess over 1200 students' perceptions of school, teachers' skills, self, and student-teacher relations in grades six through twelve, found some interesting differences in perception when students' sex and grades received were taken into account.[21] The major conclusions were as follows: (1) Girls have generally more positive attitudes about school than boys; (2) Girls' perceptions about school and themselves become increasingly more positive as they progress from grade six to grade twelve, while boys' attitudes become more negative; (3) Girls consistently report receiving higher grades than boys from grade six through grade twelve. Understandably, things get brighter and better for those who get mostly A's and B's as they progress through school.

The finding that A–B students have more positive perceptions about school is not surprising, particularly in light of the preferential treatment they usually receive from teachers. For example, DeGroot and Thompson[22] found that teachers give more praise to the youngsters who are brighter, better adjusted, and higher achievers. Less capable students were observed by these investigators to receive more disapproval from their teachers.

The finding that female students have more positive perceptions is also not surprising in view of what other studies have uncovered. Carter[23] for instance, reported that girls are more likely to get higher grades than boys of *equal ability and achievement.* In addition the results of another investigation found that boys received reliably more disapproval from their teachers than the girls.[24]

In sum, research related to students' perceptions of school indicate that, in general, perceptions become more negative as students move into the upper grades. On the other hand, if the student is a girl and bright to boot, then the total school experience is likely to be fairly positive. If, however, the student is a boy, and not so bright, then the total school experience is more likely to include negative perceptions about self, school, and teachers.

Self-Concept and Academic Achievement

As we have seen, the self is a complicated subjective system which a student brings with him to school. There is a continuous flow between the self and the stream of experiences involved in the process of living and learning at school. A student perceives, interprets, accepts, resists, or rejects what he encounters at school in the light of the way he sees himself as a person generally and as a student specifically. There is a mounting body of evidence to suggest that a student's performance in an academic setting is influenced in both subtle and obvious ways by his concept of self. For example, Roth, investigating the role of self-concept in achievement, concluded: ". . . in terms of their conception of self, individuals have a definite investment to perform as they do. With all things being equal, those who do not achieve, *choose* not to do so, while those who do achieve, *choose* to do so."[25]

In an investigation to explore possible relationships between academic underachievement and self-concept, Fink[26] studied a group of ninth-grade students, which included twenty pairs of boys and twenty-four pairs of girls. They were matched for IQ's (all in the 90–110 range), and each individual student was judged as under-achiever or achiever depending on whether his grade point average fell below or above the class median. One achiever and one under-achiever made up each pair. The self-image of each student was rated as adequate or inadequate by three separate psychologists, based on data from three personality tests, a personal data sheet, and a student essay: "What I will be in twenty years." The combined ratings of the three psychologists showed significant differences between achievers and under-achievers, with achievers being rated as far more adequate in their concepts of self. Fink concluded that there was a strong significant relationship between self-concept and academic under-achievement, and, further, that this relationship was stronger for boys than for girls. In view of the fact that boys are more likely than girls to acquire negative perceptions of themselves and school, Fink's conclusion does not seem surprising.

Later research by Campbell[27] supports the conclusions reached in the study cited above, but this time with fourth-, fifth-, and sixth-grade children. Among other things, the author found a direct relationship between self-concept and academic achievement and also noted that girls were more inclined to have a higher self-concept then boys.

Walsh[28] conducted a study involving twenty elementary school boys with IQ's over 120 who were "under-achievers" and who were matched with twenty other boys who had similar IQ's but who were high-achievers. She found that bright boys who were low-achievers had more negative feelings about themselves than did high-achievers. In addition, she noted that low-achievers differed reliably from high-achievers in (1) feelings of being criticized, rejected, or isolated; (2) acting defensively through compliance, evasion, or negativism; and (3) being unable to express themselves appropriately in actions and feelings.

In another investigation, the personality characteristics and attitudes toward achievement of two groups of fourth- and fifth-grade children differentiated in reading ability were analyzed. Subjects in this study consisted of seventy-one "poor" readers and eighty-two "good" readers equated as nearly as possible for age, sex, ethnic composition, and intelligence. As compared to the poor reader, the good reader was found to be more apt to describe himself as "well adjusted and motivated by internalized drives which result in effortful and persistent striving for success." This is in contrast to the picture presented by poor readers, who, according to the investigators, ". . . willingly admit to feelings of discouragement, inadequacy, and nervousness, and whose proclaimed goals are often ephemeral or immediate—especially in avoiding achievement."[29] The results of this study are consistent with Bodwin's,[30] who found a significant positive relationship between immature, low self-concepts and reading disabilities among students in the third and sixth grades.

In a study involving junior high students, Nash[31] developed a set of one hundred items which included three dimensions of self-perceptions assumed to be important, which included: (1) the importance of peer relationships, (2) nonconformity and, (3) satisfaction with self. Interestingly, the items which were found to be best in differentiating between high- and low-achievers were those concerned with the student's perception of the quality of his performance in school work, such as, "My grades are good," and "I am accurate in my school work."

In a significant investigation by Dyson dealing with the relationships between self-concept and ability grouping among seventh-graders, it was found that high-achieving students reported significantly higher self-concepts than did low-achieving students and that this was true regardless of the type of grouping procedures utilized in the academic program. Noteworthy is the author's final observation in which he states:

> If there is one particularly significant result growing out of this research, it is that "nothing succeeds like success." This is not a new understanding, as the old cliche indicates. The work reported here does, however, re-emphasize the importance of success in the learning situation as a contribution to positive psychological growth and it indicates that this feeling of success is probably more crucial in its effect on the student self-concept than how an individual is grouped for instruction.[32]

The results of the above study are consistent with one of the conclusions reached by Borislow[33] in his investigation of relationships between self-evaluation and academic achievement among 197 college freshman. He observed that students who underachieve scholastically have a poorer concept of themselves as students than do achievers subsequent to their scholastic performance, *regardless of initial intention to strive for scholastic achievement as a goal.* In other words, though an underachiever may say something like "I don't care if I do well or not," indicating that he isn't motivated anyway, doing poorly still leaves a mark on him. Just as success is likely to breed a "success-feeling," so, too, does failure, in spite of the assertion "I don't care whether or not I fail," breed a "failure-feeling." Indeed, it would not be unreasonable to speculate that low academic performance may make a student even more defensive and willing to claim "I don't care whether I fail or pass." Funny thing about people—sometimes those who holler loudest about *not* caring, care the most.

A monumental research effort by Brookover[34] and his colleagues involving over one thousand seventh-grade students focused specifically on self-concept of ability in school and academic achievement. They found a significant and positive relationship between self-concept and academic performance and, in addition, observed that self-concept was significantly and positively related to the perceived evaluations which significant others held of the student. This quite literally means that if persons "significant" (valued, prized, important) to a student think highly of him, then he is apt to think highly of himself.

In the second phase of a longitudinal investigation of the relationship between self-concept of ability and school achievement which began with the study cited above, Brookover[35] and his associates found that self-concept of ability was a significant factor in achievement at all levels, seventh- through tenth-grade.

In the third and final phase of this longitudinal project, which studied the same students from the time they were seventh-graders through grade twelve, the following observation regarding the relation of the self-concept of ability to achievement was made:

> The correlation between self-concept of ability and grade point average ranges from .48 to .63 over the six years. It falls below .50 only among boys in the 12th grade. . . . In addition, the higher correlation between perceived evaluations and self-concepts tends to support the theory that perceived evaluations are a necessary and sufficient condition for (the growth of a positive or high) self-concept of ability, but (a positive) self-concept of ability is only a necessary, but *not* a sufficient condition for achievement. The latter is further supported by the analysis of the achievement of students with high and low self-concept of ability. This revealed that although a significant proportion of students with high self-concepts of ability achieved at a relatively lower level, practically none of the students with lower (less positive) self-concepts of ability achieved at a high level.[36]

The research reported by Brookover and his associates is important for several reasons. One, it points out the important impact which "significant" people can have on the self-concept of a growing child. As we discussed in

Chapter One, development of the self begins early in life and is nurtured in a framework of social interaction. A substantial dimension of any person's feelings about himself is derived from his incorporation of the attributes he perceives other people assigning to him. It is through an individual's long immersion in an interpersonal stream of reflected appraisals from people important to him that he gradually develops a view of himself which he strives to maintain. And number two, the Brookover research serves to remind us that it takes more than a positive self-concept in order for there to be high academic achievement. Why should this be? Why do some students with high, positive self-concepts fail to achieve at commensurately high levels?

We have to understand that the possession of a high, positive self-concept does not *cause* high academic achievement. It appears to be a necessary and vital personal quality for one to have *prior to* achievement, but it is no guarantee that high achievement will naturally follow. A person could have a positive self-concept that is sustained and nurtured by success in nonacademic pursuits—athletics, extra-curricular participation, popularity with the opposite sex, creative expression in the various arts, and so on. If a student is motivated to do well in some nonacademic area and *does* well, he is less likely to be deflated by failure experiences encountered in the scholastic arena. Indeed, some students work very hard and diligently in nonacademic areas so as to be certain to compensate for any deficits tallied in their academic work. For example, an artist friend of mine in graduate school always tried to save as much face as possible in the wake of his sometimes mediocre academic work by reminding his friends of the "long hours he had to spend on his best paintings, and, after all, one can't be good in all things at once." The fact was, he couldn't care less about his academic performance. He did, however, care considerably about his painting skills and it was on canvas, and not in the classroom, that he was motivated "to be somebody" and to enhance and maintain his positive concept of self.

THE CHICKEN OR THE EGG QUESTION

An inevitable question in any discussion related to self-concept and achievement is the one which asks what comes first, a positive self-concept or high achievement? It is not possible to give a definitive answer to this question because the fact is, we just don't know for sure. However, even though it is not possible to say with precision which come first, good school work or high self-regard, *it does not seem unreasonable to suggest that each is mutually reinforcing to the other to the extent that a positive change in one facilitates a positive change in the other.* That is, if a child begins school with a low level of self-confidence and self-regard and experiences sufficient success, we could reasonably expect that his concept of self as far

Going to school doesn't have to hurt.

as school ability is concerned will be elevated. On the other hand, an equally plausible possibility is that if a youngster begins school with high confidence in his ability to do school work and experiences excessive failure his concept of self may be lowered. Under these conditions he will either have to shift his focus to other areas, usually nonacademic, to maintain his self-esteem, or continue to lose self-confidence and self-esteem.

A few observations by Arthur Jersild from his book, *In Search of Self*, seem a fitting conclusion to this section dealing with self-concept and academic achievement:

> Whenever the learner faces an educational situation that has significance for him as a person, the learning which takes place will involve a process of assimilation of something new into himself. It will involve a reorganization of what was there before. Of course, learning in the sense of something added may take place without such assimilation, since a child for the sake of peace may go through certain motions, undertake certain drills, in order to be able to rattle off the names of the states or do certain calisthenic stunts. There may be learning in which there is no self-involvement.

But something more important occurs when learning of a kind that makes a real difference, from the learner's point of view, has taken place. In this there is self-involvement. The experience makes a difference in the total psychology of the individual. What has been learned may have given the learner an enlarged perspective of himself, of his powers and potentialities. What has been learned may have painfully forced him to revise his conception of himself. . . . The learning may have had many other ramifications, but whether they are large or small the self picture has been changed. The learner has put patch on himself. The whole fabric of the self has, to a degree, been changed. . . .

Many other children find the educational scene so filled with failure, so full of reminders of their limitations, and so harsh in giving those reminders, that they hate school. School is such a threat to their self-picture that it is almost intolerable, but they drag themselves back to school day after day because the alternative of not going would be even more painful and threatening.[37]

Parental Variables Related to Self-Concept and Achievement

As we have seen, there is considerable evidence to suggest a link between self-concept and academic achievement. The effect that certain parental practices have on a student's self-concept and motivation for achievement in school are considerable. These include the emotional relationship between parent and child, the attitudes of the parent toward school and school achievement, and parental concern for the interest in the child's performance. In addition, there is the consideration of the importance which students assign to their parent's evaluations of their (the students') ability to do school work. For example, Brookover[38] found that practically all students in grades seven through twelve identified their parents as persons who were "significant" or "important" to them. Furthermore, when asked to indicate who was concerned about how well they did in school, parents were again named by over 90 percent of all the students. The perception of parental evaluations by students are, therefore, likely to have an impact on the self-perceptions of most students. The question is, how are these self-perceptions related to their feelings about their ability to do schoolwork and how are these feelings picked up from their parents?

Consider the following interview examples. This first one is from an interview I had with a low-achieving, low self-concept, ninth-grade girl. As we enter the conversation, it has just moved into schoolwork and the girl's parents' attitudes toward her performance. Listen carefully for the implicit and explicit ways in which her parents convinced her that she wasn't very good in math.

Counselor: How does your mom feel about your school work?
Girl: It could be better, I guess, I don't know exactly—we don't discuss it much.
Counselor: Do your parents say anything to you about your report card?
Girl: Sometimes they do.
Counselor: I noticed you did about C work last year.
Girl: Yeah, mostly I do that and sometimes not that good. I used to do better.
Counselor: Could you tell me more about that?
Girl: Well, last year I got a B in social studies and that's pretty good. Math got me though. I guess if I really tried—but I don't think I can because I've tried all I can. I'm telling you, it really gets me. My mother wasn't good in math either, but she's better in it now.
Counselor: How do you know your mother used to be poor in it?
Girl: She told me. *She says it's no wonder I'm not very good at it.*
Counselor: What does she mean by that?
Girl: Well, she says, well, I'm dumb—*"I guess I've handed it to you"* or something like that. I mean I'm real slow in math—it takes hours to get something in my head. One time my father and I were working on a problem and he lost his patience. He said I was so stupid that I should be in a special school. He was really mad.
Counselor: How did that make you feel?
Girl: Well, it hurt me. I was a little bit mad, but I got over it, *Maybe I am stupid . . .*

What follows is an excerpt of another interview I had with a different ninth-grade fourteen-year-old girl, who was also a low-achieving, low-self-concept student. The conversation was about school, grades, and feelings about ability to succeed in different subjects. As it happens, the subject area here, as in the above illustration, is math. Once again, listen carefully to the parental feedback that is gnawing away at this girl's self-confidence.

Counselor: I see you've been having some trouble with math.
Girl: Well, I don't know. My mother wasn't too good at it, my dad wasn't—I don't know, I'm just not very good at it.
Counselor: How do you know that your mom and dad had trouble with math?
Girl: Well, my mom told me the first time I got a D and I brought it home and I said, "I got a D in math," and she says, *"I'm not surprised because I wasn't exactly great in it."* And my dad, he isn't the best in it either. He said he didn't always do the best in the subject.
Counselor: How did that make you feel when you found they didn't do well in math?

Girl: Well, I don't know. My brother, he must be pretty good at it because he's an engineer. He's pretty good. *I guess I was the one that got it.* Anyway boys are better than girls in math anyway. I don't know why.

Counselor: "You were the one that got it." What does that mean?

Girl: I don't know. I guess my mom and dad passed it on to me. Maybe not, *but they aren't surprised that I do poorly in it.*

It's not difficult to see how a parent can negatively influence a youngster's feelings about his ability to do schoolwork by telling him he's stupid or by inferring that he inherited bad genes which make it impossible for him to do well. How a youngster feels about his ability to do schoolwork depends, in part, on how he perceives those who are important to him, evaluating his ability. Helper,[39] for example, found a positive relationship between the way parents saw their children and the way the children saw themselves. Children who evaluated themselves highly were likely to have parents who evaluated them highly.

Whether a parent is basically rejecting or accepting is apparently a very important aspect of a youngster's view of himself and his ability to do schoolwork. The results of a recent study, for example, involving achieving and under-achieving high school juniors and seniors found that mothers of achievers were more accepting of their children than were mothers of under-achievers.[40] Intensive case studies by Kimball[41] have demonstrated how lack of sufficient acceptance is a basic antecedent condition for the development of a low concept of self, low self-esteem, and a low-level feeling of personal security. Lack of acceptance usually leads to low security and high dependency, both of which stand in the way of a person's realizing his potential.

In terms of the actual rejection expressed by the parents of under-achievers, it may help us understand the phenomenon better if we look at the etiology of under-achievement, as it is described by Roth and Meyersburg.

The psychogenesis involves a series of very subtle devaluations of the child, stemming from the parent-child relationship. In our experience, the most frequent pattern is that of the parent who pays no attention at all to the accomplishments or failures of the child. (These students frequently exclaim, "What's the use, nobody gives a damn," in reference to their current college failure.) The life space of the child and the life space of the parent are in different realms, a state of affairs which constitutes a parental rejection. The only way a child can bring the life spaces together, albeit momentarily, is through the production of a crisis, occasionally necessitating outsiders such as police, teacher, principal, or a counselor.

Next in frequency is the parent who attends only to the child's failures and rarely to his successes. The latter are taken for granted, but the failures are punished. Thus, the contact between parent and child is through failure. If the child succeeds, he is alone, but if he fails, he is part of the concern of his parents.

Both of these early experiences lead to three devastating, incipient pathological processes: The first of these is a process of self-denigration. In order for the child to maintain some kind of identity with the parent he must learn to see himself as a failure. He must hold back his productivity and blame himself for his lacks. Hostility, he is taught, is received by him and never expressed toward others. When he does experience resentments he directs them against himself and thus supports his own constructs about himself as being worth little.[42]

There is evidence to suggest that early encouragement of independence, coupled with a warm, affectionate, accepting parent-child relationship are the most likely ingredients to produce motivation for high achievement. Indeed, in the absence of an accepting relationship between parent and child, the promotion of early independence does not produce achievement. Morrow and Wilson,[43] for example, provide support for this position in their study of the perceptions high-achieving and low-achieving high-school boys have of their families. High-achievers were found to have a favorable view of their families. They described their parents as approving, trusting, affectionate, relatively nonrestrictive, and encouraging—but not pressuring with respect to achievement. In a similar study by Davids and Hainsworth,[44] under-achieving teenage boys saw their mothers as controlling and domineering. In addition, there was a much greater discrepancy for the under-achievers than for the high-achievers between the mother's report of several child-rearing attitudes and the son's perception of her attitudes. This suggests a lack of agreement and a lack of communication between the low-achieving boy and his mother.

Clinical studies of learning difficulties have noted that under-achievement may signify not only a low self-concept on the part of the student, but a rebellion against parents as well. Perhaps what happens in some instances is that excessive pressure for achievement unaccompanied by a satisfactory relationship with parents fosters undue anxiety and resentment in the child. The anxiety could inhibit a youngster from working to full capacity, from being free to concentrate on schoolwork, and the resentment could motivate him to disappoint his parents by not meeting their expectations. Sometimes the only way a child or teenager can get back at his parents for hurting him is to *withhold* his successes. After all, what more does a child have to offer his parents except his success? Withholding success can be a powerful punishment, and one has to wonder how many school failures are traceable to that conscious or unconscious motivation.

Rather than examining parental factors related to general school achievement, several recent areas of research have sought to specify more exactly the particular kinds of parental influence which affect specific aspects of the youngster's achievement.

Bing,[45] for example, investigated a group of elementary-school children who showed marked discrepancy between verbal and mathematic ability. He found that high verbal children experienced much more verbal stimulation in the preschool years, as evidenced by such variables as amount of play time the mother had with the infant, verbal stimulation of the infant, mother's responsiveness to the child's early, early questions, and interest shown in the child's good speech habits. Although the *mothers of high verbal children were rather controlling and pressuring, the mothers of those children high in mathematical ability were less interfering and permitted greater independence.* Bing concluded that high verbal ability is encouraged by intensive interaction between parent and child, while number and spatial abilities, on the other hand, develop from interaction with the physical rather than the interpersonal environment. The development of these latter abilities apparently requires greater independence to investigate and explore one's surroundings.

Using college students as subjects Baer and Rogosta[46] found that those males showing high verbal ability were more likely to perceive their fathers as less caring and less attentive than those showing less verbal ability. They also perceived their mothers as less caring. A similar finding was noted in a study with elementary-school girls, in which those who scored high on reading achievement had less affectionate and less nurturant mothers than those less proficient in their academic skill.[47] Taken together, the findings of these two studies do not contradict those obtained by Bing, but suggest, rather, that mothers who are intrusive and pressuring also engage in a high level of verbal interaction with the child.

Although, in general, parents who value intellectual achievement for themselves stress intellectual achievement for their children, some areas of achievement are emphasized more than others. In a study of parental values for achievement in the intellectual, physical, artistic, and mechanical areas, parents who valued achievement in the artistic and mechanical areas tended also to value such achievement for their children.[48]

Before a child begins his formal schooling he is in the custody of his parents or parent-surrogates, whatever the case may be, for five or six years. In that period of time the beginnings of a self-system are molded and predispose him to view himself and school in certain ways. As you have seen, parent variables such as parental feedback and evaluation, parental

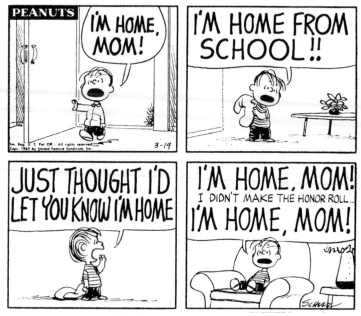

Parental standards that are too high to reach may cause unnecessary anxiety.

caring or lack of it, and parental acceptance or rejection can have a striking effect on how he views his general intellectual ability and his ability in specific subject areas. Research suggests that parents who combine caring, acceptance, and high expectations are likely to raise children who think well of themselves and who strive to do as well as they can in school.

The next question is—what are the implications of self-concept research for teaching and teachers?

Teacher Variables Related to Self-Concept and Achievement

A teacher can have an enormous influence on a student's self-attitudes, particularly as these attitudes are related to his feelings about being able to think, answer questions, and solve problems. Teachers are quickly established as "significant" persons in the lives of most students. Sometimes a teacher becomes significant to a student because he may be the only person in the whole wide world who makes that student feel like an individual of worth and value. Other teachers are significant because they are perceived as having the ultimate responsibility of evaluating a student's ability to do schoolwork and to compete with other students. Even more important, as far as the student is concerned, a teacher has the ultimate responsibility for *recording* these evaluations for both parents and posterity. A teacher can either help a student recognize his strengths and possibilities or he can remind a student again and again of his weaknesses and shortcomings. No matter how you look at it, the teacher is an important factor in the interpersonal field of forces which influence a student's developing self. Even if a child's self has been nurtured in a healthy home atmosphere, a teacher who is harsh and rejecting may interfere with the processes of otherwise healthy development. With this kind of teacher the student can no longer be his forthright self, free to inquire and develop. Instead he becomes defensive and reactive, concerned more with survival than with learning.

Let us turn now to a more specific examination of teacher variables which are most directly related to a student's academic performance and self-concept development.

TEACHER PERSONALITY

We would probably all agree that it is quite possible for two teachers of equal intelligence, training, and grasp of subject matter to differ in the extent to which they are able to encourage student motivation and learning. Part of the difference can be accounted for by the effect of a teacher's personality on the learners. What is it that students respond positively and negatively to in teachers? Your own feelings about different teachers you've had are one good source for an answer to that question. Consider what other students have had to say about teacher personality.

For example, one of the most revealing investigations related to teacher personality was based upon the opinions of 3725 high school seniors concerning best-liked and least-liked teachers.[49] A total of forty-three different reasons were listed for "liking Teacher A best" and thirty different reasons for "liking Teacher B least." Consider the four most frequently cited reasons in each category.

**Four Most Frequently Mentioned Reasons
for Liking "Teacher A" Best
Reported by 3725 High-School Seniors**

1. Is helpful in schoolwork, explains lessons and assignments clearly and thoroughly, and uses examples in teaching.	51%
2. Cheerful, happy, good-natured, jolly, has sense of humor and can take a joke.	40%
3. Human, friendly, companionable, "one of us."	30%
4. Interested in and understands pupils.	26%

**Four Most Frequently Mentioned Reasons
for Liking "Teacher Z" Least
Reported by 3725 High-School Seniors**

---

1. Too cross, crabby, grouchy, never smiles, nagging, sarcastic, loses temper, "flies off the handle." 50%
2. Not helpful with schoolwork, does not explain lessons and assignments, not clear, work not planned. 30%
3. Partial, has "pets" or favored students, and "picks on certain pupils." 20%
4. Superior, aloof, haughty, "snooty," overbearing, does not know you out of class. 20%

You will note that personality traits monopolize the top rankings after the first items which deals with teaching technique as it immediately affects students. Interestingly enough, mastery of subject matter, which is vital but badly overemphasized by specialists, ranks sixteenth on both lists.

Hart's general findings have been corroborated time and again by later studies. For example, Witty[50] in connection with the "Quiz Kids" program, received 12,000 letters on the theme, "The Teacher Who Helped Me Most." An analysis of those letters revealed that the top ranking traits were the following:

(1) Cooperative, democratic attitudes; (2) kindliness and consideration for the individual; (3) patience; (4) wide interests; (5) personal appearance and pleasant manner; (6) fairness and impartiality; (7) sense of humor; (8) good disposition and consistent behavior; (9) interest in pupils' problems; (10) flexibility; (11) use of recognition and praise; (12) unusual proficiency in teaching a particular subject.

Jersild[51] found elementary school children mentioning the following qualities as typical of the teachers they liked best: *human qualities as a person*—sympathetic, cheerful, good tempered; *physical appearance, grooming, voice*—attractive, neat, nice manner of talking; *traits as a disciplinarian or director of the class*—fair, consistent, did not scold or shout; *participation in activities*—joined in or permitted games or play; *performance as a teacher*—enthusiastic, resourceful, explained well, permitted expression of opinion. The age trend in the descriptions is worth noting; high-school students more frequently picked characteristics bearing on teaching ability, whereas younger children singled out interesting projects introduced by the teacher. At all ages children valued highly the teacher who was enthusiastic, sensitive, and understanding.

Even at the college level there is evidence to suggest that students still rank first the professor's interest in his students and their problems and his willingness to give attention to them.[52]

So far, we have been examining desirable personal characteristics of teachers as these characteristics are identified by students. For the most part, these characteristics group themselves under the general heading of capacity for warmth, patience, tolerance, and interest in students. What happens when these personal qualities are related to the more rigid test of whether having them or not makes any difference in the actual performance of students? Let's consider some evidence.

Sears,[53] for example, found that there are positive relationships between the extent to which a teacher reflects a personal interest in and willingness to listen to students' ideas and the creativity shown by students. As a further example, Cogan[54] observed that warm and considerate teachers got an unusual amount of original poetry and art from their high-school students. Reed[55] found that teachers higher in a capacity for warmth favorably affected their pupils' interests in science.

Heil, Powell, and Feifer[56] went a step further and related student achievement to interaction between different teacher and student personalities. They compared the various teacher-pupil personality combinations in terms of pupil achievement, teacher knowledge, and classroom settings. Using scores from achievement tests as their criterion measure, they found that the well integrated (healthy, well-rounded, flexible) teachers were most effective with *all* types of students. Two other identified teacher personality "types" (fearful and turbulent) were successful with only certain types of students.

Teacher personality and behavior does seem to have a kind of contagion potential in the sense that students can be influenced for better or for worse by a teacher's personal characteristics. For example, Sears[57] found that teachers who like pupils tend to have pupils who like each other. Spaulding[58] found that the self-concepts of elementary school children were apt to be higher and more positive in classrooms in which the teacher was "socially integrative" and "learner supportive." What this and other research cited here seems to suggest is that through the phychological principles of imitation and identification the teacher becomes a model for appropriate behavior and that students take on, assume, and ultimately reflect (probably unconsciously) those personal characteristics most dominant in the teacher.

The evidence seems quite clear when it comes to describing good or effective teachers on the basis of personal characteristics. Effective teachers appear to be those who are, shall we say, "human" in the fullest sense of the word. They have a sense of humor, are fair, empathetic, more democratic than autocratic, and apparently can relate easily and naturally to students

A teacher's personality may have a strong impact on a student.

on either a one-to-one or group basis. Their classrooms seem to reflect miniature enterprise operations in the sense that they are open, spontaneous, and adaptable to change.

SELF-PERCEPTIONS OF TEACHERS

We do not have to go any further than our own personal experiences to know that the way we see, regard, and feel about ourselves has enormous impact on both our private and public lives. How about "good" versus "poor" teachers? How do they see themselves?

Ryans,[59] in a monumental study of teachers' characteristics involving some 6000 teachers in 1700 schools and 450 school systems, found that there were, indeed, differences between the self-related expressions of high emotional stability teachers versus low emotional stability teachers. For example, the more emotionally stable teachers were more apt to have the following kinds of self-reports: (1) frequently named self-confidence and cheerfulness as dominant traits in themselves; (2) said they liked active contact with other people; (3) expressed interests in hobbies and handicrafts; and (4) reported their childhoods to be happy experiences.

On the other hand, teachers with lower emotional maturity scores

(1) had unhappy memories of childhood; (2) seemed *not* to prefer contact with others; (3) were more directive and authoritarian; and (4) expressed less self-confidence.

We can be even more specific. For example, Arthur Combs in his book, *The Professional Education of Teachers*,[60] cites several studies which reached similar conclusions about the way good teachers typically see themselves.

1. Good teachers see themselves as identified with people rather than withdrawn, removed, apart from, or alienated from others.
2. Good teachers feel basically adequate rather than inadequate. They do not see themselves as generally unable to cope with problems.
3. Good teachers feel trustworthy rather than untrustworthy. They see themselves as reliable, dependable individuals with the potential for coping with events as they happen.
4. Good teachers see themselves as wanted rather than unwanted. They see themselves as likable and attractive (in personal, not physical sense) as opposed to feeling ignored and rejected.
5. Good teachers see themselves as worthy rather than unworthy. They see themselves as people of consequence, dignity, and integrity as opposed to feeling they matter little, can be overlooked and discounted.

In the broadest sense of the word, good teachers see themselves as good people. Their self-conceptions are, for the most part, positive, tinged with an air of optimism and colored with tones of healthy self-acceptance. I dare say that self-perceptions of good teachers are not unlike the self-perceptions of any basically healthy person, whether he be a good bricklayer, a good manager, a good doctor, a good lawyer, a good experimental psychologist, or you name it. Clinical evidence has told us time and again that *any* person is apt to be happier, more productive, and more effective when he is able to see himself as fundamentally and basically "enough."

TEACHERS' PERCEPTIONS OF OTHERS

Research is showing us that not only do effective and ineffective teachers view themselves differently, but they also reflect characteristic differences in the way they perceive others. For example, Ryans[61] reported several studies which have produced findings that are quite similar and in agreement when it comes to sorting out the differences between how good and poor teachers view others. He noted, among other things, that outstandingly "good" teachers rated significantly higher than notably "poor" teachers in at least five different ways with respect to how they viewed others. The good teachers had (1) more favorable opinions of students; (2) more favorable opinions of democratic classroom behavior; (3) more favorable opinions of administrators and colleagues; (4) a greater expressed liking for personal contacts with other people; and (5) more favorable estimates of other people generally. In addition, good teachers expressed the belief that very few students are difficult behavior problems, that very few people are influenced in their opinions and attitudes toward others by feelings of jealousy, and that most teachers are willing to assume their full share of extra duties outside of school.

Interestingly, the characteristics that distinguish the "lowly assessed" teacher group suggested that the relatively "ineffective" teacher is self-centered, anxious, and restricted. One is left with the distinct impression that poor or ineffective teachers have more than the usual number of paranoid-like defenses. Turning to Ryans[62] again, we find that he reports that his "ineffective teachers believe a substantial portion of parents' visits to school are made to criticize the teacher or the school and that a fairly large portion of people (40–60 percent) are influenced in their opinions and attitudes toward others by feelings of jealousy." Before going further, it might be well for us to bear in mind Ryans' cautionary note:

> Certainly the research (referring to his own) has not settled the question, who is the good teacher? However, there are some interesting suggestions here—some clues that may help to identify "good" and "poor" teachers if one is willing to accept the kind of definition employed in this research. Such a definition indicates that teachers are "good" if they rank very high among their colleagues with respect to such observable classroom behaviors as warmth and kindliness, systematic and business-like manner, and stimulating and original teacher behavior.[63]

Combs has investigated the perceptual differences between good and poor teachers, and he suggests that good teachers can be clearly distinguished from poor ones with respect to the following perceptions about people:[64]

1. The good teacher is more likely to have an internal rather than external frame of reference. That is, he seeks to understand how things seem to others and then uses this as a guide for his own behavior.
2. The good teacher is more concerned with people and their reactions than with things and events.
3. The good teacher is more concerned with the subjective-perceptual experience of people than with objective events. He is, again, more concerned with how things *seem* to people than just the so-called or alleged "facts."

4. The good teacher seeks to understand the causes of people's behavior in terms of their *current* thinking, feeling, beliefs, and understandings rather than in terms of forces exerted on them now or in the past.

5. The good teacher generally trusts other people and perceives them as having the capacity to solve their own problems.

6. The good teacher sees others as being friendly and enhancing rather than hostile or threatening.

7. The good teacher tends to see other people as being of worth rather than unworthy. That is, he sees all people as possessing a certain dignity and integrity.

8. The good teacher sees people and their behavior as essentially developing from within rather than as a product of external events to be molded or directed. In other words, he sees people as creative and dynamic rather than passive or inert.

I am sure it comes as no surprise to any of us that how we perceive others is highly dependent on how we perceive ourselves. If a potential teacher (or anyone else for that matter) likes himself, trusts himself, and

How a teacher feels about a student can make a big difference in that student's attitude and performance.

has confidence in himself, he will likely see others in this same light. Research is beginning to tell us what common sense has always told us, namely, students grow, flourish, and develop much more easily when in relationship with someone who projects an inherent trust and belief in their capacity to become what they have the potential to become.

It is one thing to say that good teachers have a generally more positive view of others, but does this have anything to do with how students achieve and behave? There is evidence to suggest that it does. For example, Davidson and Lang[65] found that among the boys and girls in grades four through six those children with positive self-images were more likely to be among those who perceived their teachers as having positive feelings toward them. They also found that the more positive the perception of their teacher's feelings, *the better was their academic achievement.*

In summary, we can sketch at least five interrelated generalizations from what research is telling us about how effective teachers differ from less effective teachers when it comes to perceptions of others. In relation to this, effective teachers can be characterized in the following ways:

1.   They seem to have a generally more positive view of others—students, colleagues, and administrators.

2.   They are as prone to view others as critical, attacking people with ulterior motives, but rather see them as potentially friendly and worthy in their own right.

3.   They have a more favorable view of democratic classroom procedures.

4.   They have the ability and capacity to see things as they seem to others, i.e., the ability to see things from the other person's point of view.

5.   They do not see students as persons "you do things to" but rather as individuals capable of doing for themselves once they feel trusted, respected, and valued.

TEACHER INTERACTION STYLES

Through daily contact and interaction, the personality of the teacher affects students both positively and negatively and is basic in setting the emotional tone of a classroom. Even though there is no one *best* way to interact with students, research has shown that some ways are better than others and, further, there are specific things teachers can do to enhance *both* achievement and self-concept.

In a study related to the "self" as a factor in the classroom, Staines posed the following questions:

1. What part do teachers play in the development of the child's self?
2. Can teachers change a student's self-picture if they try to do so?
3. If they can, what methods of teaching produce what kinds of self-picture?
4. Is it possible to distinguish between teachers in the frequency and kind of comments which they make about a student's self?[66]

The basic assumption of the study was that since teachers are an important aspect of a student's environment, it is likely that they have some effect on the child's emerging self, particularly through their interaction styles.

In order to test this assumption, two elementary classes were matched for age, intelligence, and socioeconomic class. In one, teacher A deliberately set out to actively assist students to see themselves as planning, purposing, choosing individuals, responsible, and accountable. It was considered important that the student should test his purposes by carrying them through, see himself adequate and causal, and, at the same time, differentiate between his strengths and weaknesses. In order to help with this, teacher A made it a point to get to know each student and also to familiarize himself with the general area of self-concept and how it was related to behavior. In class, he was likely to make comments such as the following, all designed to help students toward a more positive view of themselves, while at the same time assisting them to be realistic about their abilities:

1. "Jack, you're tall. Help me with this."
2. "Mary, you're very good at solving addition problems."
3. "Good boy! Look at this everyone!"
4. "You're better at English than arithmetic."
5. "You're a fine one, you are."

Note the emphasis on highlighting specific strengths, assets, and skills, on helping the student sort out his strengths and weaknesses, and, as in the last statement, on commenting on his value as a total or "whole" person.

Teacher B was judged to be an equally effective teacher, but his methods were not adapted to fit within a framework which explicitly considered self-concept variables. When the twelve week experimental period was over, Teacher B's data showed that typical high-pressure teaching, with vigorous personal emphasis, with great stress on correctness and on the serious consequences of failure, and with constant emphasis on passing examinations, can lead to greater signs of insecurity. As far as achievement was concerned, the students of Teacher A produced slightly greater mean improvement than the students of Teacher B in standardized reading and number tests. If it is objected to that a teacher cannot spend his time teaching for an improved self-picture and better adjustment because of examination pressure, here is some evidence that at least equally good academic results may be obtained while helping students see themselves in a more positive light.

One of the most complete investigations related to this area of teacher interaction was conducted by Flanders,[67] who studied teacher influence styles, pupil attitudes, and resulting achievement in seventh-grade social studies and eighth-grade mathematics. He uncovered four essential elements of teacher influence in classrooms in which motivation, attitudes, and learning were superior.

1. The teacher was able to provide spontaneously a range of roles that varied from fairly active, dominative supervision to a more reflective, discriminating support.
2. The teacher was able to switch roles at will rather than pursue a single interaction style to the exclusion of other possibilities.
3. The teacher was able to bridge the gap between his diagnosis of a given situation and the course of action he should take.
4. The teacher was able to combine sensitivity and critical awareness so that, as the classroom's master observer, he was able to make reasonable diagnoses of the current conditions.

(We should keep in mind, too, that these skills, which characterized successful teachers, were superimposed upon a firm grasp of the subject matter being taught.)

Interestingly, those teachers who were *not* successful were the very ones who were inclined to use the same instructional procedures and methodology in a more or less rigid fashion. That is, there seemed to be little variation from one classroom situation to the next. In particular, unsuccessful teachers seemed to lack the ability to expand or restrict the behavior of the students through the use of their own verbal influence.

In general, the Flanders study suggests that *teachers who were able to provide flexible interaction styles, by shifting from the direct to the indirect depending on the situation were better able to create climates in which students learned more. The students of teachers who were unable to do this learned less.*

In an earlier study,[68] detailed stenographic records, observation charts, and various time charts were kept on forty-seven teachers of social studies in high school ranked as superior and forty-seven ranked well below average in teaching skills. Practically every conceivable act and every expression of teacher and pupil interaction were considered—about thirty-seven factors in all. The following are fragmentary interaction expressions which distinguished good from poor teachers. (As you read, you might try to imagine the voice inflection which accompanied each of these expressions.)

Characteristic Comments Made by Poor but Not by Good Teachers

Are you working hard? . . . Aren't you ever going to learn that word? . . . Everyone sit up straight, please. . . . I'm afraid you're confused. . . . No, that's wrong. . . . Oh dear, don't you know that? . . . Oh, sit down. . . . Say something. . . . and so on, through nearly one hundred different expressions. (Note the overtones of frustration, futility, and impatience which leak through most.)

Characteristic Comments Made by Good but Not by Poor Teachers

Aha, that's a new idea. . . . Are you going to accept that as an answer? I should like more proof. . . . Do you suppose you could supply a better word? . . . Can you prove your statement? . . . Don't you really think you could? . . . I'm not quite clear on that—think a moment. . . . Let's stick to the question. . . . Probably my last question wasn't a good one. . . . and so on, through a long list. (Note here the emphasis on challenging the student, on pushing and encouraging him to go beyond where he may be at the moment.)

There is also evidence to suggest that when a teacher is able to personalize his teaching he is apt to be more successful, particularly when it comes to motivating students to do better work. For example, Page[69] conducted an experiment with high-school and junior-high-school students and teachers in which the teachers graded objective tests of their pupils and then randomly assigned each paper to one of three groups. The group-one student was given back his paper with no comment except a stereotyped, standard comment from "excellent" if his score was high to "let's raise this grade." Every C student, for example, received his mark with the notation, "perhaps try to do still better." For those in group three, the teacher wrote a personal comment on every paper saying whatever he thought might encourage that particular student. On the next objective test, groups two and three outperformed group one. This suggests that the personalized comments had a greater effect than standardized comments and that even a very short standard comment written on the paper produced measureable achievement gains. The greatest improvement was made by the failing students in group three, who received encouraging personal notes on their papers. This study points up the motivational implications of evaluative practices that go far beyond the simple indication of right or wrong answers.

It certainly does seem to be true that teachers who reflect an active personal interest in their students' progress and *who show it* are more likely to be successful in enhancing a student's confidence in himself than teachers who are more distant and impersonal.

How about interaction styles as they are related to either "learner-centered" or "teacher-centered" approaches? In an investigation by Flanders,[70] experimentally produced classrooms simulating the two approaches mentioned above were designed. In the learner-centered classroom the teacher was acceptant and supportive of the student and problem-centered in approach. In the teacher-centered climate the teacher was directive and demanding, often deprecating in his behavior toward students. The major conclusions reached were: (1) The "teacher-centered" behavior of directing, demanding, and using private criteria in deprecating a student leads to hostility to the self or teacher, aggressiveness, or sometimes withdrawal, apathy, and even emotional disintegration; (2) The learner-centered behavior of accepting the student, being evaluative or critical only by public criteria, and being usually supportive, elicited problem-orientation, decreased personal anxiety, and led to emotionally healthy and integrative behavior.

Stern[71] reviewed thirty-four studies (largely college classes) comparing nondirective with directive interaction styles in influencing two types of learning outcomes: (a) gain in cognitive knowledge and understanding, and (b) attitude change toward self and others. In regard to cognitive gains, he concludes: "In general, it would appear that the amount of cognitive gain is largely unaffected by the autocratic or democratic tendencies of the instructor." However, when he summarizes the findings related to attitude change toward the self and others, the conclusion is somewhat different: "regardless of whether the investigator was concerned with attitudes toward the cultural outgroup, toward other participants in the class, or toward the self, and the results generally have indicated that nondirective instruction facilitates a shift in a more favorable, acceptant direction." Once more we find evidence to support the notion that, at least as far as affective or self-concept variables are concerned, a more nondirective, democratic teaching style is likely to be associated with positive changes in student behavior. As a further example of this, Tiedeman[72] found that the teacher who was disliked most by students was a domineering, authoritarian person. As a matter of fact, the older the student (hence the greater the need for autonomy?), the more intense the dislike.

Rosenthal and Jacobson[73] have shown that a teacher's *expectations* for his students' performance can be a significant determinant of how the students actually respond. For example, within each of the six grades in a particular school were three classrooms, one each of the children performing at above average, average, and below average levels of scholastic achievement. In each of these classes, an average of 20 percent of the children were identified to the teachers as having scores on the *Test for Intellectual Blooming* which suggested that they would show unusual academic gains during the academic year. Actually, the children had been picked at random from the total population of children taking the same test. Eight months after the experimental conditions were instituted, all children were retested with the same IQ test. What were the results?

For the school as a whole, those children from whom the teachers had been led to expect greater intellectual gain showed significantly greater gain in IQ score than did other children in the school! In fact, the lower the grade level, the greater the IQ gain. Apparently teachers interacted with the "brighter" children more positively and more favorably and the children responded in kind by showing greater gains in IQ. Why should there be more change in the lower grades? One reason is that younger children are generally more malleable, less fixed, and more capable of change. A second possibility is that younger elementary school children do not have firmly established reputations which can be passed on from one teacher to the next. It might not be a too far out speculation to suggest that as a student gets older, teacher's interactions with that student are determined to some extent by kind of "reputation" (good student or poor, delinquent or well behaved, "Better watch him—he can't be trusted," or "He's a good student—He'll work hard for you.") he has established.

It is not difficult to see that if a teacher expects a student to be good or poor, or well behaved or delinquent, or whatever, then he (the teacher) is likely to encourage and reinforce the very behavior he expected in the first place! Perhaps an illustration will clarify what we mean here. A colleague of mine is fond of telling of an incident which involved a student of his who frequently served as a substitute teacher. One day after teaching a fifth-grade class, this teacher came home and moaned to her husband (a principal in another school) what a terrible day it was and how unruly the children were and how she wasn't surprised that she had to holler and discipline the children so much because "After all, everyone knows how rough Mrs. Jackson's (the absent teacher) class was to teach." "Mrs. Jackson?" replied her husband. "Don't you mean Mrs. Johnson's class?" It turned out that that is exactly what she did mean, but she had gone to school that day thinking that she would be in Mrs. Johnson's fifth-grade class, which *was* hard to manage, when all along she was in Mrs. Jackson's fifth-grade class, which was reasonably well-behaved! Our substitute teacher friend was so certain that the class would leap on her "en masse" if she relaxed for even a minute, that most of her interactions were in a sharp, harsh tone of voice designed to let them know who was boss. In only a day's time the children didn't change much, but she was exhausted, thinking as she did that every noise and whisper had an ulterior motive. All we can do is speculate about what the outcome might be if this same teacher had this same class over a longer period of time and conducted it as she had that day, but we would probably not be too far afield in suggesting that eventually some of the students would begin to show some of the aggressive characteristics she thought they had in the first place and a vicious cycle of aggression and counteraggression would commence.

We might conclude from everything said so far that only normal, well-adjusted persons should be teachers. To a great extent this is true. The evidence does suggest that teachers who are warm, flexible, tolerant, interested in students, and who have a sense of humor seem better able to positively affect the self-attitudes and learnings of students than do teachers in whom these personal characteristics are less evident. The point can be made, however, that some teachers are successful precisely because of their neuroticism. For example, the compulsive-obsessional teacher who places a high premium on order, accuracy, and precision may teach students the value of order in their lives. Or, we may find another teacher with strong needs for power and domination who vigorously carries students along with his own high standards of achievement. Still another teacher may have strong self-punishing tendencies who whips himself by the long hours and hard work he puts into the job. This does not mean, however, that we should recruit more neurotic teachers or that we should feel more comfortable about our own unsolved personal hangups. Absence of self-understanding and flexibility are the two conspicuously lacking personal qualities that make it difficult for the neurotic teacher to be successful with any group except that narrow band of students who help him meet his strong personal needs.

In sum, if we as teachers, either to our students or to our own children, are to facilitate growth and learning through self-concept enhancement, we must:

1. Understand that we teach what we *are*, not just what we *say*. We teach our own self-concepts far more often than we teach our subject matter.
2. Understand that anything we do or say could significantly change a student's attitude about himself for better or for worse. Further, we must understand the implications of our role as persons who are important or "significant" to students if we are to utilize that role properly.
3. Understand that students, like us, behave in terms of what seems to be true, which means that many times learning goes on, not according to what the facts are, but according to how they are perceived.
4. Be willing not just to teach subject matter, but to deal with what the subject matter *means* to different students. In the truest sense of

the word, we must be as willing to deal with the interpretation of a subject as we are to deal with the *information* about it.

5.   Understand that we are not likely to get results simply by telling someone he is worthy. Rather, we imply it through trust and the establishment of an atmosphere of mutual respect. One good way to start is to take time to listen to what the students have to say and to use their ideas when possible.

6.   Understand that teacher behavior which is distant, cold, and rejecting is far less likely to enhance self-concept, motivation, and learning than behavior which is warm, accepting, and discriminating.

7.   Be willing to be flexible, to be direct or indirect as the situation and personality of the student demands.

Now, then, let us turn to another important variable when it comes to considering self-concept, academic adjustment, and implications for teaching practices.

Student Variables Related to Self-Concept and Achievement

A student's total academic adjustment, which includes his performance and behavior, is influenced by personality factors, individual reactions to praise and blame, personal experiences with success and failure, and differences in learning style. Let's look at each of these variables one at a time.

STUDENT PERSONALITY

Three separate experiments have reported findings which indicate that teaching methods do, indeed, interact with student personality characteristics to affect academic adjustment.[74, 75, 76] In all of these experiments some students were placed in discussion or lecture sections where expectations were clearly defined, while other students were placed in more open-ended sections where they were free to establish objectives and course procedures. In one experiment, the more highly structured sections were conducted in a warm, supportive, and permissive way. In all three studies, a certain kind of student emerged who appeared to require a high degree of structure to make optimum progress. These students were described as being personally insecure and dependent. In addition,

. . . intensely frustrated and lacking the personal security to make the best of a bad situation, this student becomes rigid, intropunitive, and vindictive in his evaluation of sections and instructors. To this student the permissive section meetings are "absolutely worthless," a place where intellectual confusion is heaped upon personal anxiety.[77]

On the other hand, there were the more personally secure students who found the permissive, open-ended class very much to their liking and who flourished under its conditions. In any case, whether a student is secure or insecure, dependent or independent, these personality dimensions do make a difference when it comes to determining whether one teaching method or another will be successful as a motivating technique.

Compulsivity and anxiety are two other student personality characteristics which apparently influence academic adjustment. For example, Grimes and Allinsmith[78] found that when teaching is structured, compulsive students do substantially better than less compulsive students. Highly anxious students do poorly in unstructured classrooms. Students who are both highly anxious and highly compulsive do their best work in structured classes.

Other evidence also points to individual differences in nonintellectual factors. Della-Piana and Gage,[79] for example, found that some pupils are more concerned about feelings and personal relationships, while others are mainly achievement-oriented. Classes made up mostly of students of the first type tend to accept the teacher whom they like and reject the teacher whom they dislike on personal grounds. Classes composed of students of the second type pay less attention to teacher warmth in estimating their acceptance or rejection of certain teachers.

STUDENT REACTIONS TO PRAISE AND BLAME

Generally speaking, praise is a more powerful motivator than either blame or reproof of the work performance of students. In one study,[80] 106 fourth- and sixth-grade children of both sexes were divided into four groups matched on the basis of intelligence and arithmetic skill. A fifteen-minute daily practice period in addition was given to the groups for five consecutive days. One of the four groups served as the control group and received its test separately without any comment as to performance. Irrespective of the score obtained, one of the three remaining groups received consistent praise; one received reproof; and one was ignored. The children in the praised group were called by name, told of their excellent results, and encouraged to improve. The reproved group was called out and criticized for poor work, careless mistakes, and lack of improvement. The ignored group received no recognition but merely heard what occurred to the other two groups. Figure 6.1 provides a diagram of the results.

As you can see, the praised group made the greatest gains and the

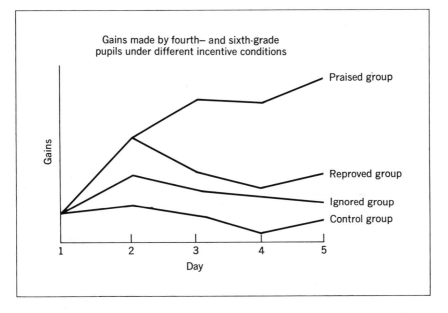

Figure 6.1 (From E. Hurlock. "An Evaluation of Certain Incentives Used in School Work." *Journal of Educational Psychology,* 1925, 16, 145–159.)

reproved group made greater gains than the ignored group. Apparently, even reproof is a sign of recognition and is better than no recognition at all!

However, the effects of praise and criticism on motivation and learning are not so simple as the above study indicates. Several other studies[81, 82] have indicated that the effects of praise or blame were related to personality differences as well. The major conclusions reached by these studies indicate that:

1.   When introverts and extroverts are grouped together (as is the case in most classrooms), either praise or blame is more effective in increasing the work output of fifth-grade pupils than no external incentives.
2.   If repeated often enough, praise increases the work output of introverts until it is significantly higher than that of introverts who are blamed or extroverts who are praised.
3.   If repeated often enough, blame increases the work output of extroverts until it is significantly higher than that of extroverts who are praised or introverts who are blamed.

It is apparent that the use of praise or blame has different effects on children with different self-concepts. It seems altogether possible that indiscriminate praise may be as detrimental to students' motivation and learning as indiscriminate blame or criticism. Praise which is won too easily or which is indiscriminately given to students, no matter what their effort or performance, quickly loses its effect. Praise, like success, means little if it is too easily won. However, if praise is honest: "You've done a fine job," or "You've done a good job, but I think you could have done better," and proportionate to the task accomplished, then it can be a sincere form of acknowledging another person's efforts.

STUDENT REACTIONS TO SUCCESS AND FAILURE

We probably do not have to go much further than our own life experiences in order to understand the differential effects of success and failure. As we discussed earlier, what is a success experience for one student is a failure experience for another. Look at it this way: each of us, like each of our students or children, has what we could call a "psychological bank account." Just as we deposit money in our savings account, we deposit successes in our psychological account. Some people have less money, therefore can deposit less and, in fact, have less to draw on in time of need. Somewhat the same is true of success. Some adults and children simply have fewer successes to deposit in their psychological accounts, and just as it is possible to go financially bankrupt, it is possible to experience psychological bankruptcy. The difference is that when we are financially bankrupt, there is always the possibility of starting over again. Not so with psychological bankruptcy; one's failures are not so easily wiped away. If we take this analogy into the school world, we can all think of students we know who pay their way through school (if they make it) on what amounts to a "psychological deficit financing plan." For the most part, they are students for whom school success is neither easily won nor easily available. Just as having enough money encourages some to invest to make more, so having enough success encourages some to invest in greater success, such as studying harder, taking more difficult courses, and the like. But there has to be an "account" to begin with.

Research has shown that a person's success experiences contribute to his setting realistic levels of aspiration.[83, 84] People who have little money will sometimes engage in wild, risk-taking ventures to get more or become uncommonly conservative in order to reduce the risk of losing what they have. Students with histories of academic failure do somewhat the same thing. They set goals either so low that no hazard is involved or so high that success is impossible. They are, to a large extent, unpredictable. If we are to help these kinds of students to be more consistent and more realistic about goal-setting, we ought to keep reminding ourselves that not all students will be motivated in the same way or interested in the same things. If we can remain aware of this, perhaps we can work harder at making success more available in more different ways and at more different levels. One way of doing this is to recognize that different students learn in different ways.

STUDENT DIFFERENCES IN LEARNING STYLES

Although little formal research on this subject has been conducted, we are beginning to understand that there are, indeed, different "styles" for learning.[85] There is no evidence that any one style is better or worse than another but if we are not careful, we may get caught in the trap of judging a learning style wrong just because it doesn't match our own. Most learning styles may be categorized as principally visual (reading), aural (listening), or physical (doing things), although it is possible that any one person may use more than one.

In the interests of effective motivation, it is important to identify each student's learning style as quickly as possible. If, for example, some students seem to learn best by reading, it may be wise not only to suggest books to them, but also to call on them more often in class to encourage them to experience more physical or verbal learning encounters. (Some students even *hope* to be called on because they lack the confidence to raise their hands.) On the other hand it may be beneficial to encourage the more physical and aural students to read more. The point is that once a student's particular "style" for learning is identified, a teacher can encourage his best use of that style and help him experience other modes of learning as well.

In sum, what is important for one student may not be important to another; this is one reason why cookbook formulas for good teaching are of so little value and why teaching is inevitably something of an art when it comes to motivating students and helping them learn. The choice of instructional methods makes a big difference for certain kinds of pupils, and a search for the "best" way to motivate can succeed only when student variables such as intellectual *and* self-concept differences are taken into account.

Self-Involvement in the Curriculum: Implications for Teaching

Nearly everything in a curriculum is charged with psychological and motivational possibilities when looked at in terms of what it might do to help students find themselves, realize their potentialities, use their resources in productive ways, and enter into relationships which have a bearing on their ideas about school and attitudes toward themselves.

Sometimes, in the quest for "the right answers," teachers fall into the trap of asking only one kind of question: the convergent kind. Of course, there can be only one kind of answer to this sort of question, and it is usually a response which sorts through, synthesizes, and integrates answers from existing data. Divergent questions, however, invite a quite different type of thinking and responding. They demand answers which are original, novel, and creative. To ask a divergent question is to ask not only "What do you *know* about this?" but also "What do you *think* about this?"

Examples of both types of questions can be drawn from the classroom. If while teaching *Macbeth*, the teacher asks, "Who killed Duncan?" then clearly only convergent thinking is involved: the student either knows the answer (from reading the play or Dan's notes) or he does not know. When the teacher asks, "Why did Macbeth kill Duncan?," the student's task is to gather appropriate data from the play and come up with a cogent answer. When the teacher asks, "What would you have done if you were Lady Macbeth?", the student is invited to think divergently, to make up alternative plots for the play based on his own feelings. Finally, if the teacher asks, "Should Macbeth have gotten away with all the murders?", he is attempting to get some sort of moral judgment, which is an open invitation to all sorts of divergent, "way-out" thinking.

Convergent, memory-type questions do have a place in the classroom, but we may seriously hinder motivation and learning if we encourage only convergent thinking. To take another example from English, divergent questions and composition assignments about literature invite the student to participate in the book, to become a character in it, to shape its plot to fit his own experience. The convergent question about the same book forces the student to come to terms with the book as it is given, a collection of information to be analyzed in some logical way. If we remain aware of these distinctions between kinds of thinking, then we can plan more purposefully, and we can also plan to make deliberate shifts from one kind of thinking to another.

Sometimes, in a teacher's anxiety to cover a certain unit of material in a given amount of time, to give his students what he considers to be crucial information and knowledge, he ends up teaching in a non-self-related manner. Many times students dislike English, or history, or social studies, or some other subject because it seems to have no personal meaning or relevance to their own lives. Indeed, many students see little relationship between what happens in school and what goes on outside of school. Can we make school more personally meaningful? Very probably so if we exploit the psychological as well as the academic content of a curriculum. Let's take some examples.

In social studies, we could encourage more inquiries into human values, needs, aspirations, and the competitive tendencies involved in economic

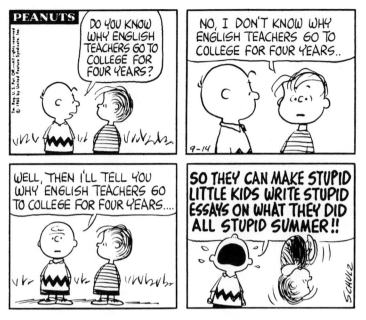

The things that students are asked to do in school are sometimes not very meaningful.

affairs. In civics, for example, rather than simply talk about the different forms of city government, the class could actually set them up in the classroom. Students could run for office, conduct campaigns, debate issues—in short, *live* the government, the election, the victory, and the defeat. Take history as another case in point. Wouldn't it be better to teach history in terms of people and their experiences rather than just in terms of events, institutions, and movements? We all know something about significant historical dates, but what do we know about the motivations of the men behind them? Or, as another example, is it possible that high-school students might get more out of Shakespeare's works by reading them not only as great literary masterpieces, but as unfolding dramas of human greed, love, and hate? How many students actually "see" *Julius Caesar* as an example of what untamed, selfish ambition can do to a man? Think a moment. How many contemporary men can you think of who reflect the personal qualities which led to Caesar's downfall? Could they be used as examples in class? I know of a class of slow-learning ninth graders who not only read *Romeo and Juliet*, but enjoyed it! A wise sensitive teacher, Mrs. Leah Graham, first exposed them to something they already knew about— *West Side Story*, the book of which was based on *Romeo and Juliet*. They listened to the music in class, and since the movie was playing at a local theater, most of the students saw the film too. True, the characters were Tony and Maria, not Romeo and Juliet; the scene was a fire escape, not a balcony; but they were in love; there were two feuding families; and it did end tragically. Thus through the simple process of exposing students to something they already knew about and liked, the teacher made the study of *Romeo and Juliet* not only possible, but of all things, fun! What could easily have been a laborious, nonmeaningful English assignment was converted into an exciting adventure as the students puzzled through the similarites and differences between the two stories. This, in the best sense of the word, is exploiting the psychological potential of a curriculum while, at the same time, enhancing its motivational possibilities.

Biographies and autobiographies offer mirrors in which students can study, among other things, their own self-reflections. Drama and fiction are filled with conflicts such as occur in our daily lives; it only remains for the teacher to point these things out, to help students see the similarities to their lives, to utilize the feelings that exist in all of us.

Physical education abounds in psychological possibilities. It can be more than basketball, swimming, and push-ups. It can be that part of a curriculum where students can learn to discover and accept their own bodies. They can be introduced to a human laboratory in which they can see acts of meanness, cruelty, and hostility on the one hand, or behavior which reflects good sportsmanship and greatness in defeat on the other. More than that, they can learn to recognize the healthy as well as the morbid features of competition. Some students may discover that winning is not so impossible after all. Others may find that to do anything well, whether in the classroom or on the game field, takes persistence, effort, hard work, and discipline. Indeed, if physical education *is* more than basketball, swimming, push-ups, and the like, then more students may carry over into life itself the sort of constructive, positive attitude about the use and care of the body which could make possible a more healthy, vigorous physical, as well as mental, existence.

Exploiting the psychological possibilities of a curriculum offers exciting new avenues for enhancing motivation and learning. This doesn't mean that we negate the importance of content, not at all. In fact, our concern about how to motivate students may be less of a problem if we can teach in a more self-related manner. In the final analysis, none of us is highly motivated to learn about those things which appear to be disengaged from and unconnected to his own personal life.

Students are always motivated, but they may be motivated in different ways and toward different ends. Some students are motivated to cut up in class, skip school, and even drop out. Others are motivated to listen quietly,

© *1965 United Feature Syndicate, Inc.*

The experiences a student has in school are not always seen as being very relevant to his life outside of school.

study diligently, and set long-term goals. This does not mean that a teacher's job is a hopeless task. Not at all. It does mean that he must be constantly aware of himself and his students as unique individuals with different ways of responding to and interpreting the world. When we consider the multiplicity of teacher, student, and self-concept variables, it is plain that there is *no one best* way of teaching any more than there is one best way of learning. Rather, there seem to be *many best* ways of both teaching and learning. It depends on the teacher, the student, and indeed, the moment. Available evidence would not support any position which suggested that successful teaching is possible only through the use of some specific methodology. A reasonable inference from existing data is that methods which are more democratic than authoritarian, which provide for adaptation to individual differences, encourage student initiative, urge individual and group participation—and stimulate "self" involvement are likely to achieve positive results in both student attitude and achievement. To encourage methods of this sort, perhaps what we need first of all are flexible, "total" teachers who are as capable of planning around people as around ideas.

THE TEACHER'S PART

A good teacher is a dramatist of ideas. He can help build bridges between the world of reality and the world of our dreams. He can make the past as vivid as the present and the future as possible as today. When you think about it, teaching is basically an existential process. It reflects the personality, outlook, ideals, and background of the teacher who, though he may claim to be objective, in reality reflects the highly subjective spirit of his work and thinking. A good teacher not only knows his subject; he can radiate it and communicate a zest which goes far beyond the content itself. To a scientist like Albert Einstein, science became an avenue to truth and the foundation of progress. To an artist like Frank Lloyd Wright, architecture was not a merely ornamental expression of man; rather it became an introduction to his innermost philosophical and spiritual needs. To a poet like Kahlil Gibran, poetry was not merely a lyrical expression, but man's encounter with a timeless reality.

It is not necessarily the teacher who knows the most, in a technical sense, who does the best with students in terms of learning and motivation. Rather, it may be that person so immersed in his work that he infects students with the kind of zest for knowing that spills outside the classroom and enables students to become, ultimately, their *own* best teachers.

In Perspective

There is substantial evidence to link both a student's school behavior and achievement to his feelings about himself. As a general statement, high self-concept students do better in school than low self-concept students, although this is not always so. The possession of a high positive self-concept does not *cause* good or high academic achievement, but it does seem to be related to it. The attitudes a student has about himself and his ability to do school work depends partly on how he was treated by people significant to him, his experiences with success and failure, his level of anxiety, and his perceptions of school and teachers.

Each student brings to school with him a certain attitude about his ability to compete and succeed, whether the school is grade school or college. A student's self-attitudes either motivate him to participate vigorously with his classmates or to sit quietly in hopes of not being called on. If the self is learned as a function of experience—and evidence from all quarters suggests it is—then, whether a student is aware of it or not, part of his accumulation of knowledge about himself is acquired in the classroom. A child ridiculed at the blackboard by an insensitive teacher in front of all his peers may learn that it's better not to raise his hand, that maybe he's not as smart as the other kids. Or a shy, uncertain child appropriately praised in the presense of his classmates for doing a good job on something may learn that speaking out, that taking a risk now and then is not so dangerous after all.

Many different experiences ultimately influence how an individual feels about himself. What happens to a youngster as he goes through school must certainly rank as one of the most important experiences in his life. Depending upon what occurs in school a child learns that he is able or unable, adequate or inadequate. The self is learned and what is learned can be taught. The question is not whether we approve of teaching for a positive sense of self in school settings, but whether the effects of schooling are positive or negative. For the young student particularly, school is not so much a vestibule to society as we adults picture it. For him it *is* society. As such, its effects are enormously far-reaching. How he does is related to how he thinks he can do, and schools play a considerable part in shaping the direction of that attitude.

[1] Prescott Lecky, *Self-Consistency—A Theory of Personality*. New York: Island Press, 1945.

[2] W. W. Wattenberg and C. Clifford, "Relation of Self-Concepts to Beginning Achievement in Reading," *Child Development*. 1964, 35: 461–467.

[3] M. C. Shaw and J. T. McCuen, "The Onset of Academic Under-Achievement in Bright Children," *Journal of Educational Psychology*. 1960, 51: 103–108.

[4] John J. Teigland and others, "Some Concomitants of Underachievement at the Elementary School Level," *The Personnel and Guidance Journal*. 1966, 44: 950–955.

[5] M. C. Shaw, K. Edson, and H. Bell, "The Self-Concept of Bright Under-Achieving High School Students as Revealed by an Adjective Check List," *The Personnel and Guidance Journal*. 1960, 34: 193–196.

[6] M. C. Shaw and G. J. Alves, "The Self-Concept of Bright Academic Underachievers: Continued," *The Personnel and Guidance Journal*. 1963, 42: 401–403.

[7] Charles F. Combs, "Self-Perception and Scholastic Underachievement in the Academically Capable," *The Personnel and Guidance Journal*. 1964, 43: 47–51.

[8] H. W. Reese, "Relationships between Self-Acceptance and Sociometric Choices," *Journal of Abnormal and Social Psychology*. 1961, 62: 472–474.

[9] Robert L. Williams and S. Cole, "Self-Concept and School Adjustment," *Personnel and Guidance Journal*. 1968, 47: 478–481.

[10] J. E. Dittes, "Effects of Changes in Self-Esteem Upon Impulsiveness and Deliberation in Making Judgments," *Journal of Abnormal and Social Psychology*. 1959, 58: 348–356.

[11] L. P. Lipsitt, "A Self-Concept Scale for Children and Its Relationship to the Children's Form of the Manifest Anxiety Scale," *Child Development*. 1958, 29: 463–472.

[12] B. R. McCandless, A. Castaneda, and D. S. Palermo, "Anxiety in Children and Social Status," *Child Development.* 1956, 27: 385–392.

[13] A. Castaneda, D. S. Palermo, and B. R. McCandless, "Complex Learning and Performance as a Function of Anxiety in Children and Task Difficulty," *Child Development.* 1956, 27: 327–332.

[14] B. R. McCandless and A. Castaneda, "Anxiety in Children, School Achievement, and Intelligence," *Child Development.* 1956, 27: 379–382.

[15] Stanley A. Coopersmith, "A Method for Determining Types of Self-Esteem," *Journal of Educational Psychology.* 1959, 59: 87–94.

[16] Stanley A. Coopersmith, "Self-Esteem and Need Achievement as Determinants of Selective Recall and Repetition," *Journal of Abnormal and Social Psychology.* 1960, 60: 310–317.

[17] J. V. Mitchell, Jr., "Goal-Setting Behavior as a Function of Self-Acceptance, Over- and Under-Achievement, and Related Personality Variables," *Journal of Educational Psychology.* 1959, 50: 93–104.

[18] S. B. Sarason, G. Mandler, and P. G. Graighill, "The Effect of Differential Instructions on Anxiety and Learning," *Journal of Abnormal and Social Psychology.* 1952, 47: 561–565.

[19] F. N. Cox, "Correlates of General and Test Anxiety in Children," *Australian Journal of Psychology,* 1960, 12: 169–177.

[20] William C. Morse, "Self-Concept Data in the University School Project," *The University of Michigan School of Education Bulletin.* 1963, 34: 49–52.

[21] D. E. Hamachek and J. Conley, "An Exploratory Study of Students' Perceptions of School, Teachers' Skills, Self, and Student-Teacher Relations in Grades Six Through Twelve." A paper presented at the American Educational Research Association Convention, Chicago, February 10, 1968.

[22] A. F. DeGroot and G. G. Thompson, "A Study of the Distribution of Teacher Approval and Disapproval among Sixth Grade Pupils," *Journal of Experimental Education.* 1949, 18: 51–75.

[23] R. S. Carter, "How Invalid Are Marks Assigned by Teachers?" *Journal of Educational Psychology.* 1952, 43: 218–228.

[24] W. J. Meyer and G. G. Thompson, "Sex Differences in the Distribution of Teacher Approval and Disapproval among Sixth Grade Children," *Journal of Educational Psychology.* 1956, 47: 385–396.

[25] R. M. Roth, "Role of Self Concept in Achievement," *Journal of Experimental Education.* 1959, 27: 265–281.

[26] Martin B. Fink, "Self-Concept as It Relates to Academic Achievement," *California Journal of Educational Research.* 1962, 13: 57–62.

[27] Paul B. Campbell, "Self-Concept and Academic Achievement in Middle Grade Public School Children," *Dissertation Abstracts.* 1966, 27: 1535–1536.

[28] Ann M. Walsh, *Self-Concepts of Bright Boys with Learning Difficulties.* New York: Teachers College Press, Columbia University, 1956.

[29] Irla L. Zimmerman and G. N. Allebrand, "Personality Characteristics and Attitudes Toward Achievement of Good and Poor Readers," *Journal of Educational Research.* 1965, 59: 28–30.

[30] F. B. Bodwin, "The Relationship between Immature Self-Concept and Certain Educational Disabilities." Unpublished doctoral dissertation, Michigan State University, 1957.

[31] Ralph J. Nash, "A Study of Particular Self-Perceptions as Related to High School Age Pupils in a Middle Class Community," *Dissertation Abstracts.* 1964, 14: 3837–3838.

[32] Ernest Dyson, "A Study of Ability Grouping and the Self-Concept," *The Journal of Educational Research,* 1967, 60: 403–405.

[33] Bernard Borislow, "Self-Evaluation and Academic Achievement," *Journal of Counseling Psychology.* 1962, 9: 246–254.

[34] W. B. Brookover, S. Thomas, and A. Patterson, "Self-Concept of Ability and Academic Achievement," *Sociology of Education.* 1964, 37: 271–278.

[35] W. B. Brookover, J. M. LePere, D. E. Hamachek, S. Thomas, and E. Erickson, "Self-Concept of Ability and School Achievement, II," Final Report of *Cooperative Research Project #1636.* U.S. Office of Education, East Lansing: Bureau of Educational Research Services, Michigan State University, 1965.

[36] W. B. Brookover, E. L. Erickson, and L. M. Joiner, "Self-Concept of Ability and School Achievement, III," Final Report of *Cooperative Research Project #2831.* U.S. Office of Education, East Lansing: Human Learning Research Institute, Michigan State University, 1967, pp. 142–143.

[37] Arthur T. Jersild, *In Search of Self.* New York: Teachers College Press, Columbia University, 1952, pp. 99–100. Used by permission.

[38] Brookover and others (1967), pp. 140–141.

[39] M. M. Helper, "Parental Evaluations of Children and Children's Self-Evaluations," *Journal of Abnormal and Social Psychology.* 1958, 56: 190–194.

[40] Thomas Hilliard and R. M. Roth, "Maternal Attitudes and the Non-Achievement Syndrome," *Personnel and Guidance Journal.* 1969, 47: 424–428.

[41] B. Kimball, "Case Studies in Educational Failure during Adolescence," *American Journal of Orthopsychiatry.* 1953, 23: 406–415.

[42] R. M. and H. Meyersburg, "The Non-Achievement Syndrome," *Personnel and Guidance Journal.* 1963, 41: 531–538.

[43] W. R. Morrow and R. C. Wilson, "Family Relations of Bright High-Achieving and Under-Achieving High School Boys," *Child Development.* 1961, 32: 501–510.

[44] A. Davids and P. Hainsworth, "Maternal Attitudes about Family Life and Child-Rearing as Avowed by Mothers and Perceived by Their Under-Achieving and High-Achieving Sons," *Journal of Consulting Psychology.* 1967, 31: 29–37.

[45] E. Bing, "The Effect of Child Rearing Practices on Development of Differential Cognitive Abilities," *Child Development.* 1963, 34: 631–648.

[46] D. Baer and T. Ragosta, "Relationship between Perceived Child-Rearing Practices and Verbal and Mathematical Ability," *Journal of Genetic Psychology.* 1966, 108: 105–108.

[47] V. Crandall, R. Dewey, W. Katkousky, and A. Preston, "Parent's Attitudes and Behaviors and Grade-School Children's Academic Achievements," *Journal of Genetic Psychology.* 1964, 104: 53–66.

[48] W. Katkovsky, A. Preston, and V. Crandall, "Parents' Attitudes toward Their Personal Achievements and toward the Achievement Behaviors of Their Children," *Journal of Genetic Psychology.* 1964, 104: 67–82.

[49] F. W. Hart, *Teachers and Teaching.* New York: The Macmillan Company, 1934, pp. 131–132, 250–251.

[50] P. Witty, "An Analysis of the Personality Traits of the Effective Teacher," *Journal of Educational Research.* 1947, 40: 662–671.

[51] Arthur T. Jersild, "Characteristics of Teachers Who Are 'Liked Best' and 'Disliked Most,'" *Journal of Experimental Education.* 1940, 9: 139–151.

[52] W. A. Bousfield, "Student's Ratings on Qualities Considered Desirable in College Professors," *School and Society.* 1940, February 24: 253–256.

[53] P. S. Sears and E. R. Hilgard, "The Effect of Classroom Conditions on Strength of Achievement Motive and Work Output of Elementary School Children,"

in E. Hilgard (Ed.), *Theories of Learning and Instruction*. 63rd Yearbook of the National Society for the Study of Education, Chicago, Ill.: University of Chicago Press, 1964, p. 195.

[54] M. L. Cogan, "The Behavior of Teachers and the Productive Behaviors of Their Pupils," *Journal of Experimental Education*. 1958, 27: 89–124.

[55] H. B. Reed, "Implications for Science Education of a Teacher Competence Research," *Science Education*. 1962, 46: 473–486.

[56] L. M. Heil, M. Powell, and I. Feifer, "Characteristics of Teacher Behavior Related to the Achievement of Different Kinds of Children in Several Elementary Grades," *Cooperative Research Project No. 352*. U.S. Office of Education, New York: Brooklyn College, 1960.

[57] Sears and Hilgard, pp. 182–209.

[58] R. Spaulding, "Achievement, Creativity, and Self-Concept Correlates of Teacher–Pupil Transactions in Elementary Schools," *U.S. Office of Education Cooperative Research Project No. 1352*. Urbana, Ill.: University of Illinois, 1963.

[59] David G. Ryans, "Research on Teacher Behavior in the Context of the Teacher Characteristics Study," in B. J. Biddle and W. J. Ellena (Eds.), *Contemporary Research on Teacher Effectiveness*. New York: Holt, Rinehart and Winston, Inc., 1964, pp. 67–101.

[60] Arthur W. Combs, *The Professional Education of Teachers*. Boston: Allyn and Bacon, Inc., 1965, pp. 70–71.

[61] Ryans, p. 88.

[62] Ryans, p. 89.

[63] Ryans, p. 90.

[64] Combs (1965), p. 55.

[65] H. H. Davidson and G. Lang, "Children's Perceptions of Their Teacher's Feelings toward Them Related to Self-Perception, School Achievement and Behavior," *Journal of Experimental Education*. 1960, 29: 107–118.

[66] J. W. Staines, "The Self-Picture as a Factor in the Classroom," *British Journal of Educational Psychology*. 1958, 28: 97–111.

[67] N. A. Flanders, "Teacher Influence, Pupil Attitudes and Achievement: Studies in Interaction Analysis," *Final Report, Cooperative Research Project No. 397*. Minneapolis: University of Minnesota Press, 1960.

[68] A. S. Barr, *Characteristic Differences in the Teaching Performance of Good and Poor Teachers of the Social Studies*. Bloomington, Ill.: Public School Publishing Co., 1929.

[69] E. P. Page, "Teacher Comments and Student Performance," *Journal of Educational Psychology*. 1958, 46: 173–181.

[70] N. A. Flanders, "Personal-Social Anxiety as a factor in Experimental Learning Situations," *Journal of Educational Research*. 1951, 45: 100–110.

[71] G. C. Stern, "Measuring Non-Cognitive Variables in Research on Teaching," in C. L. Gage (Ed.), *Handbook of Research on Teaching*. Skokie, Ill.: Rand McNally & Company, 1942, p. 427.

[72] S. C. Tiedeman, "A Study of Pupil-Teacher Relationships," *Journal of Educational Research*. 1942, May: 657–664.

[73] R. Rosenthal and L. Jacobson, *Pygmalion in the Classroom*. New York: Holt, Rinehart and Winston, Inc., 1968, pp. 72–97.

[74] W. J. McKeachie, "Students, Groups, and Teaching Methods," *American Psychologist*. 1958, 13: 580–584.

[75] D. E. Smith, "Reading Improvement as a Function of Student Personality and Teaching Method," *Journal of Educational Psychology*. 1956, 47: 47–59.

[76] L. G. Wispe, "Evaluating Section Teaching Methods in the Introductory Course," *Journal of Educational Research.* 1951, 45: 161–186.

[77] Wispe, p. 177.

[78] J. W. Grimes and W. Allinsmith, "Compulsivity, Anxiety, and School Achievement," *Merrill-Palmer Quarterly.* 1961, 7: 247–271.

[79] G. M. Della-Piana and N. L. Gage, "Pupils' Values and the Validity of the Minnesota Teacher Attitude Inventory," *Journal of Educational Psychology.* 1955, 46: 167–168.

[80] E. Hurlock, "An Evaluation of Certain Incentives Used in School Work," *Journal of Educational Psychology.* 1925, 16: 145–159.

[81] G. Forlano and H. C. Axelrod, "The Effect of Repeated Praise or Blame on the Performance of Introverts and Extroverts," *Journal of Educational Psychology.* 1937, 28: 92–100.

[82] G. G. Thompson and G. W. Hunnicutt, "The Effect of Repeated Praise or Blame on the Work Achievement of Introverts and Extroverts, *Journal of Educational Psychology.* 1944, 35: 257–266.

[83] P. S. Sears, "Levels of Aspiration in Academically Successful and Unsuccessful School Children," *Journal of Abnormal and Social Psychology.* 1940, 35: 498–536.

[84] R. R. Sears, "Initiation of the Repression Sequence by Experienced Failure," *Journal of Experimental Psychology.* 1937, 20: 570–580.

[85] F. Riessman, "Styles of Learning," *NEA Journal.* 1966, 55: 15–17.

References of Related Interest

Birney, Robert C., "Research on the Achievement Motive," in E. F. Borgatta and W. W. Lambert (Eds.), *Handbook of Personality Theory and Research.* Skokie, Ill.: Rand McNally & Company, 1968, pp. 857–889.

Bower, Eli M., and W. G. Hollister, *Behavioral Science Frontiers in Education.* New York: John Wiley & Sons, Inc., 1967, Chap. 2–5, 9, 13.

Combs, Arthur W., Chairman, American Association for Supervision and Curriculum Development Year Book Committee, *Perceiving, Behaving, Becoming.* Washington, D.C.: National Education Association, 1962.

Combs, Arthur W., and D. Snygg, *Individual Behavior* (rev. ed.), New York: Harper & Row, Publishers, 1959, Chap. 17, 18.

Greene, Maxine (Ed.), *Existential Encounters for Teachers.* New York: Random House, Inc., 1967.

Hamachek, Don E. (Ed.), *The Self in Growth, Teaching and Learning.* Englewood Cliffs, N.J.: Prentice-Hall, Inc., 1965, Parts VII & VIII.

Hamachek, Don E. (Ed.), *Human Dynamics in Psychology and Education.* Boston, Allyn and Bacon, Inc., 1968, Chap. 2–4, 10.

Jenkins, Gladys G., *Helping Children Reach Their Potential.* Glenview, Ill.: Scott, Foresman and Company, 1961.

LaBenne, W. D., and B. I. Greene, *Educational Implications of Self-Concept Theory*. Pacific Palisades, Calif.: Goodyear, 1969.

Purkey, William W., *The Self and Academic Achievement*. Englewood Cliffs, N.J.: Prentice-Hall, Inc., 1970.

Rogers, Carl R., *Freedom To Learn*. Columbus, Ohio: Charles E. Merrill Books, Inc., 1969.

Shostrom, Everett L., *Man, the Manipulator*. Nashville, Tenn.: Abingdon Press, 1967, Chap. 12.

Torrance, E. Paul, and R. D. Strom, *Mental Health and Achievement*. New York: John Wiley & Sons, Inc., 1965.

chapter seven

Toward
Developing
a Healthy
Self-Image

The voluminous literature related to the idea of the self and self-concept leaves little doubt but that mental health and personal adjustment depends deeply on each individual's basic feelings of personal adequacy. Just as each of us must maintain a healthy orientation to objective reality, so, too, must we learn to think of ourselves in healthy ways. Feelings of personal inadequacy, helplessness, inferiority, insecurity, or worthlessness tend to erode and weaken, sometimes to the point of collapse, the main pillars of one's self-structure. The growth of an adequate self-concept, free of neurotic pride, unrealistic fears, and the tyranny of irrational demands of conscience, is a critically important first step toward developing a healthy self-image. In the daily struggle to cope with the requirements of self and of reality and to deal firmly with threats, frustrations, and conflicts, we must have a firm grip on our own identity. Indeed, the admonition to "Know thyself" has been passed down through the ages as the criterion of wisdom and peace of mind until our present day where it has emerged from a religious-philosophical notion into a slogan for better mental health.

Attaining a healthy self-image with its concomitant feelings of adequacy, ableness, personal worth, and confidence is not some lofty goal beyond mortal reach, standing as a kind of poetic ideal. It is an attitude or cluster of attitudes which are learned and acquired, which means that sometimes "bad" (negative, destructive, self-defeating) attitudes must be replaced by healthier attitudes. Most people seem to want to move forward toward higher levels of physical and psychological health, although we would have to admit that there are those odd personalities who seem to get a perverse pleasure out of *un*health and suffering because it is the chief way of knowing they're alive. Sometimes a person says he would like to change his neurotic ways and have healthier attitudes about himself and others, but then says he can't change because, after all, his unfortunate childhood experiences made him the way he is. So busy is he contriving new defenses, inventing new excuses, and enjoying his own self-pity that he seldom has any energy left over for considering more constructive avenues for living. Along these lines, Maslow has suggested that:

> From Freud we learned that the past exists *now* in the person. Now we must learn, from growth theory and self-actualization theory, that the future also *now* exists in the person in the form of ideals, hopes, goals, unrealized potentials, mission, fate, destiny, etc. One for whom no future exists is reduced to the concrete, to helplessness, to emptiness. For him, time must be endlessly "filled." Striving, the usual organizer of most activity, when lost, leaves the person unorganized and unintegrated.[1]

As we noted in Chapter Two, there is little doubt but that past experiences can have a vast influence on current behavior. However, even though we cannot change what happened yesterday, we can change how we feel about it today. We cannot change past experiences, but we can change our feelings *about* those experiences, which is one step in moving toward a healthy self-image.

Self-Other Understanding as a Goal

Sometimes it is assumed that one gets to know himself by learning about man in the abstract, i.e., man as a psychological, social, biological, economic, and religious being. Necessarily, then, the "knowledgeable person" winds up knowing about a fictional man fabricated from theories, research, and other people's experiences, not the man who lives and breathes, nor the one to whom the personal pronouns "I" and "me" apply. Indeed, it is possible to major in psychology and to end up knowing a very great deal about psychology, but very little about one's self. For instance, a man may have no idea whatsoever that his fear, let's say, of getting too "involved" with a woman is related to a basically bad relationship with his mother, even though he may be very well versed in the field of psychology and able to discuss at length other men's problems and hangups with women. Clearly, such information is not wisdom, nor does it bring peace of mind, nor does positive mental health commence and prevail because of it. Self-other understanding appears to be specific knowledge about how one's unique individuality grows in an interpersonal social context. How can one arrive at a deeper understanding of himself and others as unique individuals?

A maxim of Goethe may help here. "If you want to know yourself, observe what your neighbors are doing," he said. "If you want to understand others, probe within yourself." Most of us are inclined to do exactly the opposite. We observe the other person in order to understand him, and we probe within ourselves in order to understand ourselves better. Seems obvious enough, but it doesn't often work quite that simply. Why? Normally we look at the other person objectively, but look at ourselves subjectively. We see others with the 20–20 vision of sanity and realism— no myopia here—we behold their flaws, weaknesses, self-deceptions, and even recognize their prejudices masquerading as principles.

However, when we probe within ourselves, we are not inclined to see the same personal distortions. Indeed, most of us "see" only our good intentions, our fondest dreams and hopes, our secret fears and deepest needs, and our unremitting calls for love and recognition. If we persist in distorting our self-perceptions, then we can never change anything about us which may, in the interests of a healthier more accurate self-image, need correcting. There are, however, ways to see ourselves more accurately and to know ourselves, as Goethe suggests, through "observing what our neighbors are doing."

Social Feeling as an Aid

Adler's[2] concept of social feeling provides us with a useful conceptual tool for developing a healthy self-image. What does social feeling mean? Basically, it is a notion which refers to a person's ability to empathize with another; to see, hear, and feel with him. The usefulness of this concept lies in the fact that it combines the idea of social, which is an objective reference to common experiences, with the idea of feeling, which is a subjective reference to private experiences. The synthesis of the objective "social" with the subjective "feeling" is one way of bridging the gap between "you" and "me."

Self-other understanding involves, strangely enough, self-transcendence, which calls for one to go beyond his own private motives and thoughts in order to better understand and share another person's needs and goals. Social feeling is an attempt to understand one's self through the understanding of others. It is becoming less involved with one's own hopes, fears, shame, and doubt in order to become more in tune to how the other person thinks and feels. Erich Fromm,[3] for example, has observed: "I discover that I am everybody, and that I discover myself in discovering my fellow man, and vice versa." Self-other understanding through the process of social feeling means to see one's self (insight) by participating and sharing mutual concerns with another, or more succinctly, being an "I" for a "thou" as Buber[4] would say.

How can one practice social feeling and thereby understand himself and others better? Let's look at some ways.

HONESTY AS A WAY OF FACILITATING SELF-OTHER UNDERSTANDING

This does not mean being brutally and indiscriminately frank, but it does mean showing some of yourself to another person, exhibiting some of your own feelings and attitudes. This isn't particularly easy because from early childhood most people learn to play roles which mask their feelings, as if being honest about them would only hurt others and destroy relationships. Actually, the inevitable consequence of exposing and sharing feelings is usually greater interpersonal closeness. If I am honest with you, this encourages you to be more honest with me. If you are honest with me, I am freer to be more honest with you. And so the cycle goes. Consider an example.

Although it is always desirable, being honest in our interpersonal relationships is not always easy.

Suppose a teacher has put in a relatively sleepless night and goes to class irritable, cranky, and short-tempered. He has two alternatives for handling his feelings. One, he can say nothing to the class and end up snapping at innocent students all day as if they were the cause of his sleepless night. Or, two, he could frankly admit to his irritable feelings, why they exist, and thereby give his students to respond to his honesty. Once they know that his lack of patience and irritability is for a reason, then they will have less need to be defensive and irritable themselves. Furthermore, once the students learn that their teacher has *feelings*, not all of which are pleasant or good, then they are more apt to face up to and *admit feelings within themselves* which might otherwise have remained buried. If a teacher is honest with his students, shares with them some of his own personal self, he can be much more assured of his students giving him honest feedback about the conduct of the course, its content, and him as a teacher. Carl Rogers, discussing his way of facilitating or "teaching" a class, puts it this way:

> For me, trust is *the* important ingredient which the facilitator provides. . . . He will, I hope, participate with his own feelings (owned as *his* feelings, not projected on another person). He may risk himself in expressing his problems and weaknesses. . . . The trust is something which cannot be faked. It is not a technique . . . if it is real and complete, even in a narrow area, it will have a facilitating effect upon the process of the group.[5]

In sum, honesty is one way of facilitating social feeling and healthy self-other understanding because it encourages greater freedom and openness of interpersonal exchange, the medium in which self-knowledge begins.

EMPATHIC LISTENING AS A WAY OF FACILITATING SELF-OTHER UNDERSTANDING

Another response which may be useful in developing a healthy self-other attitude is to listen. This doesn't merely mean to wait for a person to finish talking (and to spend our listening time preparing what we are going to say), but to try to see how the world is viewed by this person and to communicate this understanding to him. The sort of "total" listening we're talking about here is the kind that responds to the person's *feelings* as well as his *words*. It implies no evaluation, no judgment, no agreement (or disagreement). It simply conveys an effort to understand what the person is feeling and trying to communicate. It is an effort to communicate to the other person that we can accept the notion that his feelings and ideas are valid for *him*, if not for us.

One reason behind being a poor listener lies in the fact that it is difficult to do. We can test this out. For example, try establishing in any group discussion the ground rule that no person may present his own view until he has first satisfied the one who has just spoken that he fully comprehends what this person meant to communicate. That is, he must rephrase in his own words the total meaning of the other person's message and obtain this person's agreement that that was indeed what he said. In doing this we may find out that: (1) it is extremely difficult to get agreement between what was said and what was heard ("listened" to); (2) we frequently are remiss in our good intentions to listen; (3) when we do listen carefully, we have a hard time remembering what it was that we were going to say, and when we do remember, we find that it is a little off the subject; (4) much argument and irrational emotionality is absent from such a discussion because we spend less time responding to what we *thought* we heard or *wanted* to hear and more time responding to what was actually said, particularly when our misconceptions, if any, are cleared away.

Poor listeners are typically so preoccupied with their own sense of self-importance that they leave little room for expanding the range of their self-other knowledge. A person, whether a parent, a teacher, or a friend who talks a lot *could* have much that was meaningful to say, or he could be protecting himself from running the risk of having to change if he listened too carefully to another person's point of view.

Self-understanding is enhanced through understanding others. Understanding others is a function of one's capacity for social feeling. This capacity is both developed and encouraged by honest communication and good listening. Indeed, most of us know from personal experience that some of our most significant self-other discoveries have resulted from being in the company of persons characterized not only by their total honesty, but also by their lack of preconceptions about how they expect us to behave.

Self-other understanding, then, can be one step toward developing a healthy and accurate self-picture.

Self-Acceptance: Outcomes and Consequences

While no single definition of self-acceptance is likely to be accepted by all who use the term, it generally has reference to the extent which a person's self-concept is congruent with his description of his "ideal" self. Many self-concept studies, for example, in addition to asking subjects for *self-perceptions* also ask the subjects to go through the same set of items again and indicate how he would like to be *ideally*. Since most of us would like to be "better" than we are, the *ideal* self is usually judged to be at least as good as and almost always better than the perceived or "actual" self.

The differences between the scores for the perceived self and ideal self is the *discrepancy* score, which is obtained by subtracting the score of the perceived self from the score representing the ideal self. The larger this discrepancy score the more dissatisfied with himself and less accepting the person is presumed to be.

McCandless reviewed twelve studies designed to investigate the psychological consequences of discrepancies between the perceived self and the ideal self and concluded with the following:

> In summary, most research evidence indicates that people who are highly self-critical—that is, who show a large discrepancy between the way they actually see themselves and the way they would ideally like to be—are less well-adjusted than those who are at least moderately satisfied with themselves. Evidence indicates that highly self-critical children and adults are more anxious, more insecure, and possibly more cynical and depressed than self-accepting people. They *may* be more ambitious and driving, however. At least some evidence indicates that people experience conflict about the traits on which they have the greatest self-ideal discrepancy, and that this conflict is sharp enough to interfere with learning involving such areas. . . . There is some question whether the topic of self-ideal discrepancy is really different from the topic of positive and negative self-concepts.[6]

As you can see, research suggests that self-accepting persons are likely to have smaller self-ideal discrepancies than less self-accepting persons.

Self-Acceptance and Acceptance of Others

The notion that people who are self-accepting are accepting of others has considerable practical importance, particularly in light of the evidence suggesting that personal adjustment or maladjustment is socially learned. The self-rejecting person, if he also rejects others, is likely to be rejected by them in turn, with the inevitable consequence of reinforcing the original maladjustment. If, in counseling or psychotherapy, the self-concept can be improved and if this improvement results in increased acceptance of and by other people, then personal improvement is likely to occur. Raimy,[7] for example, has demonstrated that successful cases in psychotherapy enabled patients to acquire a more favorable view of themselves, whereas unsuccessful cases did not.

The overwhelming evidence from Wylie's[8] monumental review of the literature related to the self suggested that self-acceptance was related to adjustment. Generally, a high regard for one's self is reflected in a high level of personal adjustment. Moreover, there is evidence to show that people who are *self-accepting are more accepting of others.*[9, 10, 11] This means that if an individual thinks well of himself he is likely to think well of others, and that if he disapproves of himself he is likely to disapprove of others. Rogers[12] has noted that "when the individual perceives and accepts into one consistent and integrated system all his sensory and visceral experiences, then he is necessarily more understanding of others and is more accepting of others as separate individuals." A person who carries around a store of suppressed anger is more likely to feel hostile toward other people whose behavior, in his eyes, represents his own suppressed feelings than a person who is more open to his anger and willing to admit that his anger does exist. Or as another example, sometimes a person who feels threatened by his sexual impulses may be the first to criticize and moralize others whom he perceives as behaving in sexual ways. On the other hand, if he accepts his *own* sexual feelings he is usually more tolerant of sexual expressions by others.

Self-Acceptance as Related to Popularity

We have seen that self-acceptance is related to acceptance of others, but how is acceptance *by* others related to self-acceptance? Fey[13] made a rather interesting study of this and his research may help us answer that question. Using a group of fifty-eight third-year medical students, he obtained: (1) measures of self-acceptance, (2) acceptance of others, (3) each subject's judgment of how well he was accepted by others, and (4) an estimate of actual acceptability or popularity. Among other things, he found that the high self-accepting (positive self-concept) men were more accepting of others, estimated their own popularity higher than did the less self-accepting men, but were not *actually* any more popular.

Fey then split his subjects into groups of men who markedly overestimated their popularity (strong self-enhancing tendencies) and men who grossly underestimated their popularity (strong self-derogatory tendencies). Interestingly, he found the self-derogatory group to be significantly more popular than the self-enhancing group with an average of 6 friendly mentions each to the self-enhancers' 1.5. Fey speculated that individuals who are very self-accepting but who reject others are likely to have "defensively organized" attitudes of superiority, are insensitive to their actual group social status, tend to depreciate others, and are consequently rejected because they threaten the security of other people. On the other hand, it was found that men who have low acceptance of themselves, along with high acceptance of others, are seen as nonthreatening and therefore are more well-liked. Fey went on to speculate that the "prototypic well-adjusted person" (that is, the one with high self-other acceptance) "may not appear to 'need' friendships or to repay it . . . his very psychological robustness is resented, or perhaps it is perceived and rejected as a Pollyanna-like facade."[14] As you may have seen already, there is a striking similarity between Fey's research findings and Maslow's[15] clinical speculations discussed in Chapter One about why it is that some of us are inclined to lose our aplomb, and self-possession, even grow uneasy, anxious, and feel a bit inferior in the company of persons we regard as superior in one way or other.

In sum, self-acceptance, which we could say is a lack of cynicism about the self, appears to be associated with accepting other people. This indicates that the self-accepting person views the world as a more congenial place than the self-rejector and is less defensive toward others and about himself because of it. On the other hand, self-disparaging or self-effacing persons, particularly those who are obviously successful, are better accepted and more popular than the "prototypic well-adjusted person." There is no pat answer for why this seems to be so, but one speculation is that they pose less threat and more actively seek to please others.

Self-acceptance is an important step toward a healthy self-image. What happens, though, if one does not feel as adequate as others? Let's examine this question in greater detail.

The Inferiority Complex: Expressions and Outcomes

Allport[16] has defined an inferiority complex as a "strong and persistent tension arising from a somewhat morbid emotional attitude toward one's felt deficiency in his personal equipment." What this refers to is an attitude which a person may have about feeling less able than others. Closely allied to, but not to be confused with, inferiority, is the feeling or conviction of inadequacy. However, where inferiority, whether conscious or unconscious, implies unfavorable comparison with others, inadequacy suggests personal inability to meet the demands of the situation.

The feeling of inferiority is no stranger to most people. For example, one study found that less than 12 percent of a group of college students report that they do *not* know what it is to suffer from gnawing feelings of inferiority.[17] Consider the data presented in Table One.

As you can see, there seem to be four main types. On the whole, women appear to be worse off than men. However, when we consider that women in our culture, from the time they are little girls, are taught to be more socially sensitive than men, this is not surprising. That is, the more sensitive one is about himself in relation to the world around him, the more likely he is to spot qualities in himself which are less well developed or executed than what he may see in other people.

Table 1
College Men and Women Reporting Inferiority Feelings

Type of Inferiority Feeling	Percentage Reporting Persistent Inferiority Feelings	
	MEN	WOMEN
Physical	39	50
Social	52	57
Intellectual	29	61
Moral	16	15
None at all	12	10

Feelings of inferiority cannot be taken as an index of actual inferiority. A feeling of inferiority is a purely subjective affect related to the self, and is measured by the ratio between one's *success* and *aspirations* in a given direction. Objective facts seem to make little difference in determining whether a person feels inferior or not. The highest ranking student, or the funniest comedian, or the beauty contest winner may each suffer from a deep-seated sense of inferiority. On the other hand, the lowest student, the "unfunniest" man, or the plainest girl may not feel inferior at all. What one does or has or how one looks is far less important than how he feels about those things and what he aspires to be. For example, if a pretty girl aspires to be an excellent student, but falls short of that goal, being pretty is not likely to compensate for feeling academically inferior.

Important for us to understand is the fact that a sense of *inferiority is developmental or learned, rather than organic or innate.* This means that inferiority is in no sense necessary, and with insight into its causes and consequences, it can be handled, coped with, and in many instances, dispelled. Inferiority feelings are the result of too many failure experiences and frustrations; they are learned reactions that, if not corrected early, may eventually lead to the growth of deeply rooted attitudes of inferiority. Attitudes of this sort can dominate and condition a person to the point where he is left with a general feeling of not being able to do anything very well.

SYMPTOMS OF INFERIORITY

There are at least seven symptoms of inferiority feelings which we can be sensitive to in spotting its existence in others, or, for that matter in ourselves.

1. *Sensitivity to criticism*: An inferiority-ridden person does not like his weaknesses pointed out to him. Criticism, as viewed by him, is further proof of his inferiority and serves only to accentuate the pain associated with it.

2. *Overresponse to flattery*: The inferior-feeling person grabs at straws,

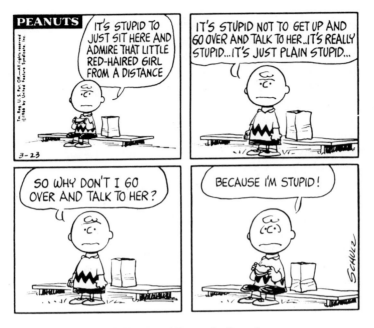

Feelings of inferiority can prevent one from doing many things he might otherwise enjoy.

particularly those constructed from praise and flattery because they help him stand more secure against his feelings of uncertainty and insecurity. The other response to flattery or praise, of course, is to stand in red-skinned embarrassment wondering, "How could anyone say anything good about me? Me, of all people!"

3. *Hypercritical attitude*: This is a frequent defense and serves the purpose of re-directing attention away from one's own limitations. Whereas overresponse to flattery is defensive in character, hypercriticism takes the offensive and is used as a way of actively warding off the implications of inferiority. For example, if I feel inferior about the quality of something I've done in relation to yours and aggressively criticize your effort, you may become so busy defending what you've done that you won't notice the flaws in *my* effort. In other words, hypercriticalness creates the illusion of superiority and relies on this illusion to belie inferiority.

4. *Tendency toward blaming*: Whenever personal weaknesses and failures are projected into others, it is relatively easy to find in them the cause of one's own failures, leading directly to the response of blaming. Indeed, some persons operate a kind of psychological "pulley system" in the sense

of being able to feel normal or adequate only if they are pulling other people *down* and themselves *up* in the process. Unless others are made to appear inferior, some persons cannot feel even normal.

5. *Feelings of persecutions*: It is only a short step away from blaming others for one's personal misfortune to the position that they are actively seeking his downfall. For example, if you fail me in a course and I can believe that you failed me because you don't like me or are against me, then I am spared the pain of having to consider that I alone am responsible. In this way, not only do I blame you for my failure but I assign you a motive for doing it—you're out to get me.

6. *Negative feelings about competition*: An inferiority-ridden person is as anxious to win in competition as anyone else, but far less optimistic about winning. He is inclined to react to competition as would a person who knows that he lacks the skills or knowledge for successful competition. The psychologically inferior person is usually among the first to complain about the breaks, his opponents' good luck, or favoritism. In some instances, the attitude toward competition is so extreme that he refuses to participate in any competitive situation and tends to shy away in a fearful and hesitant manner.

© *1967 United Feature Syndicate, Inc.*

Sometimes a person's reasons for feeling inferior or unlikeable are irrational—even to himself.

7. *Tendency toward seclusiveness, shyness and timidity*: Inferiority feelings are usually accompanied by a certain degree of fear, particularly in situations involving other people. Inferior-feeling persons prefer the cloak of anonymity, feeling that if they are neither seen nor heard their shortcomings (real or imagined) will less likely be seen. Not infrequently, students who feel less able than their peers sit near the back of the classroom because of the protection this offers. (If I'm not so easily seen, perhaps I will not so easily be called upon.)[18]

These are not mutually exclusive symptoms, but overlapping in expression and character. For example, timidity leads to avoidance of competition and also to greater sensitivity to criticism. At the same time, sensitivity to criticism can lead to blaming others or overresponding to flattery. All of these symptoms spring from a basic sense of inferiority and any one of them can serve as the catalytic agent, triggering a chain-reaction of defensive and generally self-destructive behavior.

There is still another, albeit distorted, expression of a sense of inferiority worth our consideration.

Self-Contempt as a Substitute for Self-Worth

A person who has almost, but not quite, lost his feeling of personal worth sometimes feels a strong need to condemn himself. ("I'm no good." "I can't do anything." "Others are better than me." "Look how stupid I am, etc.,") Rollo May,[19] a practicing psychoanalyst, has noted that self-condemnation may not be so much an expression of self-punishment as it is a technique to get a quick substitute for a sense of worth. It is as though the person were saying to himself, "I must be important that I am so worth condemning," or "Look how good I am—I have such high ideals that I am ashamed of myself for falling so short of them." Allport has observed:

> The very nature of the neurotic disorder is tied to pride. If the sufferer is hypersensitive, resentful, captious, he may be indicating a fear that he will not appear to advantage in competitive situations where he wants to show his worth. . . . If he is over-scrupulous and self-critical, he may be endeavoring to show how praiseworthy he really is.[20]

Self-condemnation is not so much an honest statement of one's shortcomings as it is a cloak for arrogance. This mechanism of self-condemnation can be observed in various states of psychological depression. The student, for example, who does poorly on a test can always say, generally to himself, "If I had studied more, if I had really wanted to do well on this test, I could have." Or the child who feels he is not loved by his parents can always say to himself something like, "If I were different, if I were not bad, they would love me." In the case of both the student and the child, self-condemnation is a means of avoiding a head-on confrontation with the possibility that he is not intellectually capable, in the first instance, and not loved in the other. The dynamics of self-condemnation works in such a way as to protect a person from the pain of feeling worthless. For he can always say, "If it were not for such and such a defeat, or bad habit, or lack of motivation, I would be as good as anyone else." The student who says, "I could've passed that test if I had studied harder," is really saying, "I'm really not that inadequate and furthermore it hurts to consider the possibility that I might be." An observation by Rollo May may help us understand better the hidden meaning behind self-condemnation:

> . . . the emphasis upon self-condemnation is like whipping a dead horse: it achieves a temporary life, but it hastens the eventual collapse of the dignity of a person. The self-condemning substitute for self-worth provides the individual with a method of avoiding an open and honest confronting of his problems of isolation and worthlessness, and makes for a pseudo-humility rather than the honest humility of one who seeks to face his situation realistically and do what he can constructively. Furthermore, the self-condemning substitute provides the individual with a rationalization for his self-hate, and thus reinforces the tendencies toward hating himself. And, inasmuch as one's attitude toward other selves generally parallels one's attitude toward one's self, one's covert tendency to hate others is also rationalized and reinforced. The steps are not big from the feeling of worthlessness of one's self to self-hatred to hatred for others.[21]

Strategies for Maintaining and Enhancing a Positive Self-Image

What can one do with inferiority feelings besides suffer? Feelings of inferiority are usually deeply rooted and not easily eradicated. Projection ("It's not really my fault I did this poorly on the exam—The teacher was unfair.") and rationalization ("I could have done better on the exam if I had really wanted to and studied harder.") are two frequently used mechanisms to defend against feeling inferior and have been discussed more fully in Chapter One. There is still another and it has a variety of forms and expressions.

COMPENSATION

Several types can be distinguished. *Direct action* is one kind and occurs when a person persistently attacks the *source* of an actual inferiority and attempts to remove it. When the original weakness or shortcoming is not only removed but turned into a source of strength, we think of this as *over-compensation*. For example, Demosthenes, so the story goes, not only overcame his stammer to become a normal speaker, but a great orator. Theodore Roosevelt built up his small physique, conquered his early childhood frailty, and went on to become a daredevil Rough Rider and fine lion hunter.

We speak of *substitute* compensation when a person cannot remove his handicap or shortcoming but develops other satisfactions. A Helen Keller may compensate for lack of sight and hearing through extraordinary development of tactile and intellectual ability. A physically small boy may work very hard to become a swift and elusive halfback or perhaps he excels in his studies. The somewhat unattractive woman may become an outstanding leader in social movements. The point is, in every walk of life, there are personal opportunities which do not involve setting up unreachable goals, unwisely selected activities, or the cessation of effort and hope. There are legitimate, wholesome, and necessary compensations that can add zest and meaning to any person's life.

Compensatory behavior can be a very effective means for maintaining and enhancing a positive self-image. There are, however, both *constructive* and *destructive* compensations and it may help us to be aware of the differences between the two.[22]

CONSTRUCTIVE COMPENSATORY BEHAVIOR

1. Selection of satisfying and useful fields of occupational endeavor which reflect one's strengths and interests, e.g., "I am poor with numbers, so I'll do something which enables me to use my abilities in reading and writing as in being a writer, copy-editor, or English teacher."

2. Stimulation of ambition expressed in concrete effort, e.g., "I will work very hard to develop the skills and interests I have rather than fret unduly about those things I cannot do well."

3. Attractiveness of personality if the inferiority is not excessive, e.g., "I will work on developing my interpersonal relationship skills, which may help me feel more adequate."

4. An effort to appreciate the relative advantages of one's position in life, e.g., "I'll try to appreciate those things that I have which are positive rather than worry so about those things I have which are negative."

DESTRUCTIVE COMPENSATORY BEHAVIOR

1. Decided superiority reactions, e.g., "I am bigger, or better, or more important than most." (It might be worthwhile noting here that a sense of

self-inflation and conceit does not usually come from greater feelings of self-worth. In fact, it may signal just the opposite. Self-inflation, conceit, and pompous behavior are generally signs of inner emptiness and self-doubt; a strutting display of superiority is one of the most common covers of inferiority feelings.)

2. Goals placed beyond reasonable possibility of attainment, e.g., "My below average grades in biochemistry, physics, and math aren't really that important—I still intend to go to medical school."

3. Occupation selected on a personal basis without regard to personal fitness and limitations, e.g., "So what if I've had some of heart problems? I've always wanted to be a physical education teacher and, besides, I like kids."

4. Excessive daydreaming and fantasy living, e.g., "Boy, things would be different if I were only a little bigger," or "If I only had more money then things would be different."

5. Cessation of effort; paralysis of activity, e.g., "Why try? Nothing works for me anyway."

As you can see, the ultimate effectiveness of any form of compensatory behavior is in the impact it has on our conduct.

Selection of Personal Values as Related to Positive Self-Esteem

To know that someone considers himself inferior with respect to some particular quality is insufficient information to tell us what he thinks of himself. We must also have some idea of how much he *values* this quality. What is the mechanism which determines what a person will *value* in his life? Let's see if we can understand this better.

Some years ago, Allport and Odbert[23] gathered a list of over 17,000 adjectives by which objects could be characterized. Not all of them were applicable to individuals, but an enormous number were. There is practically no end to the types of qualities an individual may consider important in evaluating himself. For example, he may consider it important to be good-looking, or nonconforming, or daring, or ruthless, or imaginative, or thoughtful, and so on and on.

Given this number of choices, which does a person choose? Why? On the whole, a person is inclined to value those things he considers himself good at and to devalue those qualities at which he considers himself poor. As an illustration of this, the quality of "good at working with your hands" was chosen by 68 percent among those who felt they possessed this skill and by only 6 percent of those who felt they lacked this quality. Self-values, we see, tend to be selected in a way that enables an individual to maintain a congenial self-picture. Rosenberg notes that:

If people are reasonably free to choose their own values, we are led to an interesting paradox of social life: almost everyone can consider himself superior to almost everyone else, as long as he can choose *his own* basis for judgment. Take four boys. One is a good scholar, the second a good athlete, the third very handsome, and the fourth a good musician. As long as each focuses upon the quality at which he excels, each is superior to the rest. At the same time, each person may blithely acknowledge the superiority of the others with regard to qualities to which he himself is relatively indifferent.[24]

One of the outcomes of a healthy, integrated self-concept is the evidence of a wise sense of values. When a problem arises, a careful, thoughtful person considers various possible avenues of action, considers the consequences of each, and then chooses the course most likely to lead to results which are most probable and most important. The discriminating person will evaluate an issue in terms of degrees rather than absolutes and will recognize that some values, for him at least, are more important than others.

Selective Interpretation of the "Facts" as Related to Positive Self-Esteem

In judging oneself, one must take account of the "facts." However, as we discussed in Chapter Two, "facts" are highly susceptible to the personal meanings we assign to them. Take a stranger who, in the face of a roaring fire, rushes into a burning house and leads to safety two previously trapped people. What he has done is certainly an objective fact. But how shall we interpret it? Does it mean that he is a fearless, courageous man so unselfish as to take little note of his own welfare? Or does it mean that he is simply too stupid and blind to recognize obvious danger when it stares him in the face? The act was clear, but whether it reflects "courage" or "foolhardiness" is a matter of interpretation.

Whenever there is sufficient lack of clarity about what a "fact" or "set of facts" mean, there is always room for a person to salvage a certain amount of self-esteem. Consider, for example, the matter of grades. One study found that although most people agree that grades are a good indication of whether they are good students, they are by no means convinced that grades indicate much about whether they are "clear-thinking and clever" or "imaginative and original."[25] In fact, it was found that nearly three-fourths of the students with D and F averages considered themselves very likely or fairly likely to be imaginative and original and to have good sense and sound judgment.

This is not a denial of reality. A "D" or "F" student *knows* that he has poor grades. There are, however, many expressions of intelligence and there is nothing in his "objective" grades to compel him to believe that he is less "clear-thinking" or "clever" than students with higher grades.

Another factor which makes it easy (or at least easier) to interpret the "facts" to fit our personal needs and thereby maintain and enhance our self-esteem is the nature of the language used to describe personal traits. For example, if one person says we are sensitive observers about human behavior and another says we are a nosey busybody, are they really describing anything different? If someone says we are ingenious and resourceful and another observes that we are cunning and cagey, is there really any difference between the two? Indeed, both you and your critic may agree that you are "too tough and aggressive," terms he engages to condemn qualities in which you may take the utmost pride. Even though you and your critic may agree on the evidence, you do not necessarily agree on the meaning.

The point is, there is scarcely any behavior which we cannot interpret as admirable in some way. In the seclusion of our mind's eye, generally free of the intrusion of alternative interpretations, we are free to review and weigh the evidence (the "facts") as our biases dictate, to shift our personal perceptions until a congenial one emerges, and to eventually settle for one which is self-enhancing.

Just as selectivity of the "facts" influences the interpretation of the meaning of evidence pertaining to the self, so too does it influence the *choice* of evidence. The type of evidence relevant to a given characteristic is widely varied. For example, by what criteria shall a person judge whether or not he is a sociable person—did he speak to a stranger? Has he gone to a party with friends? Is he among the first to speak in a crowd? Does he have many close friends but few casual acquaintances? Does he have one close friend but many casual acquaintances? Does he smile when passing someone on the street? He is not obliged to consider *all* these criteria: he can choose one, any one he wants, any one that *fits*. And he is right—the quality of, in this instance, of being sociable is so ambiguous that there is no way to prove him wrong. By his choice of criteria he may be a very friendly person. By your choice he may fall short. And the same is true of the vast range of personal characteristics that reflect a person's behavior.

Selective interpretation of the "facts," then, is one way of maintaining and enhancing a positive self-image.

Selection of Personal Standards as Related to Positive Self-Esteem

The validity of this observation is apparent in the fact that it is not simply how good a person *thinks* he is with regard to some quality, but how good he *wants to be* that counts. When you think about it, people have a wide range of options in setting standards for themselves. For example, a man can aspire to the very pinnacle of achievement, to a high level of performance, to a good level of performance, to moderate accomplishment, or even to modest success. A man may aspire to be the superintendent of a school system or to be a competent teacher within that system. The principle is all the more true of nonoccupational goals. One individual may aspire to love and care for "all mankind," whereas another is satisfied to love and care for just a few individuals he knows well. There is obviously a wide choice available in the setting of personal standards of performance in the immense sweep of areas pertaining to the self.

Given these alternatives, what personal standards do people select for themselves? We have already seen from our discussion in Chapter One that, as a general rule, a person is apt to set higher standards in those areas in which he *backs* himself to be good, or competent, or above average.[26] In Chapter Six we noted that children who experienced more failures than successes were unpredictable in setting personal standards; that is, they established standards for performance which were either too high or too low.[27] On the whole, however, research evidence suggests that most people tend to set goals that they interpret as falling within reasonable range of their potential accomplishments.[28]

Surveys of occupational aspirations tend to confirm laboratory findings related to the selection of personal standards. For example, in a study by Rosenberg[29] of college students' values, a sample of respondents was asked: "What business or profession would you *most like* to go into?" and "What business or profession do you realistically think you are *most apt* to go into?" It was found that most students had scaled down their aspirations to correspond to what they considered within their ability to fulfill. In general, a person tends to select goals (standards, level of performance, aspirations) in accord with his assessment of his qualities. This selectivity enables him to achieve his personal goals, to consider himself "good enough," and to maintain a favorable self-image.

As pointed out by Hyman,[30] the occupational attainments of people of working-class origins are lower than those raised in the middle-class environment. Does lower occupational "attainment" or "achievement" result in lower self-esteem? Not necessarily, because level of personal standards is a relative matter. For example, if a boy aspires to be a master plumber and makes it, this can be as self-enhancing for him as the boy who aspires to be a lawyer and makes it. What is important is not so much the *kind* of goal one sets, but its achievement. Accomplishment of a personal goal, whether in a physical, or intellectual, or social realm, can be a self-enhancing experience to the extent that it is personally meaningful and not too easily won.

Interpersonal Selectivity as Related to Positive Self-Esteem

One of the most consistent findings in mass communications research is that *people tend to relate to other people with whom they agree.*[31] A fundamental principle of social interaction is the idea that people, when given the choice, will tend to associate with those who think well of them and to avoid those who dislike them, thereby biasing the communications about themselves to which they are exposed in a favorable direction.

The outstanding case in point is *friendship*, which is, perhaps, the purest example of selectively choosing one's propaganda. Characteristically, not only do we like our friend, but he likes us. Indeed, it is possible that we may like him *because* he likes us. And of course friends are inclined to say friendly things, which increases the likelihood of hearing more of what we like to hear about ourselves. Friendship is at least to some extent a "mutual admiration unit," whereby each party helps to sustain the desired self-image of the other.

Indeed, one of the most important props of romantic love is the remarkable intensity of the mutual admiration. To discover that someone considers us the most wonderful girl in the world or the most talented boy is the kind of communication we very much like to hear.

What is true for friends and lovers is equally true of groups. The persistent search for social acceptance is a major enterprise of both young and old and is apparent in our active involvement in groups that accept and approve of us, thereby enhancing our self-esteem.

It is important to note, however, that interpersonal selectivity which is too cautious, too careful, and too defensive may serve to stunt personal growth. For example, the loner who has no friends, or the suspicious soul who avoids friends who might be "too honest" about him both limit the possibility of feedback which might, in fact, spur them to greater insights into themselves and their behavior. Inasmuch as the self grows best in an interpersonal stream of reflected appraisals, the opportunity for this kind of nurturance is severely curtailed when the selectivity is too guarded. *The point is, if we interact only with those who agree with us and seldom challenge us, then we are seldom forced into the position of having to re-evaluate ourselves and our positions on different issues.* Perhaps the best kind of friend is one who can, when it seems appropriate, challenge our most cherished beliefs without being threatened by the possibility of being rejected if he does.

Taking into consideration one's selective interpretation of the "facts," his selective interpretation of personal standards, and his selection of interpersonal relationships, Rosenberg has observed from his research that:

Some people are too immature to consider constructive criticism about themselves.

The communications about ourselves are thus either biased in a generally favorable direction or are so ambiguous that our own biases are free to operate. That this is the case is suggested by the responses of our adolescent subjects to the question: "What do most people think of you?" Nearly 97 percent said that most people thought well or fairly well of them, and only 3 percent said fairly poorly or very poorly. Even two-thirds of those with low self-esteem attributed such benevolent attitudes towards others. They may, of course, be right. It is possible that a vast wave of mutual love and good will engulfs the world. One cannot, however, evade the suspicion that, with the ambiguity inherent in determining another's attitudes, a great many people are giving themselves the benefit of the doubt.[32]

Situational Selectivity as Related to Positive Self-Esteem

In a society as complex as ours, a person is not always able to *create* his environment, but he is often able to *select* his environment. A primary motivation in this selectivity is an ever-present desire to maintain a congenial self-image. For the most part, we tend to expose ourselves to experiences in which we have a fair chance of success rather than those in which we may be found wanting. Occupational selectivity is a good illustration of situational selectivity. For example, one study found that, given a choice, most people naturally gravitate toward occupational situations in which their skills are likely to find expression and their talents appreciated.[33]

Situational selectivity is reflected in many areas of everyday life. For example, if a person is witty rather than deep, he may be inclined to go to parties or social gatherings rather than to lectures or discussions. If he is closed-minded rather than open-minded, he may prefer to press his own point of view rather than consider someone's else's. If he is insecure rather than secure, he may choose friends who are more nurturant than challenging. If he is good at bowling, but a poor bridge player, he will usually prefer to socialize in a bowling alley where his skill is more obvious. Similarly, it is well known that college students tend to elect subjects in which they are strong and avoid those in which they are weak. This is an effective way to avoid failure, to be sure, but it can also be detrimental to the development of a healthy self-concept. The psychology of success is

Setting a goal for one's self is important; having the courage to see it through is something else again.

such that it means little if the threat of failure is virtually absent. Winning which is guaranteed or an "A" grade with no effort contribute little to an individual's sense of personal accomplishment and self-esteem. The willingness to gamble, to "take a risk" now and then can be a healthy activity for anyone. For it is in the accomplishment of those things we were not sure we could do in the first place that the foundation for a healthy, positive self-image is laid.

And so it goes—selection of standards, friends, a spouse, an occupation, and so on are a pervasive and central outgrowth of each person's need to maintain and enhance his self-image. The maintenance of a positive self-image is thus a highly constant and ubiquitous aspect of determination of our longer-range goals and aspirations. There are, however, certain restrictions on selectivity which we should take into account.

Restrictions on Selectivity

The mechanism of selectivity is such that it operates to help shape our self-attitudes in accord with our desires and in line with our strengths. A reasonable question, then, is why all people do not have favorable self-attitudes. Some people have mild doubts about themselves, others more serious doubts, and still others have doubts so serious as to be convinced beyond question that they are worthless.

This does not mean that the principle of selectivity is wrong, but it does suggest that there are given conditions of human experience which are characterized by a narrow range of alternatives. It is in the interpersonal realm that the range of options is most severely limited. For example, while we are relatively free to choose who our friends will be, the same is not true of our parents, teachers, or classmates. If our parents reject us, or our teachers berate us, or our classmates laugh at us, we are largely deprived of option of avoiding their company or their criticism. When looked at from the point of view of interpersonal selectivity, it is not difficult to see why it is that some children run away from home, or drop out of school, or become social isolates.

Psychological research clearly shows that the self-attitudes that are the easiest to change, modify, or form are those which are least structured.[34, 35] And it is precisely in childhood that the self-image is most unstructured and unformed. Until a youngster reaches the age of about sixteen or so, his range of interpersonal alternatives is somewhat restricted by virtue of being the offspring of a particular set of parents. He must abide by *their* rules, listen to *their* appraisals, and relate as he can to such friends as there are in *their* neighborhood. These are his parents' choices, not his; of course, with no options there can be no selectivity. Hence, with parents holding a virtual monopoly on the options, the selections parents make have a particularly powerful influence on a youngster's self-esteem. For better or for worse, a child is stuck with his parents. If they choose wise options, if they love him, then he may have a substantial foundation for thinking well of himself. If they do *not* make wise selections; if they, say, live in a neighborhood where there are few children for their child to play with, he may be slow in developing social confidence; if they indulge and overprotect him, he may grow anxious and insecure; if they disparage or reject him, he may feel insignificant and unworthy.

The relative absence of interpersonal options for a growing child is no less serious than the restrictions on his situational selectivity. That is, a child's environment is largely fixed and there is not much he can do about it. For example, a bright child with intellectual potential, in a family which values things and not ideas, cannot choose to move into a family happy to answer his questions and encourage his curiosities. Similarly, there is no guarantee that one's personal whims and interests will meet the norms of the neighborhood peer group. If a child gains no recognition and applause for talents disdained by the group, he is powerless to select a different school or neighborhood.[36]

As we discussed in Chapter Five, we once again can see the enormous impact that childhood experiences and parents can have on a child's later feelings about himself. Despite the generality and power of the principle of selectivity, it is easy to see why many people *do* have low or moderate self-esteem. All in all, the evidence is consistent in suggesting that people *want* to have favorable opinions of themselves and that compensation (not to mention the other defense mechanisms described and discussed in Chapter One) and the various mechanisms of psychological selectivity are some of the strategies we use, consciously and unconsciously, to maintain and enhance positive self-attitudes.

Signs of a Healthy, Positive Self-Image

Since this chapter is devoted to a discussion of ways and means for moving toward a healthy self-image, it seems altogether appropriate that we end it on a positive note.

Increasing literature and research devoted to the problem of self-concept leaves little doubt but that mental health depends deeply on the quality of a person's feelings about himself. Just as an individual must maintain a healthy view of the world around him, so must he learn to perceive himself in positive ways. A person who has a strong, self-accepting attitude presents a behavioral picture very much the opposite of one who feels inadequate and inferior. Although there are certainly variations from one individual to another and for the same individual between situations, generally speaking, a person who has a healthy self-image can be characterized in the following ways:

1. He has certain values and principles he believes in strongly and is willing to defend them even in the face of strong group opinion; however, he feels personally secure enough to modify them if new experience and evidence suggest he is in error. (An insecure person finds it difficult to change his position for fear that it may be interpreted as weakness, or lack of ability, or compentency. "You may be right, but I'm not wrong.")

2. He is capable of acting on his own best judgment without feeling excessively guilty or regretting his actions if others disapprove of what he's done. When he does feel guilty, he is not overwhelmed by the guilt. He can say, "I made a mistake—I'll have to improve," rather than "I made a mistake—how terrible I am."

3. He does not spend undue time worrying about what is coming tomorrow, or being upset by today's experience, or fussing over yesterday's mistakes. I remember a little poem which used to hang on the wall in my grandparents living room. It goes like this:

It's easy enough to be pleasant
When Life flows along like a song,
But the man worth while
Is the man who can smile
When everything goes dead wrong.

4. He retains confidence in his ability to deal with problems, even in the face of failures and setbacks. He does not conclude, "Because I failed I am a failure," but is more likely to say, "I failed. I'll have to work harder."

5. He feels equal to others *as a person*—not superior or inferior—irrespective of the differences in specific abilities, family backgrounds, or attitudes of others toward him. He is able to say, "You are more skilled than I, but I am as much a person as you," which is different from thinking, "You are more skilled than I, therefore you are a better person." He is able to see that another individual's skills or abilities neither devalues nor elevates his own status as a person.

6. He is able to take it more or less for granted that he is a person of interest and value to others—at least to those with whom he chooses to associate. Another way of saying this is that he is not paralyzed by self-consciousness when in the company of other people.

7. He can accept praise without the pretense of false modesty ("Well, gosh, *anyone* could have done it."), and compliments without feeling guilty ("Thanks, but I *really* don't deserve it.")

Snoopy may have a point here.

8. He is inclined to resist the efforts of others to dominate him, especially those who are his peers. The resistance, in effect, is a way of saying, "I am as good as you—therefore there is no reason why I should be dominated by you."

9. He is able to accept the idea (and admit to others) that he is capable of feeling a wide range of impulses and desires, ranging all the way from being very angry to being very loving, from being very sad to being very happy, from feeling deep resentment to feeling great acceptance. It does not follow, however, that he *acts* on all his feelings and desires.

10. He is able to genuinely enjoy himself in a wide variety of activities involving work, play, creative self-expression, companionship, or, of all things, just plain loafing. An unknown author—a very wise man, no doubt —has expressed this idea in the following manner:

A master in the art of living draws no sharp distinction between his work and his play, his labour and his leisure, his mind and his body, his education and his recreation. He hardly knows which is which. He simply pursues his vision of excellence through whatever he is doing and leaves others to determine whether he is working or playing. To himself he always seems to be doing both.

11. He is sensitive to the needs of others, to accepted social customs and particularly to the idea that he cannot, willy-nilly, go about "self-actualizing" himself at the expense of everyone around him.

Perhaps we would do well to keep in mind that these are not destinations that only a fortunate few have passage to, or end states arrived at by a select number, but, rather, possibilities which any person desiring to better himself can hold as goals within his reach. Usually, motivation is more effective, and happiness more attainable, if a person concentrates on improvement rather than perfection.

In Perspective

Healthy people, research shows, see themselves as liked, wanted, acceptable, able, and worthy. Not only do they feel that they are people of dignity and worth, but they *behave* as though they were. Indeed, it is in this factor of how a person sees himself that we are likely to find the most outstanding differences between high and low self-image people. It is not the people who feel that they are liked and wanted and acceptable and able who fill our prisons and mental hospitals. Rather, it is those who feel deeply inadequate, unliked, unwanted, unacceptable, and unable.

Self and self-other understanding are not mystical ideals standing someplace "out there" as unreachable goals. Social feeling, empathic listening, honesty, and an understanding of how we use our defense mechanisms are all ways to assist in the development of greater self-awareness and self-understanding.

A person's feelings about himself are *learned* responses. Sometimes bad feelings have to be unlearned and new feelings acquired. This is not always easy, but it is possible. Sometimes this means "taking stock" of oneself—a kind of personal inventory. Or it may mean baring one's self to another person—a friend or therapist—so that the possibility for honest evaluation and feedback is more probable. And for certain, it means changing those things which one can and accepting those which one cannot.

For most persons, a positive, healthy self-image is quite within reach if they are willing to accept the risks and responsibilities for mature living.

If, as parents or as professional persons, we have a basic understanding of how a healthy self is developed and the conditions and interpersonal relations which nurture it, then we are in a position to move actively in the direction of *creating* those conditions and interpersonal relationships most conducive to positive mental health.

Perhaps the best place to begin is with ourselves.

[1] A. H. Maslow, "Some Basic Propositions of a Growth and Self-Actualization Psychology," in A. W. Combs (Ed.), *Perceiving, Behaving, Becoming.* Association for Supervision and Curriculum Development Year Book. Washington, D.C.: National Education Association, 1962, p. 48.

[2] A. Adler, *The Individual Psychology of Alfred Adler.* New York: Basic Books, Inc., 1956, pp. 135–136.

[3] E. Fromm, *Beyond the Chains of Illusion.* New York: Pocket Books, 1962, p. 186.

[4] M. Buber, *I and Thou.* New York: Charles Scribner's Sons, 1958.

[5] Carl R. Rogers, *Freedom To Learn.* Columbus, Ohio: Charles E. Merrill Books, Inc., 1969, p. 75.

[6] B. R. McCandless, *Children: Behavior and Development* (2nd ed.), New York: Holt, Rinehart and Winston, Inc., 1967, p. 280.

[7] V. C. Raimy, "Self-Reference in Counseling Interviews," *Journal of Consulting Psychology.* 1948, 12: 153–163.

[8] Ruth C. Wylie, *The Self Concept.* Lincoln, Neb.: University of Nebraska Press, 1961.

[9] Ruth C. Wylie, "Some Relationships between Defensiveness and Self-Concept Discrepancies," *Journal of Personality.* 1957, 25: 600–616.

[10] R. W. Levanway, "The Effect of Stress on Expressed Attitudes toward Self and Others," *Journal of Abnormal and Social Psychology.* 1955, 50: 225–226.

[11] E. L. Phillips, "Attitudes toward Self and Others: A Brief Questionnaire Report," *Journal of Consulting Psychology.* 1951, 15: 79–81.

[12] Carl R. Rogers, *Client-Centered Therapy: Its Current Practice, Implications, and Theory.* Boston: Houghton Mifflin Company, 1951, p. 520.

[13] W. F. Fey, "Acceptance by Others and Its Relation to Acceptance of Self and Others, A Re-evaluation," *Journal of Abnormal and Social Psychology.* 1955, 50: 274–276.

[14] Fey, p. 275.

[15] A. H. Maslow, "The Jonah Complex," *Humanitas.* 1967.

[16] G. W. Allport, *Patterns and Growth in Personality.* New York: Holt, Rinehart and Winston, Inc., 1961, p. 130.

[17] Allport, pp. 130–131.

[18] A. A. Schneiders, *Personality Dynamics and Mental Health.* New York: Holt, Rinehart and Winston, Inc., 1965, pp. 227–228.

[19] Rollo May, *Man's Search for Himself.* New York: W. W. Norton and Company, 1953, pp. 98–101.

[20] G. W. Allport, *The Individual and His Religion.* New York: Crowell-Collier and Macmillan, Inc., 1950, p. 95.

[21] May, p. 100.

[22] E. A. Strecker, K. E. Appel, and J. W. Appel, *Discovering Ourselves* (3rd ed.). New York: Crowell-Collier and Macmillan, Inc., 1958, p. 249.

[23] G. W. Allport and H. S. Odbert, "Trait-Names: A Psycho-Lexical Study," *Psychological Monographs.* 1936, No. 211.

[24] M. Rosenberg, "Psychological Selectivity in Self-Esteem Formation," in C. W. Sherif and M. Sherif (Eds.), *Attitudes Ego-Involvement and Change.* New York: John Wiley & Sons, Inc., 1967, pp. 28–29.

[25] Rosenberg, pp. 26–50.

[26] William James, *Psychology: The Briefer Course.* New York: Harper & Row, Publishers, 1961, pp. 43–83.

[27] P. S. Sears, "Levels of Aspiration in Academically Successful and Unsuccessful School Children," *Journal of Abnormal and Social Psychology.* 1940, 35: 498–536.

28 Rosenberg, p. 41.

29 M. Rosenberg, *Occupations and Values*. New York: The Free Press, 1957.

30 H. H. Hyman, "The Value Systems of Different Classes: A Social Psychological Contribution to the Analysis of Stratification," in R. Bendix and S. M. Lipset (Eds.), *Class, Status and Power*. New York: The Free Press, 1953, pp. 426–442.

31 D. Cartwright and A. Zander, *Group Dynamics: Research and Theory*. New York: Harper & Row, Publishers, 1968, pp. 45–62.

32 Rosenberg (1967), p. 47.

33 E. Ginzberg, S. W. Ginsburg, S. Axelrad, and J. L. Herma, *Occupational Choice*. New York: Columbia University Press, 1951.

34 M. Sherif and C. W. Sherif, *An Outline of Social Psychology* (rev. ed.). New York: Harper & Row, Publishers, 1956.

35 B. Berelson, "Communications and Public Opinion," in B. Berelson and M. Janowitz, *Public Opinion and Communication*. New York: The Free Press, 1950, pp. 448–462.

36 Rosenberg (1967), p. 48.

References of Related Interest

Aronson, E., "Who Likes Whom and Why," *Psychology Today*. August 1970, 48–50, 74.

Babladelis, G., and S. Adams (Eds.), *The Shaping of Personality*. Englewood Cliffs, N.J.: Prentice-Hall, Inc., 1967.

Bugental, J. F. T. (Ed.), *Challenges of Humanistic Psychology*. New York: McGraw-Hill, Inc., 1967.

Clarizio, H. F. (Ed.), *Mental Health and the Educative Process*. Skokie, Ill.: Rand McNally & Company, 1969.

Grebstein, Lawrence C. (Ed.), *Toward Self-Understanding*. Glenview, Ill.: Scott, Foresman and Company, 1969.

Grossack, Martin M., *You Are Not Alone*. Boston: Christopher Publishing House, 1965.

Hamachek, Don E. (Ed.), *The Self in Growth, Teaching, and Learning*. Englewood Cliffs, N.J.: Prentice-Hall, Inc., 1965, Parts V, IX.

Hamachek, Don E. (Ed.), *Human Dynamics in Psychology and Education*. Boston: Allyn and Bacon, Inc., 1968, Chap. 11–13.

Maslow, A. H., *Toward A Psychology of Being* (2nd ed.). Princeton, N.J.: D. Van Nostrand Company, 1968.

Matson, F. W. (Ed.), *Being, Becoming, and Behavior*. New York: George Braziller, 1967.

McNeil, E. B., *Human Socialization*. Belmont, Calif.: Brooks/Cole, 1969.

Moustakes, C. E., *The Self: Explorations in Personal Growth*. New York: Harper & Row, Publishers, 1956.

Rogers, C. R., *Being, Becoming, and Behavior*. Boston: Houghton Mifflin Company, 1961.

Sanford, N., *Self and Society*. New York: Atherton Press, 1966.

Shapiro, D., *Neurotic Styles*. New York: Basic Books, Inc., 1965.

Shostrom, E. L., *Man, the Manipulator*. New York: Abingdon Press, 1967.

Southwell, E. A., and M. Merbaum (Eds.), *Personality: Readings in Theory and Research*. Belmont, Calif.: Brooks/Cole, 1964.

Stein, M. R., A. J. Vidich, and D. M. White (Eds.), *Identity and Anxiety*. New York: The Free Press, 1960.

Smith, H. C., *Sensitivity to People*. New York: McGraw-Hill, Inc., 1966.

Stoodley, B. H. (Ed.), *Society and Self*. New York: The Free Press, 1962.

White, R. W., *The Abnormal Personality* (3rd ed.). New York: The Ronald Press Company, 1964.

Index